CONTEMPORARY SOCIAL RESEARCH

Volume 6

DOING SECONDARY ANALYSIS

DOING SECONDARY ANALYSIS

ANGELA DALE, SARA ARBER
AND
MICHAEL PROCTER

Routledge
Taylor & Francis Group
LONDON AND NEW YORK

First published in 1988 by Unwin Hyman

This edition first published in 2026
by Routledge
4 Park Square, Milton Park, Abingdon, Oxon OX14 4RN

and by Routledge
605 Third Avenue, New York, NY 10158

Routledge is an imprint of the Taylor & Francis Group, an informa business

British Library Cataloguing in Publication Data
A catalogue record for this book is available from the British Library

ISBN: 978-1-041-07377-2 (Set)
ISBN: 978-1-041-05359-0 (Volume 6) (hbk)
ISBN: 978-1-041-05371-2 (Volume 6) (pbk)
ISBN: 978-1-003-63246-7 (Volume 6) (ebk)

DOI: 10.4324/9781003632467

Publisher's Note
The publisher has gone to great lengths to ensure the quality of this reprint but points out that some imperfections in the original copies may be apparent.

Disclaimer
The publisher has made every effort to trace copyright holders and would welcome correspondence from those they have been unable to trace.

Doing Secondary Analysis

Angela Dale, Sara Arber and Michael Procter
Department of Sociology, University of Surrey

London
UNWIN HYMAN
Boston   Sydney   Wellington

Published by the Academic Division of
Unwin Hyman Ltd
15/17 Broadwick Street, London W1V 1FP

Allen & Unwin Inc.,
8 Winchester Place, Winchester, Mass. 01890, USA

Allen & Unwin (Australia) Ltd,
8 Napier Street, North Sydney, NSW 2060, Australia

Allen & Unwin (New Zealand) Ltd in association with the
Port Nicholson Press Ltd,
60 Cambridge Terrace, Wellington, New Zealand

First published in 1988

British Library Cataloguing in Publication Data

Dale, Angela
Doing secondary analysis. — (Contemporary social research series; v.17).
1. Social Sciences — Statistical methods
I. Title II. Arber, Sara III. Procter, Michael IV. Series
300'.72 HA 29
ISBN 0-04-312041-5
ISBN 0-04-312042-3 Pbk

Library of Congress Cataloging-in-Publication Data

Dale, Angela, 1945–
Doing secondary analysis. (Contemporary social research series)
Bibliography: p.
Includes index.
1. Social surveys. 2. Social sciences — Statistical methods. 3. Social surveys — Great Britain. 4. Social sciences — Research — Great Britain.
I. Arber, Sara L., 1949–. II. Procter, Michael, 1941–.
III. Title. IV. Series.
HN29.D34 1988 300'.72 87-17422
ISBN 0-04-312041-5 (alk. paper)
ISBN 0-04-312042-3 (pbk. : alk. paper)

Set in 10 on 12 point Times by Word Capture Limited, Salford and printed in Great Britain by Billing and Sons Ltd, London and Worcester.

Contents

Acknowledgements

This book has benefited from both the witting and unwitting support and assistance of a great number of people. First, colleagues in the Department of Sociology, particularly past and present members of the Stratification and Employment Group, have contributed to the research on which this book draws. We would especially like to acknowledge the role of Nigel Gilbert in the series of projects to make the GHS accessible to the research and academic community and for his continued support; also, Gill Jones (now at Thomas Coram Research Unit), Claire Bamford and Judith Glover for comments on draft chapters. Roger Burrows (now at NELP), Alan Clarke and Christian Heath have made valuable comments and suggested clarifications.

Both Karen Dunnell of OPCS and Howard Newby of the University of Essex were kind enough to find time to read and comment on the draft text which has benefited a great deal from their constructive suggestions and points of information. We have also received helpful comments from Janet Finch of Lancaster University and Hilary Graham of Warwick University. All the staff at the ESRC Data Archive have given us a very great deal of help, ranging from answering telephone queries to reading and commenting on drafts of the text – we are particularly grateful to Eric Tanenbaum, Marcia Taylor, Randy Banks and Ann Hockey. We would also like to thank Andy Heath from SIA, Major Lestor from SPSS, John Fox of the City University and Stephen Tagg from the University of Strathclyde, all of whom have read and given us comments on parts of the text.

We are very grateful to Martin Bulmer for his encouragement and helpful suggestions throughout the process of producing this book and also to Gordon Smith of Unwin Hyman who has smoothed out numerous problems *en route.*

Finally we would like to acknowledge the role of the Economic and Social Research Council in supporting a number of research projects from which this book draws. Without this support the book could not have been written.

Glossary of Abbreviations

ASCII	American Standard Code for Information Interchange
BES	British Election Study
BSAS	British Social Attitudes Survey
CHES	Child Health and Education Survey
CPAG	Child Poverty Action Group
DE	Department of Employment
DHSS	Department of Health and Social Security
DOE	Department of the Environment
EBCDIC	Extended Binary Coded Decimal Interchange Code
ESRC	Economic and Social Research Council
FES	Family Expenditure Survey
FFS	Family Formation Survey
FIS	Family Income Supplement
GHS	General Household Survey
GSS	General Social Survey
ICPSR	Inter-University Consortium on Political and Social Research
JANET	Joint University Academic Network
JUVOS	Joint Unemployment and Vacancies Operating System
LFS	Labour Force Survey
LS	Longitudinal Study
MSC	Manpower Services Commission
MORI	Market and Opinion Research International
NCDS	National Child Development Study
NLS	National Longitudinal Survey
NOMIS	National On-line Manpower Information System
NOP	National Opinion Polls
NORC	National Opinion Research Centre
OPCS	Office of Population Censuses and Surveys
PAF	Postcode Address File
PC	Personal Computer
PSS	Packet Switching System
PUMS	Public Use Microdata Samples (US Census)
RAM	Random Access Memory
RNR	Relative Net Resources
SCPR	Social and Community Planning Research
SIR	Scientific Information Retrieval
SOEC	Statistical Office of the European Community
SRA	Social Research Association
SSRC	Social Science Research Council
WES	Women and Employment Survey
WIRS	Workplace Industrial Relations Survey

Preface

As the title suggests, this book is about how to *do* secondary analysis. Secondary analysis is increasingly recognized within the social sciences as an important research tool, and yet there has, to date, been very little published work on the methodology of secondary analysis as opposed to survey research in general. With the limited funding available in the current financial climate, one of the most important ways in which social research can maximize its impact is to build on the work already done by others, particularly where that work has been funded by government sources. However, if it is to produce a worthwhile contribution to knowledge and understanding, secondary analysis must not be used as a short-cut to quick results. It is important that the secondary analyst takes as much time and trouble over defining the research problem and understanding categories of data as would be required by any other method of research.

This book is therefore aimed at those who are embarking upon social research and may not yet have realized the potential that is available through secondary analysis. It is also aimed at those who are established users of other methods of social research but for whom secondary analysis could provide an additional dimension to their research. We hope, too, that those who are already familiar with secondary analysis will find that issues of concern to them are discussed and perhaps some additional light is shed on problems that they may have encountered.

The book focuses particularly upon the secondary analysis of large-scale government survey data. The surveys carried out by the UK Office of Population Censuses and Surveys (OPCS) provide an enormous wealth of high quality data for the secondary analyst, but also present some of the most difficult problems of analysis. We are not, however, concerned simply with giving a recipe of procedures for the novice to follow. We take the position that the secondary analyst needs to do a good deal of preliminary thinking about the research process and the implications of using data that has[1] been collected for other purposes. Because the secondary analyst joins the research process at a point when the primary analysis has probably finished it is important that she[2] becomes fully aware of the nature of the data to be used, its method of collection and any limitations that this imposes on analysis and subsequent interpretation of results.

The first section of the book, therefore, is devoted to the preliminary thinking that needs to precede any contact with secondary data. Chapter

1 discusses the variety of data available for secondary analysis and the ways in which it has been produced. It concludes by questioning the assumption that survey data has an objectivity that makes it qualitatively distinct from other kinds of research data and that the survey method is necessarily linked to one particular epistemological position. In Chapter 2 we work through the kinds of questions which the secondary analyst should be asking of the data source and also of herself at the very initial stage of the analysis process. In this chapter we discuss many of the issues that the originator of the data would have had to answer but which the secondary analyst may be tempted to overlook. The chapter finishes by considering the particular uses which may be made of data from large-scale government surveys. It is argued that these need not be bound into the traditional world of survey research so often characterized as belonging to the public domain of men but can also be used to serve the interests of women. Chapter 3 considers those features that are unique to secondary analysis, but looks also at the benefits to be gained and the costs that may be incurred by using this method. The chapter discusses some of the ethical issues involved when data is used for purposes other than those for which it was collected. In doing so, it emphasizes the role of secondary analysis in enabling data to be re-analysed and results debated, thereby acting as a safeguard against systematic misinterpretation or misuse. A rather more hidden benefit of secondary analysis is the way in which it can avoid additional intrusion into the private lives of citizens.

One of the focuses of the book is on the potential of hierarchical, household-based data for social research. In Chapter 4 we explain the distinction between this form of data and the more usual 'rectangular' data collected in surveys. Using the General Household Survey (GHS) as an example, we explore some of the topics that can be researched by using this kind of data and which have previously required specialized surveys.

The remainder of the book is concerned with the practical issues of secondary analysis – the day-to-day problems encountered in *doing* secondary analysis. Therefore Chapter 5 begins with the assumption that a decision has been made to use secondary analysis of survey data and works through the stages of locating and ordering a suitable dataset. Although most illustrations use British surveys held at the UK Data Archive at the University of Essex, the principles that lie behind them apply to using data from archives in any other country. It goes without saying that secondary analysis of survey data will need some computing facilities and Chapter 6 explains the various kinds of computers available and provides an introduction to the terminology that surrounds the world of computing. In Chapter 7 we offer some background information on the types of computer packages available for analysis and point out the more fundamental differences behind the variety of approaches to data management and manipulation.

Having reached Chapter 8, the secondary analyst should be equipped with a dataset to analyse, and knowledge of both the hardware and software to facilitate this. Therefore this chapter outlines procedures for reading and checking the data once it has arrived from the Data Archive. These include methods of checking that the data is intact and complete, setting up a system file and a procedure for deriving new variables. Examples given use SPSS^x as the analysis package. However, as Chapter 4 has already made clear, not all data is organized into simple rectangular files and some of the most exciting research may be generated by the use of household surveys which collect information from all household members and which can be used to establish intra-household relationships. Chapter 9 discusses the choices to be made about units and levels of analysis when working with hierarchical data and provides a framework for understanding the types of variables that can be derived from hierarchical surveys. This is followed in Chapter 10 by a practical outline of how the types of derived variables discussed in the previous chapter may be created by the secondary analyst. These examples are all based upon the database management system SIR and examples are drawn from the GHS.

Finally, Chapter 11 pulls together the separate strands that have been discussed throughout the preceding chapters by providing an exemplar that takes the reader through each stage of the process of secondary analysis, from defining the theoretical area of interest to generating the preliminary analyses. The exemplar used is drawn from a 'real' project carried out by the authors and focuses on the substantive area of income inequality and household assets.

Although this book is very much a joint piece of work, with all chapters receiving contributions from all of the authors, the main responsibility for Chapters 4 and 9 lies with Sara Arber, Chapters 6 and 7 with Mike Procter, and the remainder with Angela Dale.

Notes

1 According to the 2nd edition of *Modern English Usage* (Fowler, 1965, p.119): '*data* is a Latin Plural . . . Latin plurals sometimes become singular English words (e.g. *agenda, stamina*) and *data* is often so treated in US'. In our judgement, twenty years later, and in the context of social research, *data* is best treated as singular.

2 As Coxon (1982, p.viii) so aptly puts it: 'the observant reader may notice that the user is referred to throughout the book as "she". This is deliberate – it avoids the ugly "he or she" form, and any remaining unease exemplifies just the point which professional guidelines on gender usage aim to make.'

1

An introduction to secondary analysis

'In recent years the idea of secondary analysis of survey data . . . has inspired a major movement in social science.' Thus Hyman (1972, p.1)[1] opens his classic book on secondary analysis. In the USA this movement may be dated from 1957 when the Roper Public Opinion Research Center became designated as a general archive for survey data and, in the same year, a funding proposal for a Library Center of Survey Research Data was made to the Ford Foundation (Hyman, 1972). Secondary analysis was used, however, long before this date with the volumes on *The American Soldier* (Stouffer *et al.*, 1949) an early example of the way in which data collected to provide factual information for the US Army could be re-analysed for an academic audience (Hyman, 1955). More recently, the Inter-University Consortium for Political and Social Research (ICPSR) became established at the University of Michigan in 1962. This is claimed to be the largest archive in the world, holding more than 17,000 files of machine-readable social science data, from more than 130 countries (Kiecolt and Nathan, 1985).

In Britain, the establishment of the SSRC Survey Archive (now the ESRC Data Archive) at the University of Essex in 1967 has done much to facilitate the use of secondary data sources. The brief of the Archive is to 'collect and preserve machine-readable data relating to social and economic affairs from academic, commercial and governmental sources, and to make that data available for secondary analysis' (ESRC Data Archive, 1984). The rationale behind this brief is that this data represents an enormous resource in terms of both human effort and funding and therefore ought to be preserved as a knowledge bank and made available to others. The Data Archive holds more than 3,000 data sets, a vast repository of material, although even that does not completely exhaust all the material which can become the subject of 'secondary analysis'. The range of studies, relating not just to the UK but with world-wide coverage, is documented in the two-volume Catalogue produced by the Archive (Taylor, 1986). A free quarterly Bulletin gives news of the latest acquisitions and provides a means of sharing recent developments that are relevant to secondary analysts all over the world.

Despite this, secondary analysis has not become the established method of research among social scientists in Britain in the way that it has in the USA. The more extensive use of secondary analysis in the USA, as well as the greater emphasis on survey methods, is bound up with the sociological traditions that make empirical quantification more highly regarded in North America than in Britain. By contrast, the reluctance to embark upon secondary analysis by British sociologists must be seen as part of a traditional disdain for surveys – which, as Marsh (1979b; 1982) points out, tends to characterize the survey as inherently positivistic and therefore epistemologically flawed. That there is no one to one relationship between a research method and an epistemological position has been well established (Bryman, 1984; Platt, 1986) and the assumption that the survey can be used only within a positivistic framework has been effectively rebutted (Marsh, 1979b; 1982). It therefore follows that the secondary analyst does not have to embrace any particular epistemological position and there is no necessary conflict between using both survey methods and less structured techniques to research a problem. Marsh argues very ably that there is no inherent contradiction between good sociology and good survey research. One of the purposes of this book is to extend that argument to demonstrate that secondary analysis can also be used to produce good sociology.

Silverman (1985), describing the polarity which is so often found between macro and micro research, and between structural and interactional perspectives, stresses the need to synthesize both approaches. Although this book is written mainly with reference to surveys, we take the position that, with many research problems, an adequate understanding can only be gained through the use of qualitative methods together with the more structured approach of the survey.[2] While the survey provides an analytic framework, it may be richly enhanced by the insights and understandings gained from less structured forms of interviewing or from ethnographic work. Secondary analysis can provide a means by which the benefits of the survey, particularly its ability to provide a national-level dimension, may be combined with other methods to bridge the traditional dichotomy of qualitative and quantitative research (Glenn, 1978). It may also provide the basis for major research projects that have importance to both theory (Erikson, Goldthorpe and Portocarero, 1982; 1983) and policy formation (Layard, Piachaud and Stewart, 1978; Elias and Main, 1982). Secondary analysis has a role, not just in research, but also in teaching. A readily accessible and well-documented dataset can both enable students to carry out their own analysis in an area of substantive importance and also provide a medium for teaching data analysis, statistics and computing. The General Social Survey (GSS) has long been used in this way in the USA (Cutler, 1978) and in Britain the *Exploring British Society Series* (Arber, Gilbert, Dale and Rajan, 1984) has provided an undergraduate teaching package based around four substantive areas using data from the General Household Survey.

Secondary analysis: a definition

Hakim (1982, p.1) defines secondary analysis as 'any further analysis of an existing dataset which presents interpretations, conclusions or knowledge additional to, or different from, those presented in the first report on the inquiry as a whole and its main results'. In similar vein, Hyman (1972, p.1) describes the secondary analysis of survey data as 'the extraction of knowledge on topics other than those which were the focus of the original surveys'. Thus the term 'secondary analysis' implies a re-working of data already analysed. As such, it may appear to offer little by way of originality and seem to be an unlikely method of revealing new and exciting findings. The following pages will attempt to make clear, however, that 'secondary analysis' can open doors that would not otherwise be accessible to academic social researchers, and can offer far more than a simple re-analysis of somebody else's data.

Secondary analysis must, by definition, be an empirical exercise carried out on data that has already been gathered or compiled in some way. However, the shape and form of the data represents a source of variation which, in turn, affects the scope for analysis by those wishing to use it. For example, the method of data collection, the form in which the data is stored, the substantive area covered by the data and whether or not it is representative of a larger population are just some of the factors that influence the scope for secondary analysis.

Although the term 'secondary analysis' is most often used in connection with survey data, any machine-readable data may be deposited at the ESRC Data Archive and many other data forms may become the subject of secondary analysis. Hakim (1982, Table 1.1) lists six sources of quantitative social data that may be used for secondary analysis. These range from aggregate data, as produced by the population censuses, through microdata[3] represented by sample surveys, to datasets derived from administrative and public records. The main focus of this book will be on the secondary analysis of microdata derived from surveys.

In order to clarify the distinction between primary analysis and secondary analysis, we may consider a small sample survey carried out by a social researcher, with the data collected, analysed and written up within the same project. This is clearly an example of primary analysis. However, if this survey has been financed by the ESRC, the researcher will be required to deposit a copy of the data file and documentation at the ESRC Data Archive. From this Archive it may be obtained by another researcher, who decides that the data could usefully be re-analysed for an entirely different piece of research. After filling in the Data Archive's application forms and signing an undertaking to meet the conditions of use stipulated by the Archive, the second researcher will be sent a data tape and documentation on the survey. She will then be ready to embark immediately upon her analysis, using the data already collected by the first researcher. Such is the nature of social science that it is almost impossible for any one research project to exhaust the analysis potential of a dataset. The analysis carried out by the second researcher is 'secondary' analysis, falling firmly within the definitions supplied by both Hakim and Hyman.

However, it is not always possible to make such a neat division into 'primary' and 'secondary' analysis and in this book we shall extend our discussion to the further analysis of data by anyone other than those responsible for its original commissioning or collection. By extending the definition in this way we incorporate the further analysis of multi-purpose surveys and the analysis of data collected specifically for use by others. In the examples selected for discussion there is no attempt to cover the entire range of material available for secondary analysis – sources available in Britain have been extensively reviewed by Hakim (1982) with examples of the ways in which they have been successfully used. The *ESRC Data Archive Catalogue* (Taylor, 1986) provides a listing of holdings in the UK, with short descriptions of each study, and the ICPSR annual *Guide to Resources and Services* lists the contents of the most extensive American archive, located at the University of Michigan. Further discussion of American data sources is found in Hyman (1972), who also gives a list of archives in North America and Europe. A more recent discussion of data sources available for public use in the USA is given by Stewart (1984) and Kiecolt and Nathan (1985), who also supply a list of archive addresses. In the following section we discuss a selection of data sources, ranging from those designed specifically for analysis by others to those carried out with no view to their use by others. Summaries of the sources discussed in this chapter are given in Figures 1.1 and 1.2.

Figure 1.1 *Sources of microdata discussed in Chapter 1. (All abbreviations are given in the Glossary on p.xi.)*

		MICRODATA		
Method of collection	*Purpose*	*Example*	*Agency*	*Sponsor*
Sample survey:	Secondary analysis (academic)	GSS	NORC	National Science Foundation, USA
		BSAS	SCPR	Numerous: mainly ESRC/charity
	multi-purpose/ descriptive (government)	GHS LFS FES	OPCS	a variety of government departments
	explanatory (government)	FFS WES	OPCS	DHSS DE
	explanatory (academic)	Social Mobility Inquiry Class Structure (Newby) Social Obligations (Finch)	--- SCPR SCPR	ESRC ESRC ESRC
Cohort study:	prospective/ explanatory	NCDS	National Child-ren's Bureau	DHSS/DE/ DOE/ESRC
		NLS	US Bureau of the Census	US Dept of Labor
Combined sources:				
Census + official records	descriptive + explanatory (government)	Longitudinal Study	OPCS	Government depts.
Historical records	descriptive/ explanatory (academic)	Haraven (US) (Amoskeag)	---	numerous: private and charitable

Figure 1.2 *Sources of aggregate data discussed in Chapter 1*

	AGGREGATE DATA	
Method of collection	*Example*	*Sponsor*
UK Population Census, 1971, 1981	Small Area Statistics	OPCS
Administrative records	World Handbook Series of Political and Social Indicators III	University of Yale USA
Local employment office records	NOMIS	MSC
Records from benefit offices	JUVOS	DE
Compiled from numerous sources	Domesday Project Community and National Disks	BBC/Acorn Computers/ Olivetti

Sources of data for secondary analysis

Perhaps the first example of a data source established explicitly for secondary analysis is the General Social Survey (GSS) carried out by the National Opinion Research Center (NORC) based at Chicago. This annual survey has been running since 1972 and is specifically designed to provide a time series that allows the changing social attitudes of a representative sample of US citizens to be charted. The survey content is designed in consultation with academic and other researchers, and many questions replicate classic studies – for example, Stouffer's work on civil liberties (Stouffer, 1955). Because it is designed for use by others, the NORC staff refrain from extensive analysis of the data until one year after it has been made available to other researchers (Glenn, 1978). Its success in encouraging secondary analysis may be evident from the fact that more than 1,000 publications have been produced using data from the first nine years of the survey (Smith, 1982, 1983). Research topics include attitudes towards abortion (Evers and McGee, 1980), changing attitudes to crime and punishment (Stinchcome *et al.*, 1980), structural changes in occupational mobility (Hauser *et al.*, 1975), and the relationship between social class and parental values for children (Wright and Wright, 1976).

In Britain, the British Social Attitudes Survey (BSAS) is the first data source specifically planned for secondary analysis. It is designed to fulfil the role played by the GSS in the United States, by providing a time series of data, freely available to the research community, on the nation's attitudes, values and beliefs. Begun in 1983, it has core funding for at least five years, and is a nationwide sample survey carried out by Social and Community Planning Research (SCPR). In the Foreword to the 1984 report, Sir Claus Moser writes: 'The main point of the survey after all is to provide a publicly available dataset which *others* can utilise.' He goes on: 'That is why a selection of microfiche tables is contained in the hardback edition, why questionnaires containing all marginal totals are contained as appendices in both editions, and why the data will be lodged in the ESRC Data Archive as soon as each volume is published' (Jowell and Airey, 1984). The survey, therefore, has been specifically designed with a view to its re-analysis by other social researchers. It is 'free-standing' in the sense that it should be possible for a secondary analyst to use the data on the basis of the documentation supplied. It may also be assumed that the expertise that went into setting up the survey, sampling, deciding upon question wording and coding responses, is encapsulated within the dataset and, through the medium of the data, is also made available to the secondary analyst.

The BSAS published reports summarize the main findings of each survey, but for those who want to extend the analyses further the data is readily available from the ESRC Data Archive. In this instance, those who use the data may, formally, be designated 'secondary analysts'; they are re-analysing data that has been collected and analysed by another agency but they are, none the less, using the data for the purpose for which it was collected – the analysis of British social attitudes. The survey set out to be descriptive rather than explanatory – it attempted to record the attitudes held by a representative sample of the British public to a series of social issues. Therefore, those social researchers who obtain the survey data tape and carry out further analyses themselves are, in a sense, extending the original analyses.

From a survey designed for analysis by others, we can move to consider the Government-sponsored surveys run in the UK by the Office of Population Censuses and Surveys (OPCS). These may be divided somewhat arbitrarily into surveys designed for descriptive or explanatory purposes (Hyman, 1955; Bone, 1981), although one survey may support both types of analysis. The General Household Survey (GHS), although very complex, is essentially a multipurpose descriptive survey designed to provide statistics for those government departments that sponsor it. The GHS provides base-line figures and monitors trends for a number of government departments – for example, data on health status and the extent of absence from work due to sickness are provided for the Department of Health and Social Security, estimates of household burglary for the Home Office, data on marital history and family formation for the Population Statistics Division of OPCS, and information on housing standards for the Department of the Environment (see Bulmer, 1986, Chapter 5, for a brief overview). Descriptive statistics, mainly in the form of complex tabulations, are produced by OPCS both for its annual GHS Report and also for the use of its government clients, but little analysis of an explanatory kind is carried out. Once the survey is deposited at the ESRC Data Archive (about 18 months after fieldwork is completed) it becomes available for secondary analysis by the academic community, who are likely to extend its use into hypothesis testing within a variety of different theoretical frameworks.

The Labour Force Survey (OPCS, 1986) is also unequivocally descriptive in its origin and primary purposes. Although it has an international dimension – it supplies data on employment and unemployment to the European Community – it also provides the Department of Employment with population estimates of labour force participation at both national and regional level. This survey, which became annual from 1983, is also lodged at the ESRC Data Archive, where its large sample size (76,000 households in 1984) and detailed occupational coding give it enormous potential for secondary analysis.

The Family Expenditure Survey (FES) is principally a consumer expenditure survey, the main purpose of which is the calculation of weights for the Index of Retail Prices (Kemsley, Redpath and Holmes, 1980). However, the FES also collects income details from household members and, like the GHS, falls under the heading of a 'multi-purpose' survey, providing data for the Central Statistical Office, the Treasury, the DHSS and the Department of Transport on topics as diverse as the distribution of income, fuel consumption, benefit take-up and vehicle ownership. Like the GHS and LFS, the FES is also continuous and designed principally to monitor trends.

In many cases, academic researchers will be analysing these government surveys in a way that has not been done before, and using an analytic framework that was not planned when the data was collected. The problems that this raises will be discussed in the next chapter.

In contrast to the 'descriptive' surveys, there are a number of Government sponsored surveys, conducted by OPCS, which fall clearly into the explanatory mode. These are often ad hoc or 'one-off' surveys – for example, the Family Formation Survey by Karen Dunnell (1979), and *Smoking Attitudes and Behaviour* by Alan Marsh and Jil Matheson (1983) – and usually relate to a specific topic that is of current policy interest. They are commissioned not just for the purpose of providing background data but also with the aim of increasing understanding within the area of concern. For this reason, they are set up with an awareness of the various explanatory models which may be used in analysis, and explore in considerable depth a carefully circumscribed topic. For example, the OPCS Family Formation Survey (Dunnell, 1979) was concerned not just with collecting factual information on women's histories of marriage and child-bearing but with seeking explanations for changes in these patterns. For this reason, information was sought on the circumstances in which each of these events (marriage and child-bearing) took place. However, such an approach necessitates that the researcher responsible for the survey has established an analytic framework which is reflected in the specification of the problem, the form of the questions, and the interpretation of the responses. Although the secondary analyst is free to develop an entirely different analytic framework, the original framework will, to some extent, impose limitations on the alternatives that can be used.

Another recent government ad hoc survey, carried out jointly by OPCS and the Department of Employment, is the Women and

Employment Survey (WES) (Martin and Roberts, 1984a). Fieldwork for this survey was begun only after a great deal of preliminary in-depth questioning, to decide the appropriate concepts to use and the issues that were of importance to the women in the sample. The research was instigated by the Department of Employment in order to explore 'the issues which are germane to understanding why and when women take paid work, with what consequences, and how this relates to the wider issue of their role in the family' (Martin and Roberts, 1984a, p.2). Previous research had identified this gap in knowledge and understanding and the survey was set up to remedy it. On completion of the preliminary analyses, the dataset was deposited at the ESRC Data Archive. In contrast to continuous government surveys such as the GHS and the LFS, the WES approached its topic from the perspective of the women concerned. Although it has become a valuable source of data for supporting feminist arguments, the survey itself did not take an explicitly feminist perspective;[4] rather, it aimed to identify the concepts relevant to the population studied. For example, as preliminary qualitative work (Schlackman, 1979) had shown that the concept of 'not working' may take on quite different meanings to women in differing situations, Martin and Roberts rejected the conventional categories of 'unemployed' and 'economically inactive' as a basis for analysing women not in paid work and established a five-point continuum ranging from 'unemployed', through 'temporarily economically inactive' to 'permanently economically inactive' (Martin and Roberts, 1984a, Table 7.2). The fact that the originators of the survey were able to use an essentially interactionist methodology to establish the coding frames to be used is noteworthy, and will be referred to again in the next chapter. The Women and Employment Survey, therefore, was developed to answer some quite specific questions located within a carefully formulated theoretical framework. Although available for re-analysis, it has already been extensively analysed by the originators and others commissioned by the Department of Employment to carry out specific pieces of research (Dex, 1984; Joshi, 1984). The Women and Employment Survey has also been used in conjunction with the US National Longitudinal Survey for comparative analyses between Britain and the USA (Dex and Shaw, 1986). Although neither survey was set up to be comparable with the other (cf. the Labour Force Surveys of the European Community, which are specifically designed to enable international comparisons), Dex and Shaw were able to draw comparisons on the basis of the work-history aspects of the two surveys.

Rather akin to the Women and Employment Survey in conception and analysis are the many academic surveys that are deposited at the

ESRC Data Archive. These, too, have been carried out to answer a particular research problem and have generally been approached from a predetermined theoretical framework. The initiators of these surveys are usually also responsible for analysing and writing up the results. One of the best known examples of academic surveys is the 1972 Nuffield social mobility inquiry (Goldthorpe, 1980), carried out by the Oxford Mobility Group. This study of occupational mobility among 10,000 men aged 20 to 64 and resident in England and Wales has been the subject of much secondary analysis and is still, fourteen years later, being effectively used (Goldthorpe and Payne, 1986a).

Another academic survey, with a very clear theoretical framework that informs both the structure and content of the questionnaire and the analysis and interpretation of results, is that of Marshall, Rose, Vogler and Newby (1988) at the University of Essex. This study explores the impact of economic recession on class processes in contemporary Britain. It comprises a survey of 1,770 adults in Britain, and is linked to the International Project on Class Structure and Class Consciousness, organized by Erik Olin Wright.

Rather different from most academic surveys is that carried out by Janet Finch as part of a project on family obligations. This is particularly interesting because survey methods are used to tap those obligations that people express towards relatives outside the nuclear family (Finch, 1987). As its purpose is to capture exactly what people regard as 'socially acceptable', it manages to capitalize on the fact that respondents are likely to produce answers that are 'socially acceptable'. Thus, one of the most common bugbears of survey designers can be turned to good advantage.

However, not all microdata available for secondary analysis comes from cross-sectional sample surveys. A cohort study may use all, or a sample of, individuals born during a particular time period. Thus the National Child Development Study (NCDS) used all births occurring in Britain in one week in 1958 (Davie, 1966), and the National Survey of Health and Development drew a sample of all children born in Britain in one week of 1946 (Atkins *et al.*, 1981). In each of these cohort studies the respondents are re-surveyed at varying intervals, thereby enabling a longitudinal database to be set up. The value of longitudinal data lies in the fact that it allows causal mechanisms and processes to be researched, something that is not possible with cross-sectional data where information about the same individual is only available at one time point. British sources of longitudinal data relating to class and health, and reports of research using it are discussed in Blaxter (1986). Chapter 3 discusses cohort studies in more detail.

Longitudinal data does not always have to be collected by means of a special survey. A British data source which has been compiled from a number of primary sources, is the OPCS Longitudinal Study (Fox and Goldblatt, 1982). The LS is based on a 1 per cent sample of individuals drawn originally from the 1971 Census. Those recording their birth on any one of four dates within each year are included; the study is updated annually with new births on each of these four dates. This method of selection approximates to a systematic sampling scheme. Additional data about these selected individuals is linked to the census material; this data comes from public records on births, deaths, immigration and emigration, cancer registers and registers of entry into long-stay psychiatric hospitals. Linked again to those individuals from the 1971 Census is their data from the 1981 Census (Brown and Fox, 1984). This study, then, although based upon pre-existing material, forms a data source that is considerably more than the sum of all its parts. It is described by the authors of the first report as 'a continuous, multi-cohort study following random samples of individuals through time' (Fox and Goldblatt, 1982, p.6). While the primary task of the 1982 Report is specified as showing the ways in which 'data brought together in this way can be used to analyse mortality and to indicate the advantages it offers over more traditional national mortality statistics', its second aim is 'to advertise the study and to encourage its use outside OPCS' (ibid., p.4).

The material in the LS has been combined for both descriptive and explanatory purposes; one of its important features is that it enables *prospective*[5] studies to be made. The Census represents a record of the population at the time of collection, with the data relating to specific events obtained from vital registration records. Once the linkages have been made between all these items for each individual, a unique data source exists, which has enormous explanatory potential. Because of both the longitudinal and prospective aspect of the LS, it allows causality to be incorporated into the research design and, therefore, gets away from the restrictions of cross-sectional surveys, which are confined to measuring associations. Thus the causality of the relationship between unemployment and mortality can be clarified by using this data source (Moser, Fox and Jones, 1986). The LS is not available from the ESRC Data Archive. In fact, the data itself is only available for analysis through the Office of Population Censuses and Surveys (OPCS). This is because the nature of the information which it contains means that it cannot be adequately 'anonymized' and therefore all analysis must be carried out by OPCS in a strictly controlled way. However, potential users of the LS are welcomed by the Social Statistics Unit at the City University in London, which provides support for academic users.

In many ways those who use the LS may be considered analysts of a *primary* data source – the linking of a number of existing items of data results in a *new* database, which has not hitherto been available for analysis in that form. The essential point, however, is that the LS has been formed through the individual linkage of a variety of types of official data and, thereby, has been established as a resource for use by government and other approved researchers.

Historical records can also be used to produce a source of microdata for secondary analysis. A data source that has been compiled from existing records in a rather similar way to the LS is the Amoskeag study by Tamara Haraven (1982). This fascinating dataset represents an enormous effort undertaken by a team of researchers from Clark University, who were allowed access to employee records held by the Amoskeag textile mills in Manchester, New Hampshire, USA. From these and from other public records it has been possible to compile a database that relates to all household members over an extended time period and covers many aspects of their employment, finances and family events. Analysis of this database may be considered as 'secondary' as it represents further analysis of existing material, although the data has not been previously available in this form.

Although the dataset produced by Haraven illustrates the way in which 'secondary analysis' cannot be defined in any precise way, there is one unifying feature common to all the data sources referred to so far. Whether the data is pre-existing but not previously analysed, previously analysed but for a different purpose, or originally in a different form but brought together to produce an essentially new dataset, in all cases there exists a body of data already collected and available for use by others.

All the data discussed so far have been micro-data: that is, data that relates to an individual person and can be used to draw comparisons between individuals within the database. While the primary focus of this book is on microdata, it is also possible to use aggregate[6] data for secondary analysis, either as published statistics, or in a form that can be read by computer and analysed by the researcher (Figure 1.2). Hyman (1972) suggests that Durkheim's classic study of suicide (Durkheim, 1952) is one of the earliest examples of secondary analysis using published statistics. A more recent example of machine-readable aggregate data is the Small Area Statistics of the British Population Census for 1971 and 1981 (see Hakim, 1982, pp.45–94 for a full description) available from the ESRC Data Archive and other sites. The data files of the SAS contain information on total population, sex, age, country of birth, marital status, economic activity, employment status, occupation, housing tenure, density and amenities, all of which can be aggregated to the level of enumeration district, ward, local authority, county, standard region, health district or parliamentary constituency.

Also available from the Archive is the *World Handbook of Political and Social Indicators III, 1948–1977.* This holds aggregate political, economic and social data for 155 countries during this 30-year time period, compiled in machine-readable form for the purpose of secondary analysis. Another form of aggregate data covering employment and unemployment, job vacancies and placements is known by its acronym NOMIS (National On-Line Manpower Information System). This provides very detailed local area statistics throughout Britain, which are regularly updated and accessible to researchers through a computerized link with the University of Durham. This database has been established with support from the Manpower Services Commission (Townsend *et al.*, 1986). The Department of Employment's JUVOS (Joint Unemployment and Vacancies Operating System) unemployment statistics provide another source of aggregate labour market data. These are counts of claimants at benefit offices and are aggregated either to Jobcentre area or post-code sector and are available from the ESRC Data Archive.

The BBC Domesday Project provides a source of aggregate data peculiar to the United Kingdom. Nine hundred years after the original Domesday book was compiled on the orders of William the Conqueror, the BBC decided to assemble another record of life in the United Kingdom in the 1980s. All the information collected is stored on two interactive laser videodisks – the National Disk and the Community Disk, which are played on a special videodisk player. The Community Disk is organized around 24,000 Ordnance Survey maps and provides 150,000 screen pages of text and 20,000 photographs. The National Disk contains a similarly massive amount of information, much of it drawn from material held by the ESRC Data Archive. More than 3,000 tables were supplied by the Archive, drawn from the GHS, FES, LFS, BES and WIRS. Data is organized into four main groups (culture, economy, society and environment) and is rapidly accessed interactively as displays on the video monitor. Using the latest technology available a vast amount of material on the economy and society of the United Kingdom is available, not just for academic use but for schools, libraries and the public in general.[7]

What makes data suitable for secondary analysis?

There is no reason why statistical data should be the only material available for secondary analysis. Research data is obtained not only through surveys and official records but also from documentary analysis, by tape-recording interviews and by video-recording. The Oral History Archive at the North West Regional Studies Institute at the University of Lancaster holds a collection of biographies relating to the nineteenth and twentieth centuries, which are available as transcripts to social historians and other researchers. Similarly, both audio and video recordings of naturally occurring events and sequences are shared among the academic research community and may be subject to repeated examination and analysis (Atkinson and Heritage, 1984; Heath, 1986). However, while all these data sources may be regarded as relatively 'free-standing' and amenable to secondary analysis, the prospect of re-analysing the transcripts from an unstructured interview or ethnographic field-notes raises problems of a kind not encountered in the earlier examples.

In marked contrast to the formal survey where the survey itself is the research instrument, in qualitative research that involves ethnography or in-depth interviewing the researcher becomes the research instrument, with all the 'results' being filtered through her perception and understanding of the social situation in which she is working. The data produced by this means is not only highly dependent upon the researcher but cannot be distanced from her in the way that survey data can. While the prospect of secondary analysis of this kind of data raises immediate issues of confidentiality and anonymity, we may also question whether it is possible for another researcher to use an interview transcript to reconstruct an in-depth interview without first-hand knowledge of the context of the interview, or whether another researcher can re-analyse the field-notes of an unknown colleague. Research of this kind sets out to capture an understanding of a process through a methodology that immerses the researcher in the chosen topic. In these circumstances, it seems unlikely that the re-analysis of either interview transcripts or field-notes by an outsider could give more than a partial understanding of the research issues.

Generally, then, the analysis process of the qualitative researcher involves not just the organization and interpretation of collected data, but also requires an understanding, derived from participating in social interactions, that cannot entirely be recorded on tape or paper. By contrast, in survey-based research, an understanding and knowledge of the substantive area will have been used to inform the construction of the questionnaire, with the result that this knowledge is built into the process of survey design and data collection. Although this means that survey data can be considerably more 'free-standing' than qualitative[8] data, none the less to be successful the secondary analyst must be able to use and interpret the data with the knowledge and insight that went into its original collection.

The juxtaposition of these two different research methods in a discussion of secondary analysis may lead to an initial assumption that survey data must be more objective and more 'scientific' than that produced by qualitative research, especially where it can be demonstrated that responses to surveys are largely independent of the interviewer. However, any such comfortable assumptions can be quickly dispelled.

Although it is true that using structured questionnaires and interviewers who are trained in standard procedures should produce reliable responses, this is only one aspect of the entire research process. The use of the term 'findings' to describe the results of quantitative research reinforces the idea that there are objective 'facts' that are waiting to be gathered (Irvine, Miles and Evans, 1979). In fact, hidden from view in survey research, although more explicit in qualitative work, is the way in which at every stage of the research process decisions are made, either explicitly or by default, which influence the 'data' that is 'produced'. Thus Oakley and Oakley (1979) have pointed to the exclusion of housework from official statistics on employment, and the variety of ways in which 'unemployment' may be defined is the subject of continuing debate. Marsh (1979a) has shown the way in which subtle changes in question wording can produce quite different responses when an opinion is being sought. Thus any claim that data based either upon surveys, interviews or observations can be entirely objective and unbiased cannot be substantiated once we begin to ask such questions as:

Who defines the topic of the research?
Does it set out to provide evidence to substantiate a particular viewpoint?
Whose definitions are used?
What are the implicit assumptions behind the questions?

This is not, of course, to imply that only data that is neutral, objective and value-free has any worth; it is unlikely that such data can ever be achieved. Rather, it is simply to make the point that, while in some kinds of research the subjective elements are readily apparent, in survey-based research they are likely to be hidden from view and can therefore be easily overlooked. Thus data of all kinds and however obtained must be seen as social products that have been 'produced' rather than 'collected', with research results that are 'creations', not 'findings' (Irvine, Miles and Evans, 1979).

Although the extent to which data is free-standing influences its amenability to secondary analysis, it does not mean that data which is 'researcher-independent' is any more objective or neutral than data based upon observation or in-depth interviewing. The Longitudinal Study and the General Household Survey will be used to provide examples to illustrate this point.

In terms of the apparent independence and objectivity of the data, the Longitudinal Study may be seen to epitomize both. The data is drawn from 'official' records, including Census returns, and may therefore appear to be free from the influence of the subjective interpretation or value-laden preconceptions of a researcher. However, although the data used in the LS is largely determined by its availability, intervention on content is none the less present. For example, government has ultimate control over the topics included in the Census, although consultation with interested bodies may influence decisions. The decision not to ask a question on ethnic origin in the 1981 Census was the subject of strong pressure from ethnic minority groups. Social norms and values may also influence the 'creation' of official statistics, such as the cause of death. Thus Atkinson (1978) argues that the cause of death recorded by a coroner is socially constructed and as such is not a static and universally shared category. Reinforcing this point, Armstrong (1986) charts the emergence in the early 1950s of the category of 'sudden infant death' into the records of the Registrar General. He concludes that, for medicine, official statistics 'represent a composite picture of "reality" in that they portray in a unified form a series of individual events. The singular event is related to the total picture through the process of assignment whereby each death is placed at a point on the overall montage. Assignment, however, would appear to be a constantly changing and seemingly haphazard procedure' (Armstrong, 1986, p.229). Thus the data in the LS, although officially generated and not dependent upon the vagaries of a particular researcher, is none the less influenced by the circumstances under which it is produced.

The continuous government surveys are also designed to achieve consistency through time, at least in their core sections, despite changes of OPCS personnel, mobility within the civil service, ministerial re-shuffles and changes in the political party in power. However, many of the questions asked in the General Household Survey are included because they are of direct relevance to political decision-making; conversely, areas in which the government has no concern or interest are not covered. For example, government interest in movement from renting into owner occupation makes housing tenure a key section, and provides little incentive to introduce questions on tenants' management schemes for publicly owned property. Thus, while the core sections of the General Household Survey remain relatively constant, particular items may be expanded or reduced depending upon the concerns of the government of the day. Although by comparison with academic surveys there may be a less obvious theoretical framework, none the less the topics included in government surveys are those accepted as of significance to officialdom. Therefore, by the selection of some topics and the omission of others, these surveys can prescribe the agenda that is available to secondary analysts. Some of these themes will be expanded in the next chapter.

Notes

1 A paperback edition was produced in 1987 by Wesleyan University Press, Connecticut, USA, with a new introduction and subject index but otherwise unaltered.

2 Burrows (1987) provides a discussion of the realist approach which sees the integration of both structuralist and ethnographic approaches as essential. For a detailed discussion of the relationship between qualitative and quantitative methods in social research see Fielding and Fielding (1986); also Denzin (1978) and Silverman (1985).

3 Microdata is data that relates to an individual unit, which may be a person, a household or an organization.

4 It is often argued that survey methods cannot adequately represent women in social research; feminist research would not, therefore, normally use survey-based material. This issue is discussed in some detail in Chapter 2.

5 A prospective study collects data at a number of different time points and at each time point the data relates to the current situation of the respondent. This contrasts with retrospective data, which is collected at one time point but refers to a number of earlier time points.

6 Aggregate data is produced from microdata by aggregation into categories. The categories may be countries, travel-to-work areas, or any other category for which data may be aggregated.

7 Further information on the Domesday project can be obtained from Broadcasting Support Services (Domesday), PO Box 7, London W3 6XJ.

8 Exceptions arise in conversational and video analysis where naturally occurring sequences are recorded and are available for analysis by others.

2

A sociological perspective on secondary analysis

The previous chapter argued that, although it was neither practicable nor necessary to attempt to construct a watertight definition of 'secondary' analysis, none the less it could be readily typified and thereby described. In this chapter we shall consider some of the questions that the secondary analyst needs to ask, both of the data source and also of herself, before embarking upon analysis. We then consider some of the criticisms frequently levelled at survey-based research and the way in which these may be challenged, using exemplars from the secondary analysis of large-scale national government surveys to do so.

Secondary analysis of survey data

Picture the would-be secondary analyst who obtains a copy of the ESRC Data Archive Catalogue and sits down to find out what material is available on her chosen topic. After a time she alights upon an (entirely fictitious) survey entitled *The child-care requirements of non-working mothers*. The Catalogue gives the name and academic institution of the depositor and informs the enquirer that the sample consists of 2,000 'housewives' drawn from a probability sample within five major cities. The majority of the data was collected by use of a pre-coded interview schedule, although a certain number of open-ended questions were coded later: a typical social survey.

Our incipient secondary analyst fills in all the forms sent to her by the Data Archive and in due course receives her data tape and accompanying documentation. The documentation consists of a copy of the interview schedule, the instructions issued to the interviewers, and also the notes on coding procedures, as well as information on the way in which the data is held on the computer tape.

By the simple expedient of filling in a few forms and paying for the costs of producing the data tape, this secondary analyst has at her fingertips a data source that took one year and £100,000 to collect! Moreover, the original survey was carried out by members of a well-respected academic department, and so the data should be of good quality. Having written an SPSS^x set-up file with which to read the data (she may even be fortunate enough to receive this with her data), the researcher is, with a little luck, in a position to specify the analyses that she wishes to make and to generate some results.

By comparison with the primary analyst – the researcher who conducted the survey – the secondary analyst has been able to sidestep all the time-consuming and difficult problems of obtaining funding for the survey, working out an interview schedule, carrying out a pilot study, briefing interviewers, sorting out coding problems, devising categories for the open-ended questions, coding the data and getting it into a form that can be read by computer. While these may be seen by some as mundane run-of-the-mill procedures to which those who carry out surveys have routinely to attend, they serve a *crucial* role in the research process. They not only form the interface between the respondent and the researcher, but also ensure that the researcher has thought through the issues, clarified the concepts to be used and, through the process of the fieldwork, become familiar with the respondent's understanding of the issues and interpretation of the interview questions.

Preliminary considerations

Having neatly sidestepped all these tasks, the secondary analyst must, in order to use the available data sensitively and with validity, confront a different, but equally important set of issues. Stewart (1984) suggests six different kinds of question that those embarking upon secondary analysis should ask themselves. These questions form the basis of those listed below:

1 First, what was the purpose of the study? Was it an academic study designed to explore background issues? Was it a very quick poll aimed at capturing attitudes at one point in time? What was the conceptual framework that informed the study?

The study may have been a fact-gathering exercise that was concerned with drawing together as much information on one particular topic as possible. Alternatively, the researcher may have been trying to establish an explanatory framework and has sought information on a range of topics believed to be significant. Therefore, the purpose of the study – whether descriptive or explanatory – as well as the topic, becomes of relevance to the secondary analyst.

Where a study has used a particular theoretical perspective to explore an issue, the questions asked will relate not just to the subject of investigation, but also to other areas that may be expected to have explanatory value. For example, a study of school truancy, if it is merely a fact-gathering exercise, may collect data on who plays truant, which type of schools are most affected and the number of days off school. However, if the study is interested in explaining the reasons behind truancy, and the researcher is concerned to test the hypothesis that the reasons lie within the school – in the teacher-pupil relationship and the discipline procedures used – then these will form additional areas about which detailed information is gathered. A secondary analyst who wants to use this data to explore truancy using a model that postulates the importance of relationships between home and school and the extent of parental involvement in a child's education, is likely to find that a number of key questions have been omitted. Therefore, if the data has been collected in order to answer a specific hypothesis, it may not lend itself to re-analysis using a different explanatory model.

With either a descriptive or explanatory survey the analyst may find it necessary to derive new variables by combining information from a number of items of data. This is one of the distinctive features of secondary analysis (Hyman, 1955, p.67) and is discussed in some detail in later chapters.

2 What information has been collected? Does it cover the range of issues in which the researcher is interested? What categories have been used for classifying, say, occupation or marital status? Does the data incorporate the distinctions required by the secondary analyst?

The questions asked here will, to some extent, be answered by knowing the purpose of the study and the theoretical framework employed. However, it is essential for the secondary analyst to study with care the documentation relating to the survey and to establish exactly the topics that it covers. This involves obtaining not just the interview schedule but also the instructions to interviewers, the coding frames used and, if possible, the results of the pilot study and any qualitative work that was done as a preliminary exercise. For example, if the researcher is concerned with making a detailed investigation of the occupational structure, then it is essential to find out beforehand what classification has been used and to ensure that it is adequate for the required purpose. It is similarly important to know the basis upon which categories such as 'self-employed' and 'manager' have been assigned, if distinctions of employment status are likely to be important. If the secondary analyst thinks that she may need to distinguish between people who are legally married and those who are cohabiting, then, again, it is necessary to check that the survey to be used incorporates such a distinction. This often entails thinking through, with great care, each stage of the analysis in an attempt to foresee the likely analytical requirements.

3 What sampling frame was used, and what is the sampling unit–that is, has the survey sampled individuals, or households, or employers? What are the potential biases in the data? What is the response rate?

The sampling frame will be chosen to give, as accurately as possible, a listing of the population to be surveyed. In UK surveys, which take the individual as the sampling unit, the Electoral Register is often used to obtain a complete listing of the adult population. However, a survey that samples households, for example the General Household Survey, may use the Postcode Address File (PAF), which lists addresses rather than individuals. While sampling frames are generally chosen as the best available to draw a particular sample, all have their weaknesses. For example, the Electoral Register is between six and eighteen months out of date during the period it is available for sampling. Also, particular groups of the population tend to be under-represented: while about 4 per cent of adults were estimated not to be on the 1981 register, this rose to 25 per cent of those who had moved in the last six months and 14 per cent of citizens of New Commonwealth[1] countries eligible to vote (Todd and Butcher, 1982; Butcher and Dodd, 1983). However, for household-based surveys the Electoral Register may be used as a sampling frame of addresses rather than of individuals which may go some way towards overcoming these problems. The Postcode Address File overcomes the problem of under-representation of specific sub-groups, because it samples addresses, not people and, unlike the Electoral Register, does not depend upon self-registration; it is also frequently updated and has a 98 per cent coverage rate of all private households in Great Britain (Butcher, 1986). (It is, however, restricted to addresses that receive an average of less than 25 items of mail per day, which results in the inclusion of some small firms and the exclusion of some private residences that also serve as business premises.) As it is held on computer tape, the required sample can be drawn very easily.

The Workplace Industrial Relations Survey 1980 and 1984 (Daniel and Millward, 1983; Millward and Stevens, 1986) takes the place of work as the sampling unit and collects information from a maximum of three management representatives (two in 1980) and three employee representatives (two in 1984). For both surveys, the most recently available Census of Employment was used as a sampling frame. It is notoriously difficult to obtain a satisfactory sampling frame of employers – the Census of Employment has the disadvantage that it is likely to be out of date by the time it becomes available (the 1981 Census of Employment was two and half years old when it was used for the 1984 Workplace Industrial Relations Survey (WIRS)); also it does not include workplaces that have no employees paying tax under PAYE (pay as you earn).

Knowledge of the sampling frame used can give the secondary analyst an indication of the extent to which the population sampled is likely to correspond to the 'true' population and the sampling unit used can indicate the kinds of analyses that are appropriate to that dataset. For example, a household-based survey such as the Labour Force Survey, although recording details of employment, cannot adequately support an analysis of *employers' use* of fixed contract labour, although it can provide an estimate of the number of contract workers, the occupations which they fill and their personal characteristics. By contrast, an employer-based survey can focus directly on the ways in which employers use contract workers.

It is always important to know the limitations of the data that is being used. Although we may fall back on the slogan that 'any data is better than none', this is not a very adequate excuse for using poor data, and it is an even less adequate reason for failing to identify and assess the impact of the weaknesses. In some cases, by identifying biases, allowance can be made for their likely effect; if this cannot be done, it may be possible to draw upon another data source to complement the first one.

For example, because of differential non-response, household surveys tend to under-represent elderly people, unmarried men and the self-employed and to over-represent families with dependent children (OPCS, 1981; Rauta, 1985). If this were likely to be important to the results of the research (in fact, it very rarely has a significant effect), then additional information could be obtained from other sources to enable the extent of the misrepresentation to be assessed. Methodological work has been carried out by OPCS on the Family Expenditure Survey to find out whether its response rate of 66–74 per cent causes bias in the results. This was done for both 1971 and 1981 by matching addresses sampled by the FES with those in the Census. Thus, the addresses for which no response was obtained in the FES could be checked against Census information to enable the characteristics of the non-respondents to be assessed. This confirmed the extent of under-representation of households containing elderly people, those with several cars, and the self-employed (Redpath, 1986). Although this sort of work cannot be done by the secondary analyst (only OPCS has access to Census returns and addresses sampled in the FES), the results are published and readily available to FES users. OPCS reports on the General Household Survey also indicate the extent to which the characteristics of the respondents differ from those generated by the latest Census returns (OPCS, 1983). Similarly, OPCS carry out a Census Post-Enumeration Survey (Britton and Birch, 1985) following each decennial Census, where a sample of households is surveyed in order to check the validity of the information collected by the Census (Britton and Birch, 1985). It is perhaps paradoxical that a sample survey may be used to check results from a Census, but the highly trained interviewers who carry out the survey are able to assess the areas where the self-completion methods of the Census lead to errors.

However, in some circumstances differential non-response may give substantially misleading results, which are only picked up if checks are made against other sources. The Family Expenditure Survey collects data on the amount spent on alcohol and tobacco, among many other items. Population estimates derived from the FES show expenditure on alcohol at nearly 50 per cent less than the reported income from sales of alcohol recorded by the National Income Blue Book (Kemsley, Redpath and Holmes, 1980). Through exhaustive methodological work it was found that, although some of this difference is due to under-reporting by the respondent, most is caused by non-response bias and the fact that, as a survey of private households, the FES excludes public houses and hotels. Those occupations in which alcohol consumption is highest (judged by the incidence of deaths from cirrhosis of the liver) are those occupations that are either likely to be excluded from the FES sample (publicans) or those where the respondent is likely to be absent from home when the household is sampled (for example, fishermen and deckhands). It is estimated that these groups, comprising about 5 per cent of the adult population, account for 30 per cent or more of total alcohol consumption, with a further 20 per cent being consumed by 1–2 per cent of the population with a serious drinking problem who are therefore unlikely to be available for interview (Wilson, 1981).

A further study of non-response bias was carried out by OPCS, using a postal survey of young people who had participated in a government-sponsored Youth Opportunities Programme (YOP). The results of the methodological study suggested that, although non-response bias existed in the sense that the 'successful' (measured by current employment status) were more likely to respond than the 'unsuccessful', the effect on the final results was likely to be minimal (Elliot and Thomas, 1983).

However carefully a questionnaire is worded and however well-trained the interviewers, these kinds of bias occur and must be borne in mind. But, for the government surveys, the methodological work done by OPCS means that the secondary analyst who takes the trouble to find out has access to very valuable estimates of bias effects and the likely impact these have on the data collected. In surveys where the response rate is high (both the GHS and LFS have response rates of about 82–85 per cent) non-response bias is a less serious problem than in the FES and other surveys where response is considerably lower.

4 The secondary analyst needs to establish the credentials of the data which she is going to use. Who was responsible for collecting the data? What is the quality of the data?

However good the the credentials of the agency responsible for collecting the data, there must always be a degree of healthy scepticism about both the reliability and the validity of the data. In fact, the more professional the data collection, the more likely it is that the shortcomings of the data will be recognized and assessed. OPCS publish a biannual series of *Survey Methodology Bulletins* (available from OPCS for a small subscription), which report in-house research into topics that include the effects of non-response, question wording tests for the next Census, the use of particular sample designs, an assessment of interviewer variance effects, and an evaluation of the use of the Postcode Address File as an alternative sampling frame to the Electoral Register. Although the British Social Attitudes Survey, carried out by SCPR, has been the vehicle for methodological comparisons of cross-sectional versus panel data (Lievesley and Waterton, 1986), this kind of methodological work is beyond the means of most of the academic researchers and social and market research organizations who make their data available for secondary analysis.

In the final analysis, it is necessary to recognize that the construction of a survey database is a socially negotiated exercise. This is well demonstrated by yet another OPCS methodology study, which measured the amount of variation among coders in assigning respondents to occupational categories. This concluded that 'The probability of two expert coders agreeing on the appropriate social class of any informant is as low as 90 per cent' (Elliot, 1982, p.49). Additional variability may be introduced if there is a lack of precision in the wording of questions relating to occupation and yet more arises through the difficulty that respondents have in describing their own occupations precisely.

5 Is the survey nationally representative? Will it support generalizations about the population sampled? Are any weighting procedures needed?

One of the main reasons for using secondary analysis is because it is the only feasible way of obtaining a nationally representative sample. It is becoming increasingly difficult for social scientists to carry out their own large-scale surveys. The cost of mounting a national sample survey, together with the reductions in funding available to the social sciences, make this a rare option for academic researchers. If it is important to the analyst that her research findings can be generalized, then the secondary analyst should check that the sampling frame and the sampling procedure used allows this. The ESRC Data Archive Catalogue (Taylor, 1986) gives details of sampling methods and response rates for the surveys that it holds, and additional documentation available usually includes a copy of the questionnaire and coding frames; any further queries can be addressed to those who carried out the data collection.

If the secondary analyst is not concerned about generalization and is happy to use a survey that is confined to one particular city or geographical region, then it becomes important to do some background research into the historical and geographical features of that area that may have had an impact upon the data. Census returns for the area, in the form of Small Area Statistics, may provide a valuable means of checking whether or not the survey appears representative of the population sampled. Similarly, labour market data obtained using NOMIS (see Chapter 1, p.14) may be used to provide local parameters on employment and unemployment.

It is very important that the secondary analyst finds out whether the survey requires any weighting procedures to be applied. For example, the Workplace Industrial Relations Survey 1984 gave a higher probability of selection to larger workplaces and used a weighting system to restore the number of cases within each size band to their proportions according to the Census of Employment (Millward and Stevens, 1986). If the secondary analyst overlooks the need to use a weighting procedure, the results obtained may be quite misleading.

6 When was the data collected? Is it still relevant, or have there been substantial changes that make the data source of little value?

For much academic research the fact that the data is five or six years old may not detract from its value. Many theoretically interesting issues concern structures of society that are not liable to short-term change and fluctuation; for example, a model that represents a set of relationships linking economic conditions and voting behaviour may be expected to hold irrespective of the date of the survey. However, those wanting to carry out research of relevance to social policy (for example, on the effect of legislation restricting the power of trade unions), may find it essential to use recent data. Market researchers will place paramount importance on using current data and, for this reason, are unlikely to find much benefit from secondary analysis.

Whatever the importance attached to the age of the data, the analyst should always take into account the political and economic circumstances that may have influenced the results of the survey. For example, a researcher concerned with divorce should be aware of the legislative framework existing at the time of the survey, as well as the prevailing social mores of the period. A particular time period can also have more direct effects on the data collected. The miners' strike of 1974, with the resulting 'three-day working week' for many employees, had a considerable impact upon the income data collected by surveys carried out during that period. Those interview schedules that asked for 'usual' earnings if the most recent pay packet differed from normal were able to cope with this contingency – others were not!

Preliminary questions relating to the proposed analysis

Having listed those questions which should be asked about the data to be analysed, it may also be useful to suggest another set of questions, which the secondary analyst should ask *herself* before beginning work.

1 Is secondary analysis an appropriate method for tackling the research problem?

This raises fundamental points, many of which will be discussed more fully later. The reason for including it here is to acknowledge the fact that secondary analysis is only one method among many and may not be appropriate for all kinds of research. Considerable creativity may be employed in the derivation of a new variable to produce measures which were not included in the original questionnaire (see Chapters 8–11), but there are, none the less, limitations to this, and it may be important to recognize the possibility that secondary analysis is not going to permit you to measure adequately the concepts of importance in your research.

2 What theoretical framework will be used in analysing the data? What are the hypotheses to be tested? What are the questions to be answered?

There is little to prevent the secondary analyst approaching a dataset with a complete absence of both theoretical concepts and understanding of the issues to which the data relate. There is no *requirement* on the secondary analyst to do any of the preliminary thinking that has to be done before designing an interview schedule; nor is there any need to have first-hand experience of the issues covered by the survey.

The relationship between theory and data is one that has always troubled sociologists. C. Wright Mills (1959) adopted the term 'abstracted empiricism' to describe the trend that he saw in American sociology in the 1950s towards increasingly sophisticated quantification, which was replacing the traditional role of theory. He refers to 'the blindness of empirical data without theory and the emptiness of theory without data' (ibid., p.77) and attacks vigorously his fellow social scientist Lazarsfeld for equating 'theory' with the 'variables useful in interpreting statistical findings' and 'empirical data' with such 'statistically determined facts and relations as are numerous, repeatable and measureable'. These sharp warnings are, perhaps, particularly relevant to the secondary analyst who may be tempted to view her ready-made survey data as 'manna from heaven'.

Clearly it is important that the secondary analyst approaches the research with a carefully thought-out conceptual framework, if worthwhile results are to be achieved. It is also important, and perhaps more difficult, to ensure that there is a close relationship between theory and data: there is little value in adopting a theoretical framework that cannot be operationalized.[2] This relationship between theory and data is vital to the success of secondary analysis and will be focused upon more closely in Chapter 4.

For purely practical reasons, particularly when using large government surveys, the number of available variables is such that it is very difficult to do any useful analysis unless one has a clear idea of the research problem. This is not, however, to argue that all secondary analysis must necessarily be confined to hypothesis testing and confirmatory analysis. The expansion of exploratory methods of data analysis in recent years (Tukey, 1977; Hartwig and Dearing, 1979; Marsh, 1988) has provided an alternative way of thinking about data that moves away from the formalities of hypothesis testing based upon statistical summaries such as correlation coefficients and tests of significance. Instead, it allows for exploration of the data structure and advocates graphical expression that reveals rather than conceals any irregularities or deviations in the data. However, the apparent lack of structure of exploratory data analysis is put into perspective by Hartwig and Dearing:

> This is not to say the exploratory data analyst is adrift without a compass in a sea of data. Just as explorers both of earth and space have a guiding rubric, so does the exploratory data analyst. The great explorers of man's physical surroundings struck a delicate balance between following a charted course and remaining open to the unexpected, and so it is with the exploratory data analyst. (Hartwig and Dearing, 1979, p.77)

Exploratory data analysis should not, therefore, be confused with data dredging (Selvin and Stuart, 1966) where the cross-tabulation of every variable accompanied by a request for 'STATISTICS ALL' must not only be seen as a waste of time but should also conjure up 'the image of disappearing Alaskan trees' (Coxon, 1977, p.6). Such methods produce vast amounts of quite unmanageable computer print-out which lead the analyst to search blindly for statistically significant associations between variables, which will invariably be found, but which are unlikely to lead to any advancement in the social sciences.

3 Has the secondary analyst acquired a good knowledge of the substantive area under investigation?

It is to be hoped that an interest in the substantive area will be the propelling factor behind the planned research, but, if not, it is essential to acquire a good grounding in the subject material if the specification and interpretation of analyses are to be meaningful. There is no doubt that it is possible for researchers with very little substantive knowledge to engage in secondary analysis, but the results of such work are unlikely to stand up to scrutiny by those with greater experience of the area and may also fail to build upon work already done. Although a thorough review of all publications in the research area is always important, reports based upon qualitative research may have a particular role to play in giving insight and understanding of the conceptual problems involved and the issues of interpretation that may arise. Mills (1959, p.80), again writing on the topic of 'abstracted empiricism', gives a timely warning of the danger of doing a hasty review of the literature *after* data analysis and of using it to surround an empirical study with a 'cloak of theory'.

4 Does the secondary analyst understand the meaning of the categories used and the methods of coding open-ended questions?

This question leads on directly from the previous one; an understanding of the meanings behind the categories used is likely to produce much better analyses than if no effort has been made to understand the way in which responses are coded. The process of assigning responses to categories plays a crucial role in the interpretation and negotiation that, at least implicitly, goes on between the respondent, the interviewer and the coder. It is during this process that the 'reality' of the respondent is turned into a numerical category in a data file.

Braverman (1974, p.430) points to a distancing from 'reality' that can occur when he writes, 'it is only in the world of census statistics, and not in terms of direct assessment, that an assembly line worker is assumed to have greater skill than the gardener or groundskeeper, the machine feeder greater skill than the longshoreman, the parking lot attendant greater skill than the lumberman or raftsman'.

This is an important point, and much recent criticism of the use of the Registrar General's occupational classification for women has been based upon an apparent distancing from the 'reality' of women's work by the process of assigning occupations to the categories used in official statistics; thus occupations that, on most objective criteria, are highly skilled, tend to be classified as semi-skilled when predominantly held by women (Craig *et al.*, 1982; Dale, Gilbert and Arber, 1983). Cavendish (1982) describes in detail the tasks involved in assembling car components. All the women doing these jobs were classified as semi-skilled, whereas male charge-hands, whose work, Cavendish claims, required much less skill, were not only accorded a higher status and level of pay than the women but would also have been categorized as skilled manual workers by the Registrar General.

This point is further illustrated by the way in which official surveys often categorize the 'self-employed'. In order to establish those who are 'self-employed without employees', the defining principle used in both the GHS and the LFS (if the respondent is unsure) is either how the respondent is described for tax purposes or who pays National Insurance contributions. If this categorization is then accepted at face value as representing the 'self-employed', the unthinking secondary analyst, who assumes that all the self-employed are members of the petty bourgeoisie and therefore own their own means of production and also have control over the labour process, is likely to be making generalizations that are not supported by reality (Dale, 1986a). For example, the fact that 7 per cent of West Indians are classified as self-employed (Brown, 1984) needs to be understood in the light of the additional knowledge that one-half of them are in the construction industry and are likely to be selling their labour to an 'employer'. Many women home-workers are classified as self-employed by official surveys, and it is likely that the recent growth of out-workers (also classified as self-employed, OPCS, 1980) owes more to expediency on the part of employers than to a growth in the petty bourgeoisie. In fact, Hakim (1984, p.148), reporting on the results of the 1980 Workplace Industrial Relations Survey, concludes that homeworkers 'have few or none of the advantages of employee status with no evidence of advantages of self-employment either'. In this instance, the exploration of the category 'self-employed' was provided by a government survey that was specifically designed to clarify the contractual relationship of those who worked either in or from their own home. Thus, the agencies of which Braverman complains may also act as the means whereby anomalies and inconsistencies can be highlighted and remedied.

Even though it may be possible for the secondary analyst to extract 'facts' at the click of a terminal key, these facts cannot be turned into a sociologically informed analysis without the preliminary knowledge and understanding with which to interpret them.

If worthwhile and meaningful results are to be produced by the secondary analyst, as much preliminary thinking, background reading and theoretical development needs to go into the study as would be required if it were a primary survey. Further, the results need to be understood in the context of other studies that approach the issues by using qualitative methods.

The secondary analysis of government survey data

Having discussed in general terms some of the preliminary considerations needed before embarking upon secondary analysis, we shall now look in more detail at specific issues associated with using national-level government survey data. Because of its extensive but largely untapped potential for secondary analysis, we shall discuss some of the ways in which this data can be used imaginatively and effectively within the sociological tradition, and also the limitations of such data. In doing so, we shall explore some of the worries voiced by feminist researchers about the use of survey data (Graham, 1983; Oakley, 1981) and other critics of this research method (Cicourel, 1964; Galtung, 1967). It will be argued that it is often possible to achieve the most fruitful research by linking together and fully utilizing both survey data and qualitative data (Fielding and Fielding, 1986).

Most government surveys in the UK are carried out by OPCS, using trained field staff who conduct highly structured interviews, usually in the home of the respondent. The structured form of these official surveys has a number of consequences for secondary analysis. The first is that the data collected is relatively independent of interviewer effects: OPCS go to great lengths to ensure that interviewer effects, although not absent, will at least be consistent. To achieve this, the questionnaires must be well-tested, the interviewers well-trained and given detailed instructions on the interpretation of answers and when and how to prompt the respondent, and the coders must also be given clear coding procedures. All these instructions are documented and available to the secondary analyst; therefore, the process of negotiation that goes on between interviewer and respondent has, to a considerable extent, been formalized and recorded. The second consequence is that most surveys are largely confined to 'factual' questions and do not explore in depth complex and emotional issues.

The effect of these two factors – formalizing recording procedures and confining the survey to 'factual' questions – makes the task of the secondary analyst considerably easier. In a survey that asks: 'How long have you lived in this accommodation?', the extent to which the researcher or interviewer can influence the answer is limited (Moser and Kalton, 1971). The objections raised by Cicourel (1964, p.113) to 'questionnaire items [that] define social scenes in hypothetical terms which assume that both the meanings of the propositions and the differential responses are invariant to situational interpretations of "rules" and the actor's stock of knowledge at hand', may in the final analysis be correct, but cannot be accepted as an argument for abandoning all use of structured questionnaires. This is not, however, to argue that no inconsistencies can creep into the compilation of the data or that the data recorded can ever be regarded as 'objective facts'. It is worth noting that the Census Post-Enumeration Survey (Britton and Birch, 1985), conducted by OPCS as a means of checking the validity of the Census data, found the greatest mean gross error rate in response to the question on the number of rooms in the accommodation. It may be thought that 'number of rooms' is invariant and not liable to social negotiation. However, a lack of clarity in the definition of a 'room', or an unwillingness by respondents to read the definition, as well as regional and individual differences in the use of rooms, leads to the error rate reported. While this effect results largely from the self-completion methods of the Census, none the less, interviewer effects are also important sources of variation and the methodological literature on them is extensive (Hughes, 1976; Moser and Kalton, 1977; Denzin, 1978; Hyman, 1954). Marsh (1982, Chapter 5) gives a detailed discussion of the ways in which researchers can overcome many of the acknowledged problems deriving from the different social worlds of the interviewer and the respondent. It is sufficient here to make a few basic points.

First, the interview is a social situation, where one important role of the interviewer is to put the respondent at ease and establish a friendly atmosphere, while at the same time being aware of the dangers of 'over-rapport' (Hyman, 1954; Moser and Kalton, 1977). Responses given in this specific social setting may differ from those which would be given under entirely different circumstances (Hughes, 1976). Secondly, the interview is conducted verbally, although there may be self-completion sections. Clearly, the extent to which the respondent understands English and shares a common meaning system will influence the nature of responses. Interpreters are often used for non-English-speaking respondents, but this will inevitably have an influence on the outcome of the interview; where GHS interviewers use an interpreter who is not part of the respondent's household, only the shortened, proxy version of the schedule is completed. Thirdly, questions that require the interviewer to record a description that is coded later (for example, occupation and industry) may be subject to a selective filter by the interviewer (despite the fact that interviewers are given precise instructions about the probes to be used), and the later coding of this information has been shown to result in a 10 per cent coder variation (Elliot, 1982). These are all methodological hazards well known to those who work with surveys and which need to be borne in mind by users of survey data, particularly where they have not, themselves, experienced the process of interviewing and recording information. However, none of these factors of itself negates the secondary analysis of the data; rather, such qualifications need to be thoroughly understood before embarking upon the research.

A further effect of the 'free-standing' nature of the data collected by these government surveys is that the data tends to be primarily descriptive and fragmentary in nature. A highly structured interview is not an appropriate medium through which to explore meanings or beliefs and rarely provides a means of capturing the complexities of a respondent's life (Blumer, 1956; Hughes, 1976). It is fragmentary because information is recorded as discrete answers to discrete questions and must therefore compartmentalize data into that relating to 'education', 'health' or 'income', rather than producing an explanation of the way in which these all interrelate for the individual in question. None the less, the secondary analysis of such data need not be purely descriptive and confined to discrete aspects of the respondents' lives. The statistical relationship between variables can be examined within a model that assumes an interrelationship, with interaction effects between variables.

From the discussion above it is apparent that, although observations may be counted and recorded, trends plotted and relationships established, cross-sectional survey data is unlikely to provide an adequate answer to all those questions that sociologists may wish to ask. These include such questions as:

What does it feel like to live on this income level?
What are the reasons for the relationship between gender and frequency of doctor consultations?
What kinds of family tensions are generated by long-term unemployment?
What are the reasons for non-takeup of supplementary benefits?

Such questions would usually be best answered by qualitative methods, although it is arguable that, with sufficient qualitative work at the developmental stage, even these questions are amenable to survey research. However, survey material of the kind usually available for secondary analysis may be particularly valuable in providing an indication of the extent and distribution of the topic of concern – low income families, or levels of unemployment – and also in enabling structural relationships to be established within which answers obtained from qualitative research can be interpreted and understood.

The use of government surveys for conceptual work

Although often collected primarily for descriptive purposes, the government surveys discussed here may form the basis for conceptual work on widely used and fundamental social indicators such as social class and occupation (Burgess, 1986). The detailed nature of many of the questions (for example, on occupation, income and consumption) and the size and representativeness of the sample make it possible to use these data to develop and test new and perhaps more appropriate social indicators. For example, existing ways of categorizing occupations, particularly the Registrar General's classification, were developed for men and therefore reflect the divisions of skill typically associated with jobs held by men. In a project using the General Household Survey, the traditional skill divisions by which the Registrar General's classification allocates individuals to classes were ignored and, instead, women were re-classified on the basis of a concept of 'labour market power', which incorporated variables relating to income, fringe benefits and educational qualifications (Dale, Gilbert and Arber, 1985). By this method, women's occupations[3] were found to group together in a way that broke through many of the traditional divisions of skill and crossed the manual/non-manual divide. For example, shop assistants, classified as non-manual workers by the Registrar General, were found to be similar in 'market power' to cleaners, hospital orderlies and packers. Women working in manufacturing industries, despite being classified as semi-skilled by most government surveys, were shown to differ significantly from those in other groups of 'semi-skilled' occupations. The distribution of women in these classes, derived from a measure of labour market power, could then be compared with traditional Registrar General's classes. In this work, evidence from participant observation (Pollert, 1981; Cavendish, 1982; West, 1982) was invaluable in giving a better understanding of the reasons behind the occupational groupings which had been derived from empirical measures of labour market power.

Extending this kind of conceptual work further, Roberts (1986) and Barker and Roberts (1987) have used Census data drawn from the OPCS Longitudinal Study to incorporate information on women's occupations, the number and age of their children, their housing tenure and husband's class into a number of women's 'work positions'. These totally new categories provide another, quite original way of classifying women's occupations, which is far removed from anything in the minds of those who planned the original survey or Census schedules.

Thus, although it is often assumed that the secondary analyst has no control over the way in which data is categorized, this may not necessarily be a barrier to research but, given the availability of variables that can serve as 'building blocks', may form a spur to the sociologist who finds the existing categorizations unsatisfactory.

A feminist perspective on secondary analysis

In these last two examples it is noteworthy that the subject of research has been women. Surveys in general are often criticized for (a) being male-oriented, in concentrating on the 'public' world of men; (b) for misrepresenting women's lives by the 'variable-centred' method of the survey (Graham, 1983); (c) for assuming that men and women form equivalent social units (Graham, 1983; Hughes, 1976; Galtung, 1967); and (d) for assuming a dominant (male) role of the interviewer against a subordinate (female) role of the interviewee (Oakley, 1981). These criticisms raise some important issues for secondary analysts and will therefore be considered in some detail.

1 SURVEYS AND THE PUBLIC WORLD OF MEN

It is undoubtedly true that the first surveys were carried out by men (Booth, 1889; Rowntree, 1902) and that subsequent development of survey methods was mainly a male preserve (Bowley, 1915). However, this does not necessarily mean that surveys can only represent men's interests. The criticism that surveys, by focusing on issues such as employment, housing and income, represent the 'public' world of men rather than the 'private' world of women is in danger of perpetuating the idea that women 'naturally' belong to a private and domestic world. In fact, there is no necessity for the survey to be confined to researching a 'public' sphere. Although it is true that government surveys do not include housework within the definition of 'employment' (Oakley and Oakley, 1979), the use of time-budget surveys has proved to be a method of adapting the survey to take into account the time spent both within the home and outside it, by all household members (Gershuny *et al.*, 1986). Furthermore, even official government surveys are concerned with 'female' topics such as abortion and sterilization, contraception and child-birth (OPCS, 1986); disabled people living at home (Martin and Bone, 1986); and the extent to which household tasks are shared between spouses (Martin and Roberts, 1984a).

Although it may be argued that this data is produced to answer problems that trouble government rather than explicitly to benefit the women who provide the data, these two factors are not necessarily mutually exclusive. More important, because the results of these surveys are not only published in report form (e.g. *Women and Employment: A Lifetime Perspective*) but are also available for secondary analysis,[4] they provide an opportunity for others to ensure that the data is fully used for purposes that promote the interests of women or whatever group makes up the study. Data from most of the government sources mentioned has been used by the Family Policy Study Centre and the Child Poverty Action Group (CPAG) to highlight policy issues of particular relevance to women – for example, social security reform, family poverty, the care of elderly dependants (Family Policy Study Centre, 1983, 1986; CPAG, 1984). Systematic analysis of the inequalities between men and women within the occupational structure is possible through secondary analysis of the Labour Force Survey. Although the LFS is unequivocally concerned with the 'public' world of work, because it includes questions on casual or temporary work, and home working (OPCS, 1982), it is able to support research on a national basis into the inadequacies of women's paid work by comparison with men's in a way that would not otherwise be possible. Through secondary analysis of the LFS, the differential access of men and women to internal labour markets can be demonstrated and, in particular, the way in which women working part-time systematically fail to gain access to jobs with promotion prospects (Dale, 1987b). Such research is able to reinforce and give a national dimension to studies of local labour markets that have suggested the processes through which the structuring of the labour market may take place. Thus, the very fact that government surveys *do* often assume an equivalence between men and women means that databases are available by which to draw comparisons based upon gender.

2 THE VARIABLE-CENTRED APPROACH OF THE SURVEY

The charge that surveys fragment the complexities of life into 'discrete, clean-cut and unitary variables' (Blumer, 1956; Procter and Abell, 1985) has already been mentioned. This fragmentation is felt to particularly misrepresent the lives that women lead (Graham, 1983). Clearly, surveys do tend to iron out the uncertainties of life and present a rather more clearly defined picture than might be obtained by qualitative methods. It would be foolish to claim that a structured survey can ever fully represent the complex social life of any individual, family or household. But to assume that, because of this, survey data can have no useful role to play in the research process is as unhelpful as to argue that there is no role for research methods that are not quantifiable or that cannot be generalized. What must be recognized is that if research is to achieve the maximum in terms of explanation and understanding it is unlikely to depend solely upon any one method. It is important, therefore, that those who use a particular methodology realize its strengths and limitations and use it appropriately. The survey method does, inevitably, deal with discrete variables and may not be an appropriate medium for exploring feelings, or complex relationships. However, if used appropriately, there is no reason why, with careful preliminary work, the variables used in a survey cannot reflect accurately the experience of life – both men's and women's. For example, the qualitative work (Schlackman, 1979) that preceded the construction of the questionnaire used in the Women and Employment

Survey (Martin and Roberts, 1984a) had a considerable influence on the final schedule and ensured that the categories used in the variable construction corresponded as closely as possible to the realities of the women's lives.

3 SURVEYS TREAT MEN AND WOMEN AS EQUIVALENT SOCIAL UNITS

The survey is also criticized for assuming that individuals can be treated as units (Galtung, 1967), although there is no necessity for a survey to take the individual as a unit of analysis; the household-based surveys such as the GHS and FES use the household as the unit of analysis, distinguishing also families within the household. By the use of data-management packages such as SIR (Scientific Information Retrieval), it is now possible to analyse relationships between different individuals within the same household. Thus the research design can take account of the fact that people do not act in isolation from those with whom they live and can begin to develop ways of measuring interactions. Clearly, not all interactions are amenable to survey methods, but the relationship between employment status of household members can be analysed, and the way in which this leads to occupational inequality between men and women can be shown (Dale, 1986b). Thus, by taking the household as the unit of production (Redclift and Mingione, 1985; Pahl, 1984) and assuming that members of the same household are not equal or equivalent but have differential access to paid work, inequalities may be revealed rather than obscured. Household surveys are further criticized because 'they tend to treat households as bundles of equivalent individuals and not as men and women occupying different and unequal positions within both the home and the wider society' (Graham, 1983, p.139). Although it is true that household level surveys rarely distinguish the distribution of resources within the household, this is largely because this has not been a question of particular interest to those who conduct or finance surveys. As it is now possible to record differences in time use by household members (Gershuny *et al.*, 1986) so it should be possible to develop a methodology by which to record use of domestic space, or the allocation of other resources between household members.[5] It is, then, more appropriate to blame those responsible for the survey design rather than the survey method itself for many of these shortcomings. Growing recognition of the importance of intra-household inequalities within policy-making circles (Platt, 1987) gives rise to hopes for a reappraisal of the design of household surveys in order to incorporate this dimension explicitly.

None the less, it is argued that the survey can only record the *structure* of the gender relations within the household, and not the *impact* of them.

Thus Graham writes: 'In obscuring the relationships which mould women's lives, the survey method masks the nature and patterns of power which derive from these social relationships' (Graham, 1983, p.140). While the survey can never be the most appropriate methodology for all kinds of research, it may none the less serve a valuable role for women if it can record accurately the structure and extent of gender-based inequalities within society, although, as Graham makes clear, it is important that the power which resides within gender relations is not lost from view.

4 THE ROLE OF INTERVIEWER VERSUS RESPONDENT

Finally, the argument that the interviewer adopts a superior (male) role to that of the subordinate (female) interviewee (Oakley, 1981) can surely not withstand an examination of the way in which most social surveys are conducted? Despite the use of the male pronoun in many textbooks, men do not have a prerogative of survey research, either in the formulation of the questionnaire or in carrying out the interview. Half of the OPCS social survey officers and more than half of the interviewers are women. In a household-based survey, the interviewer is allowed into the home by the interviewee and is, therefore, in the position of a guest, dependent upon the good nature of the interviewee – who may be either male or female. Although it is true that the interviewer formulates the issues and asks the questions, the interviewee holds the ultimate power of refusal. In the following chapter it will be suggested that the formal approach of the survey may, in fact, protect the respondent from revealing detailed personal information that may later be regretted and also provides the respondent with an opportunity to refuse to answer intrusive questions.

In summary, we would argue that secondary analysis can provide a valuable method by which to research issues relevant to both men and women. Clearly, it is not a method that is suitable for all research problems and an important first step for any social researcher is to identify the methods that are going to be most appropriate to the problem under investigation. Where secondary analysis of survey data is identified as an appropriate method, its value may be enhanced by incorporating evidence from qualitative methods into the analysis. There is no need for qualitative and quantitative methods to be seen as adversarial or mutually exclusive. The link between macro and micro analysis forms the theme of the final section of this chapter.

The relationship between survey and qualitative research

So far, it has been emphasized that the secondary analyst needs to be fully acquainted with the substantive area of analysis and that qualitative studies (in-depth interviewing, ethnography, participant observation) can provide an invaluable means of gaining insight and understanding of the relationships established by survey research. While survey-based methods are traditionally thought of as suitable for 'confirmatory analysis' and qualitative methods for 'exploratory work', there is little reason to make a rigid differentiation between the roles that they can play. The confirmatory role of the survey derives from the assumption that, by using a representative sample and testing a hypothesis-based model, the probability of the observed relationships occurring through chance can be assessed and the results generalized to the population at large (Moser and Kalton, 1971). However, there is no necessity for the secondary analyst to use this particular mode of research. Although it is necessary to establish what the research problem is, exploratory methods of data analysis, referred to in the previous chapter, may form an alternative to hypothesis testing. In either case, there is likely to be a two-way process between data and theory, with initial analysis of the data leading to a modification of the original theory (if the confirmatory mode of analysis is used), and with interpretation tempered by an awareness of the research of others who use different methods and different theoretical perspectives.

An example to illustrate the way in which survey and qualitative research can interact is described below. Particular manufacturing industries are characterized by low wages among manual workers – notably textiles, footwear, clothing and leather. From the New Earnings Survey 1983 (Department of Employment, 1983) it is apparent that, for both men and women, these industry groups have average hourly earnings that are low by comparison with most other groups. At the same time, the 1981 Labour Force Survey (OPCS, 1982) shows that, of those women of Indian and Pakistani ethnic origin in employment, a very high proportion work in the manufacturing sector (particularly in these four industries) but that women of this ethnic origin also have rates of unemployment more than double the national average of 9 per cent for all women in 1981. The reported figures can lead one to build a hypothesis based upon the relationship between unemployment and wage rates, which incorporates the additional effect of a female workforce with very little bargaining power. However, to establish whether or not there was any causal linkage between these observations, and to tease out the processes through which they might operate, would probably need an in-depth study of employers of the kind carried out by Craig *et al.* (1985) into the factors determining wage rates in small firms. This kind of in-depth work can, in turn, highlight the areas where survey data can usefully test relationships at a macro level. Thus, an analysis can be slowly and carefully built up, on the one hand keeping an open mind about unpredicted relationships in the data and on the other ensuring that whatever the theoretical framework used it is underpinned by evidence from other studies, both qualitative and quantitative. Fielding and Fielding (1986) give examples of the way in which qualitative and quantitative research can work together, drawing upon their research on the police.

Qualitative research can also enhance the value of secondary analysis of large-scale surveys by providing greater depth of information, particularly by suggesting the underlying processes that are responsible for the observed relationships. A great deal of the material available for secondary analysis is cross-sectional, which makes it impossible to distinguish the direction of causality between associations; for example, women who work part-time are more likely to provide care for a sick or elderly dependant than women working full-time (Martin and Roberts, 1984a, p.133). However, this may be either because they are obliged to give up full-time jobs to do this or, alternatively, that women who are not in full-time work are more likely to offer, or be expected, to care for a dependant. Although this could be asked as a retrospective survey question, the results of such a question are likely to be unreliable and, by presenting a simple dichotomy, may also fail to disentangle the complexities of the decision.

A similar problem that occurs with cross-sectional data is that such data cannot be used to assess the extent to which relationships observed at the time of the survey are still influenced by events long since past. As cross-sectional data is most often used for secondary analysis it may, again, be useful to look at other sources, whether qualitative or longitudinal survey data, to obtain further insights. For example, research that uses cross-sectional data to establish the relationship between married women's work participation and the presence of a sick or elderly dependant in the household is unable to assess the continuing effect on labour force participation of time spent caring for an elderly relative who has since died. These women would appear in the survey as having no elderly dependent relative. Although a retrospective question may be used in a cross-sectional design, this presents problems of recall and post hoc rationalization. It is valuable, therefore, to explore other sources of information in order to gain an indication of whether cross-sectional data may give misleading results. An in-depth study by

Yeandle (1986) of the work and family histories of fourteen middle-aged women showed that, although only three were currently caring for an elderly dependant, a total of eight women had been responsible for the care of an elderly dependant at some time during their married lives. Several of the women felt that their present employment situation was still affected by their previous caring commitments. Thus, this research can provide an indication, although not quantifiable, of whether results from cross-sectional data may be misleading. Neither data source can establish with certainty what effect an earlier period of caring has on current employment – this can only be achieved by using true longitudinal data.[6] Sampling limitations and sample size make it impossible to generalize from the study by Yeandle, and her use of retrospective questioning makes it possible that post hoc rationalizations were influencing responses. None the less, the study is valuable to the secondary analyst using cross-sectional data, as it alerts her to the possibility that earlier, unrecorded periods of caring may be affecting the current employment position of some women and that caution is needed in interpreting results.

From the preceding discussion it is apparent that, whatever research method is used, longitudinal data has a vital role to play in establishing the causal ordering of social processes and in recording change at an individual rather than an aggregate level.

Conclusions

This chapter has tried to show the range of secondary analysis that is available to the sociologist and the ways in which such analysis may be used to do sound and interesting research. It has also raised some questions and provided some answers for those embarking upon secondary analysis for the first time. Although survey data provides by far the largest source of material available for secondary analysis, there is no reason why it must be used strictly within traditional methods of hypothesis testing; it may alternatively be used in an exploratory way or for developing new ways of measuring concepts such as social class. If used with an awareness of its limitations and an understanding of the basis on which it was collected, it is able to provide an important descriptive and analytic framework within which to understand the social processes operating within the world.

Notes

1 The term New Commonwealth refers to all Commonwealth countries except Australia, Canada and New Zealand. Pakistan left the Commonwealth in 1973 but is generally included with the New Commonwealth in a category termed 'New Commonwealth and Pakistan' (NCWP).
2 This argument is challenged by realist modes of concept formation that accept that empirical observation may be generated by real phenomena that are not empirically observable or testable (Burrows, 1987).
3 The GHS coded occupations to the detailed 223 category Occupational Unit Group (OPCS, 1970) until 1977, after which date they were coded to a higher level of aggregation. Detailed coding recommenced in 1985.
4 The Autumn 1986 Equal Opportunities Commission Research Bulletin (EOC, 1986) deals with methodological issues in gender research and, in particular, the secondary analysis of the Women and Employment Survey (Dex, 1986).
5 Pahl's work (1983) on the unequal allocation of money within households provides the foundation for methodological development.
6 An example of a British longitudinal study that provided evidence of the *effect* of husbands' unemployment benefit on the employment status of their wives is found in Moylan, Millar and Davies (1984).

3

Benefits and costs of secondary analysis

Hyman (1972, p.2) quotes Newton as saying 'If I have seen further, it is by standing on the shoulders of giants'. This seems to epitomize the single most important benefit of secondary analysis. Although all knowledge builds upon the work of others who have gone before, secondary analysis enables this to happen in a much more direct and practical sense than is usually the case. The economic aspects have already been mentioned; enormous savings of both money and time are to be made (Hyman, 1972; Kiecolt and Nathan, 1985), but, more fundamentally, the benefit of the years of expertise that have gone into establishing organizations such as OPCS or SCPR in Britain, and the National Opinion Research Center in the USA, are available to the secondary analyst for little more than the cost of the data tape that holds the material.

This chapter will be concerned with the specific advantages that can be gained by secondary analysis and also with the reverse side of the coin – the costs and disadvantages. As benefits and costs are often interlinked, and weighted differently depending upon specific circumstances, no attempt will be made to compile two separate lists, but, rather, to focus on those features that are distinctive to secondary analysis.

The more obvious financial savings that secondary analysis can provide are of particular value to the lone researcher who wishes to use quantitative methods but has no source of funding, or to the research student who does not have the resources to carry out the primary data collection necessary to answer a particular research problem. However, secondary analysis can do much more than just save the researcher the time and expense of conducting her own survey.

The national government surveys provide one of the most widely used sources of secondary data and form an important theme of this book. Therefore it is appropriate to begin this chapter by considering the specific benefits that these datasets offer the social researcher and also the disadvantages associated with their use. Following this, some further examples will be provided of the way in which secondary analysis can enable specific kinds of research that might otherwise be impossible. The final section will consider the ethical issues associated with secondary analysis and ponder on the costs and benefits to both the researcher and the researched.

Benefits and costs of secondary analysis of government surveys

The large-scale national government surveys represent very high quality data with careful questionnaire design, fieldwork and methodological development. Because of their relative consistency over time, their large sample size and national representativeness, surveys such as the Family Expenditure Survey and the General Household Survey have been widely used by economists for many years, particularly for trend analyses, and are now becoming more extensively used in other disciplines of social science.

The continuous government social surveys ask of their respondents questions that are primarily 'factual'. Some (for example, size of household, housing amenities and possession of consumer durables) are of a kind frequently collected by market research organizations or local authority surveys. Others ask for information that is regularly recorded by employers, doctors or the Inland Revenue (for example, number of children, dates of birth and marriage, earnings, tax and national insurance deductions, income from property or investments). However, although this information may already be recorded by various agencies, it is not available for analysis in an anonymized form, and neither are the various pieces of information linked together to give the detailed picture that is available from the government household surveys. It is only through surveys such as the GHS and FES that it is possible to obtain this range of information, for all sections of the population, in the form of microdata that can be analysed at the level either of the individual or of the household. The availability of these large-scale datasets for secondary analysis therefore presents a unique opportunity to the academic community.

Users of these large datasets may also receive a variety of forms of support and information from the ESRC Data Archive. For example, regular data-use workshops are held on specific datasets; the Archive produces a regular newsletter for users of the GHS, and also runs a 'Bulletin Board Service', which enables users of a range of datasets to hold teleconferences and send each other mail. Further information on this range of services is available from the ESRC Data Archive at the

University of Essex. Similarly, the Inter-University Consortium for Political and Social Research (ICPSR) at Michigan provide information, training and support facilities for social scientists who use its data archive.

The diversity of research that can be supported by the large government surveys is shown by the subjects of some research projects for which the General Household Survey has been used in recent years:

Inter-generational mobility of Irish immigrants (Hornsby-Smith and Dale, 1988).
The life course of individuals in the family (Murphy, 1983).
The household structure of the elderly (Dale *et al.*, 1987).
Changes in the youth labour market, 1974-1981 (Payne, 1985).
Stratification in youth (Jones, 1986) .
Co-habitation in Great Britain (Brown and Kiernan, 1981).
Gender and class inequalities in health (Arber, 1988)
Equity and efficiency in the allocation of the personal social services (Bebbington and Davies, 1983).
Alternative measures of social class for women and families (Dale, Gilbert and Arber, 1983).
The causes of poverty (Layard *et al.*, 1978).

A similarly wide-ranging list of research projects based upon the Family Expenditure Survey could also be compiled; in both cases, the surveys are able to support extensive and detailed analysis of a wide range of topics. However, from some of the research topics listed above it is also apparent that the GHS may be used as a means of defining and studying small sub-groups within the population.

Using government surveys to analyse sub-groups

Social researchers are often interested in very specific sub-groups of the population – for example, those who were born in the Republic of Eire and have migrated to Britain; cohabitees; those who are covered by private medical insurance; those who rent property from Housing Associations; those who hold two jobs. However, there is often no available sampling frame for the group to be studied (e.g. cohabitees, Irish immigrants), thus making it very difficult to carry out one's own survey and often leaving secondary analysis as the only practicable alternative. In some cases, government surveys provide the sampling frame by which OPCS selects respondents for smaller and more intensive studies of sub-groups. For example, the 1981 Labour Force

Survey was used to generate a sample of home-based workers for the *1981 National Homeworking Survey* (Hakim, 1987a).

The sample size of the GHS is sufficiently large to provide a representative sample of many sub-groups, although in some cases it may prove advantageous to combine data over several years. Because of the continuity of questions over time, this is usually possible. For example, in a study of the early retired, using the GHS, data was combined over a three-year time period in order to gain a sufficiently large sample size (Laczko *et al.*, 1988). (If data is combined over several years it is important to ensure that the period covered is not one during which any considerable changes were affecting the group in question).

Even where the main thrust of the research is an in-depth study of a particular sub-group, it is often important to be able to locate this sub-group within the population as a whole and to ascertain the extent to which it differs from that population. For example, while it might be assumed that Irish immigrant men are found to a disproportionate extent in manual labouring jobs, an in-depth study of the occupational barriers encountered by this group of men would be greatly enhanced by prior knowledge of the way in which their occupational distribution differed, if at all, from that of the population generally. Secondary analysis, then, can be particularly useful to the researcher making a small in-depth study who needs to locate it within a national context. Often data on particular sub-groups is only available through secondary analysis of nationally representative surveys.

However, although secondary analysis may provide a valuable means of studying small sub-groups, particular attention needs to be paid to the sampling frame used and the response rate, as both may in some cases cause results to be unrepresentative. For example, where the sampling frame is based upon private households, a study of the very old may under-represent the most infirm, who are disproportionately likely to be in institutional care and therefore outside the sampling frame. Problems may also arise if the sampling frame used systematically under-represents a certain section of the population. We have already drawn attention to the way in which the Electoral Register under-represents some sections of the population (Chapter 2, p.22) particularly people from New Commonwealth countries, or the highly mobile. Selective non-response among sub-groups such as the self-employed may also give rise to inaccuracies of analysis.

These household surveys are valuable because they provide the possibility of research on a number of relatively inaccessible sub-groups, but there is, none the less, the danger that the research agenda may be inadvertently constrained to accommodate those issues that are accessible through secondary analysis. Thus potentially important debates may be neglected while attention is concentrated on maximizing the findings from those areas for which data does exist.

For example, while the General Household Survey contains a detailed section on family formation and cohabitation, information on these subjects was, until 1986, asked only of women. This rendered any national-level research on the marital history of male lone parents impossible to carry out, although comparable data for women is readily available and one-parent families have formed the subject of a considerable amount of research (Popay *et al.*, 1983). Another example from the GHS concerns questions on the use of private consultations with a doctor. Between 1974 and 1982 questions on whether doctor consultations were made under the NHS or privately were dropped from the interview schedule. Had this data been available, it might well have formed the subject of a research project to analyse trends in use of private health care during that period of time. There are no other national-level data sources that would allow use of private health care to be analysed in relation to occupation, stage of life-cycle, income and health status. Although it may be difficult for the researcher to overcome these gaps in available information, it is none the less important that they are recognized and do not form a hidden influence upon the research process.

The secondary analysis of government surveys, by providing a data source of unsurpassed size, scope and quality, which can be used to make inferences about the population as a whole and also about certain subsections of the population, raises issues that go beyond those usually encountered in secondary analysis of academic surveys. Because this data is collected by government, for use by government, it carries with it a credibility that may be lacking in many other data sources, and those who use it may find that publications based on its analysis carry more weight than might otherwise be the case. While it is easy to accept unquestioningly the definitions and concepts of the survey, and to use the officially collected data to represent complex concepts such as 'personal income' or 'level of consumption', we would reiterate the arguments made in Chapter 2, that the secondary analyst should question both the basis upon which data is collected and also the meanings that can be attributed to the data.

Comparative studies

Secondary analysis can also provide a means by which comparative research may be possible. Comparative analysis, whether nationally, cross-nationally or over time, often requires considerable resources of both time and money, which are likely to present problems to those without access to large funding organizations. Therefore, for many researchers, secondary analysis provides the only possibility of doing this kind of work. Within Britain, the Economic and Social Research Council has initiated a comparative study of six localities under the title 'Social change and economic life'. Each locality study contains an employer's survey, a work-attitudes survey and a household-based survey, with a common component in each to enable comparative analysis. At a total cost of more than £1,000,000 and involving a number of years of careful planning as well as more than 30 team members, this kind of study is not an option likely to be considered by many researchers! However, as with all ESRC-financed surveys, this data will be available for secondary analysis from the ESRC Data Archive soon after the end of the research programme.

Comparative cross-national research poses even more problems; the sheer organizational task of getting together a group of co-operating researchers in a number of countries and agreeing on a questionnaire in which the question wording has the same meaning for respondents in each country is daunting, to say the least. To get such an undertaking funded is likely to be even more difficult. Many of these issues are discussed in Shanas and Madge (1968), with reference to the Danish, British and American study of old people made in the early 1960s (Shanas *et al.*, 1968). A more recent project that has managed to overcome these obstacles has been initiated by Erik Olin Wright and forms a major international study of class structure in twenty different countries. The British survey has been conducted in Britain at the University of Essex, with funding from the ESRC (Marshall *et al.*, 1988; Rose *et al.*, 1987). Data from most of the countries participating in this project will be deposited at the ESRC Data Archive and should form an important data source for secondary analysis.

Even where surveys have been designed to provide comparability between countries it is frequently the case that national legislation on data protection does not allow that data to be 'exported' to users in other countries. For example, the Statistical Office of the European Community commissions from member countries an annual Labour Force Survey designed to enable international comparisons to be made. A standard questionnaire schedule and coding framework is discussed and agreed by all member states, and regular publications based upon the data are produced in Luxembourg. However, data protection legislation does not allow SOEC to release these data tapes to a user in another country. This forms a major obstacle to the aspiring secondary analyst who is interested in this material, but, although SOEC is not allowed to release the tapes, this restriction does not apply to the member country that collects the data. Individual countries are subject to their own national legislation with respect to the release of data. Some countries (for example, France) are willing to allow this data to be used abroad, but others (Norway, Sweden) insist upon all analysis being carried out within the country of origin.

If access to data is allowed only in this restricted form, then co-operative research with a resident of the country concerned may allow the comparative element to be retained. This can often prove to be a very fruitful form of working, as it means that the collaborators can provide for each other the detailed knowledge of their own data that would not otherwise be available. Examples of this kind of co-operative research have resulted in studies of temporary employment in Britain and Germany (Casey, 1988) and a comparison of the effectiveness of Equal Opportunities legislation in Britain and the USA (Dex and Shaw, 1986). The latter study used the British Women and Employment Survey and the American National Longitudinal Study (this latter survey is discussed in more detail later in this chapter). By a choice of two age-cohorts and careful selection of variables, as well as some time-consuming re-coding of occupation and industry codes, the authors were satisfied that they had achieved sufficient comparability for meaningful results to be achieved.

The Luxembourg Income Study (Rainwater, Smeeding and Schmaus, 1985) is a cross-national database set up under the sponsorship of the government of Luxembourg. It draws upon seven different national data sources to which researchers may have access, but which is not distributed. It provides comparative measures of income, taxation and benefits, household and family composition and labour market data. Data for the UK is drawn from the Family Expenditure Survey, and that for the USA from the Current Population Survey. The database may be accessed by a telecommunications network from Europe and the USA, or SPSS^{x} data requests can be mailed to Luxembourg on magnetic tape or floppy disk and the results mailed back. Alternatively, researchers may visit the Center for Population, Poverty and Policy Studies in Luxembourg and carry out their own analyses.

Perhaps one of the most successful and ambitious comparative surveys is the World Fertility Survey, begun in the early 1970s under the aegis of the International Statistical Institute at Voorburg, Netherlands. The aim of the project was to assist participating countries to collect internationally comparable data to describe and explain the fertility of their population (Scott and Chidambaram, 1985, p.9). The work has resulted in the production of standard magnetic tapes for forty-two countries, stored and distributed by the World Fertility Survey archive and used by more than 300 institutions world-wide (ibid., p.15).

Analysing trends over time

Time series data, whether cross-sectional or longitudinal, are again almost impossible for the academic researcher to collect. While it may be possible to sample successively over a three-year or even five-year period, anything longer requires a greater financial commitment than most academic researchers are likely to achieve. Some of the most notable longitudinal studies have arisen from a policy concern that has received funding by government. In Britain, longitudinal methods have been most often used in health-related research, particularly where factors influencing the development of children have been of interest. Their particular value lies in the fact that they are prospective as opposed to retrospective and, therefore, do not rely upon the quality of a respondent's memory. Longitudinal studies in Britain relevant to health issues have been comprehensively reviewed by Blaxter (1986), although not all the data sources that she cites are available from the ESRC Data Archive.

One of the major longitudinal surveys that is readily available to the secondary analyst is the National Child Development Study. This consists of data from a cohort of 17,000 people born in one week in March 1958 (Davie, 1966). The origins of the survey are found in a study of perinatal mortality designed to examine the social and obstetric factors associated with early death or abnormality among the children born in Britain during that specific week. Since then, there have been four sweeps, when the cohort was aged 7, 11, 16 and 23 and, at the time of writing, funding is being sought for a further sweep, which would also collect data on the children and the parents of the cohort members (Shepherd, 1986). Again, this survey has been immensely expensive and has received substantial funding from central government. Because it uses a birth-cohort sample, it enables changes within this cohort to be traced over time, with the knowledge that those factors likely to produce period[1] effects (for example, the statutory school-leaving age or the national level of unemployment at a specific time) will be relevant to all the sample (Fogelman, 1984). Although use of a single cohort does *not* permit us to assess changes *between* cohorts (for example, the increasing proportion of women working at different ages for successive cohorts, Martin and Roberts, 1984a, p.120) this problem may be overcome when comparable data is available from other cohort studies. Two studies, the National Survey of Health and Development (Douglas, 1964; Wadsworth, 1986), which drew a cohort of children born in the first week of March 1946, and the Child Health and Education Survey (CHES), which used a cohort born in 1970 (Butler *et al.*, 1982, 1985), both allow comparisons to be made, although unfortunately neither of these studies is currently available from the ESRC Data Archive.

In the USA, examples of longitudinal surveys are far more plentiful than in the UK. One of the best known is the National Longitudinal Survey of Labor Market Experience, carried out at the Center for Human Resource Research at the Ohio State University, under a contract from the US Department of Labor (Center for Human Resource Research, 1981). This data not only permits true longitudinal analysis of the same individuals over an extended time period but, by including two cohorts, allows analysis of the way in which labour market activity varies with cohort as well as age. The first interviews took place early in 1966, with reinterviews at yearly intervals until 1973, followed by a combination of telephone interviews and personal interviews at rather less regular intervals until 1983. Two cohorts of both men and women were taken; men were aged 14–24 or 45–59 in 1966, and women were aged 14–24 or 30–44.

Retrospective data of the kind contained in the Women and Employment Survey enables comparisons to be made between cohorts within the same survey (Martin and Roberts, 1984a; Dex, 1984, 1987). Work-history information was collected from a sample of women aged 16–59 in 1980. In order to trace cohort effects, the sample was divided into groups based upon their birth-dates and then each group was analysed separately. By this method it was possible to demonstrate the way in which successive cohorts of women were taking less time out of the labour market during child-bearing (Dex, 1984). Had the women all belonged to the same cohort this effect could not have been seen.

Another kind of comparison over time can be made by using successive cross-sectional surveys. Both the British Social Attitudes Survey (Jowell and Airey, 1984) and the US General Social Survey (Smith, 1983) are designed to record attitudes of a nationally representative cross-section, of, respectively, the British and American non-institutionalized populations. Because they do not sample the same individuals each year, it is not possible to disentangle age, cohort and period effects in the way in which longitudinal data allows.[2] None the less, by examining the attitudes on, for example, abortion, over a 12-year time span it is possible to assess the extent to which they have changed in aggregate, and the variation in change among different social groups (Stinchcome *et al.*, 1980). To the extent that the US and British questionnaires are comparable there is also scope for cross-national comparisons over time, although any such analysis would need to bear in mind the different political and legislative framework operating in the two countries.

The General Household Survey can also be used to give a cross-sectional time-series. Data is available annually from 1971 and, although new sections of the interview schedule are added and old ones deleted, there remains none the less a core section that is relatively unchanged from year to year. A dataset based upon a 10-year span from 1973–82 has been prepared at the University of Surrey; it provides a means by which changes over time in the characteristics of British households can be tracked – for example, in the composition of households, income relativities of different social groups and participation in the labour market (Dale *et al.*, 1987).

Where no ready-made time-series exists, it may be possible to find several different archival sources and link them together. For this to be done, it is preferable that the surveys used should define the same or a very similar population and also share similar questions. An example from the USA measured change in women's sex-role attitudes between 1964 and 1974 (Mason, Czajka and Arber, 1976), using five different sample surveys. Because there was not uniformity in the sample population and the sampling methods used, pairs of samples, matched to each other as nearly as possible, were analysed in turn. Secondary analysis of an earlier survey can also be combined with a primary survey to give a time dimension. The Women and Employment Survey (Martin and Roberts, 1984a, p.176) repeated some questions on women's attitudes to work and domestic responsibilities that had first been asked in a survey carried out in 1965 by Audrey Hunt (1968). They showed that, while in 1965 only 13 per cent of women thought that a married woman with no children ought to go out to work if she was fit, this had risen to 33 per cent by 1980 (Martin and Roberts, 1984, p.176, Table 12.11).

Similarly, the BBC Time Diaries, collected by BBC Audience Research in 1961, 1974/5 and 1983 have provided comparative material for a study of time use. These asked respondents to record in considerable detail how they had spent the previous day. They have been analysed by Gershuny *et al.* (1986) to provide comparative material with an ESRC-funded study of time-budgets, carried out by SCPR in 1983 in collaboration with Gershuny and Miles. Used together, these surveys provide a unique means of comparing how time use has changed over a twenty-five year period.

Serendipity

Secondary analysis of existing data can provide an opportunity to establish relationships that were entirely unforeseen at the time of data collection. Thus, the link between lung cancer and smoking was established through the analysis of medical records made available to researchers, although the records were not collected with the intention of making such a causal association (British Association Study Group, 1979). In this example, secondary analysis provided a quite fortuitous means of establishing relationships retrospectively.

Replication and debate

One of the most important benefits to be gained from secondary analysis is the facility to replicate studies and to re-analyse the same data from different perspectives and within different theoretical frameworks. Data used by Brown and Harris (1978) to develop a model to explain the occurrence of clinical depression in women has been re-analysed by McKee and Vilhjalmsson (1987) with the result that a worthwhile debate has been begun over the appropriateness of particular statistical techniques and the interpretation which can be placed upon them (Brown, 1987).

The same data sources may also be used by those concerned with similar issues but taking quite different approaches to the research problem. Layard, Piachaud and Stewart (1978) used the GHS in a study of the causes of poverty, prepared as evidence to the 1974 Royal Commission on the Distribution of Income and Wealth. At one point in the report (p.82) they consider whether extending higher benefit levels to the long-term unemployed is likely to have an adverse effect on labour supply and conclude that it is unlikely. Bradshaw, Cooke and Godfrey (1983), using data from the Family Finance Survey (a survey based upon the FES, but confined to families with resources at or below 140 per cent of the Supplementary Benefit level) conclude that, in terms of relative disadvantage, there is a case for extending a long-term benefit to the unemployed. By contrast, Minford (1985) uses data from the GHS and a number of other sources in a book that argues for the introduction of a maximum level of unemployment benefit at 70 per cent of net income from work, and the tightening of procedures for giving benefit to the long-term unemployed. Thus, in the context of arguments from quite different ideological standpoints, similar data sources can be used to reach opposite conclusions.

Although data of the kind collected by structured surveys may be represented as 'knowledge' that should be made freely available and that provides the basis for understanding the structure of society, it is none the less impossible to abstract data from its context and assume that it will always reveal a consistent story. This is further illustrated by Kincaid (1979), using the work of Fiegehan *et al.* (1977) on the Family Expenditure Survey. The FES forms the main basis on which official levels of poverty in Britain are measured but, depending upon the technical assumptions made in calculating income levels and supplementary benefit entitlement, estimated levels of poverty in 1971 could vary between 4.9 and 8.5 per cent of the population. However, because these datasets are available through the ESRC Data Archive, they can be re-analysed and the results debated in academic journals in a way that is not possible with interview transcripts. The ability to replicate research provides a mechanism that should ensure that survey data is not systematically misinterpreted or used against the interests of any one group. The possibility of replication by secondary analysis always allows findings to be challenged and debated.

The foregoing discussion has painted a generally favourable picture of the benefits to be gained from secondary analysis, although attention has been drawn to the need for an awareness of the shortcomings and limitations of using data which has been collected for other purposes. One of the key areas where the secondary analyst may seem, at least superficially, to be at an advantage over those who collect their own data is in the ethical considerations that attach to all social research. From the preceding discussion, it is clear that the ethical issues involved in secondary analysis of survey data are quite different from those of the qualitative researcher, whose data is not readily accessible for re-analysis and re-interpretation. None the less, we argue below that important ethical issues exist, which the secondary analyst should address.

Ethical issues of secondary analysis

At first glance, the secondary analyst has an anonymized, ready-made dataset that requires none of the moral considerations that are a constant worry for the qualitative researcher carrying out interviews in the field (Bulmer, 1982) or the survey researcher concerned about issues of privacy and intrusion (Bulmer, 1979). Generally, microdata supplied for secondary analysis are anonymized, often by collecting into broad groupings data on geographical location, so that it becomes impossible to piece together attributes in order to identify any one individual or household. This 'broad-banding' can offer to most social researchers a very acceptable means of overcoming problems of anonymity – although it may provide a major headache to geographers who seek precise information on residential location.

Thus, the secondary analyst has no need to confront decisions about intrusion into the home of a potential respondent (SCPR Working Party, 1979), to decide on whether to offer advice and sympathy to her respondent and so jeopardize the supposed objectivity of the interview (Oakley, 1981), or whether she should reveal her own personal circumstances to the respondent (Finch, 1984). Because she is one stage removed from the data collection, it is very easy for the secondary analyst to be completely unaware of the issues that so concern field researchers. But this is a mistake.

In order to contrast the dilemmas encountered by those who carry out face-to-face interviews with those of the secondary analyst, we shall first give a few examples raised by researchers using both qualitative and quantitative methods, and then consider the relationship of the secondary analyst to the primary analyst. Finch (1984), in the context of research with playgroup mothers and clergy wives, draws attention to the willingness of women to disclose very personal and private information about themselves during the course of in-depth interviewing by another woman. By doing so, they put themselves in a vulnerable and potentially damaging position vis-à-vis the interviewer. Finch argues that, because of the trust which her respondents placed in her, it was important that the research was not used to undermine the collective interests of the women – for example, in the case of the playgroup mothers, by making them appear inadequate or incompetent as mothers. Oakley (1981) describes a dilemma about whether to provide information and advice to women whom she interviewed during pregnancy – fearing that it might jeopardize the 'objectivity' of the interview. Ritchie (1986) reports a situation where she had to decide whether to disclose the name of a respondent who was suicidal in order that social workers could give her help. All those who have carried out their own interviews have had to decide how hard they should push in order to achieve an interview; whether they should abandon an interview if they feel it is disturbing the respondent; whether they are intruding unnecessarily into the privacy of the respondent. Although there are standard advice and ethical codes to cover all these situations, the worker in the field often finds that her particular situation does not fit neatly into a textbook example.

To some extent, these dilemmas are less likely to be encountered by those who use formal interview techniques. This is partly because the structured survey is less likely to be used as a means of exploring sensitive or highly personal issues. None the less, surveys such as the GHS do ask respondents for information on sterilization or birth-control methods, divorce and death, any of which may, for some people, touch upon raw nerves. However, the very formality of the question-wording in such surveys may give the respondent some protection from the need to produce more than superficial answers, and in this sense, the 'clinical' approach of the survey can serve to protect the respondent from revealing more than she might wish. This formality also means that the respondent is less likely to give the kind of potentially damaging or revealing information that emerges from in-depth interviews. The formal interview may also provide more accessible escape routes for the respondent. First, it may be easier to evade a question during a structured interview than in an in-depth interview, when detailed elaboration is often required after initial responses (Graham, 1983); also, survey respondents find it relatively easy to refuse particular questions – about 10 per cent of adult respondents either refuse or do not know the answer to one or more of the questions on income that are asked in the General Household Survey. In this formal situation, respondents clearly feel able to conceal information which suggests that, whatever the hierarchical relationship between interviewer and interviewee (Oakley, 1981), the latter is not totally powerless in the hands of the former! In this respect the moral/ethical problems of survey research may be rather less difficult than those of qualitative research.

To this extent, then, the analyst of survey data, whether primary or secondary, may feel confronted by fewer moral dilemmas than the qualitative researcher. However, it has been suggested earlier that in many kinds of qualitative research it is the researcher herself who represents the research instrument. Generally, the person who carries out the interviews also analyses them and writes up the research for publication. In this situation, where the same person is responsible for the research process from beginning to end, it is realistic to give the interviewee guarantees of the way in which the data will be used and to ensure that the interests of the respondent are not undermined or misrepresented (Finch, 1984). The concept of 'informed consent' is one that is included in many ethical guidelines and rules of conduct governing research practice. Generally, this is summarized to mean that 'a potential respondent should be told truthfully why, and for whom, the research is being undertaken and how the results will be used' (SCPR Working Party, 1979, p.78). This may be feasible for those who have sole control over all stages of the research process (although there is still scope for misuse and misinterpretation of the final publication, particularly if it reaches the attention of the media (Roberts, 1984)), but it is much more difficult to guarantee if the research is a team project and the interviewer is not responsible for analysis and publication. Thus, those who do in-depth interviewing are likely to have greater control over the way in which their data is used than those who conduct surveys using highly structured interviews.

In the case of large-scale government surveys, it is practically impossible for the interviewer to do more than indicate the kinds of use to which the data will be put. Thus, OPCS represent the General Household Survey as 'providing government departments with facts and figures about life in Britain . . . covering such topics as housing, employment, education, health and leisure' (extract from an advance letter by OPCS, 1986). However, the interviewers who carry out surveys for OPCS and other similar organizations have no voice in the use to be made of the data they collect. Although they can pass on the official message from their employing organization, they cannot, for example, assure pensioners that the income information that they give will not be used to justify cuts in pensions, or promise mothers that a change to means-tested child benefits will not be introduced as a result of research using the GHS.

If these problems arise with primary analysis, it is immediately clear that the uses to which a secondary analyst may put the data can never be identified by the interviewer making doorstep contact, and therefore the respondent cannot be fully informed of the way in which her responses may be used. Secondary analysts of most government surveys are asked to submit a formal application, through the ESRC Data Archive, to the agency responsible for the survey. This procedure, however, can only ensure that the data is not used for a purpose that is totally inappropriate – it is not designed to influence the policy line behind the research, or the theoretical framework of the analyst. The Ethical Guidelines of the Social Research Association (SRA) point out that 'no information is devoid of possible harm to one interest or another. Individuals may be harmed by their participation in social inquiries or group interests may be damaged by certain findings' (SRA, 1985, p. 88). The Guidelines go on to suggest that, while individuals may be protected by anonymity as members of a group or as members of society itself, they cannot be exempt from the possible effects of decisions based upon research (SRA, 1985, p.103). The conclusion that appears to follow from this is that, while Finch (1984) may ensure that the collective interests of her respondents are protected because of the common bond that she established with them, which may have made them more ready to reveal information, this is not a precondition that can be placed upon all research data in a blanket fashion. The way in which data from the GHS may be used to support quite contrasting arguments of social policy demonstrates the impossibility of ensuring that interests are not liable to be damaged through participation in this kind of survey – although there is, of course, no reason to assume that the same policies would not be put forward irrespective of the availability of statistical data.

A further point of interest found in the SRA Guidelines is the exhortation to social researchers to minimize the inconvenience caused to people by social inquiries. One method of achieving this, it is suggested, is by making greater use of existing data. This, of course, is an important benefit of secondary analysis, for it enables the researcher to obtain her data without causing any additional intrusion into the private lives of citizens.

The balance of interests between citizens, data users and the community formed one of the main concerns of the UK Data Protection Committee, which reported in 1978 (Report of the Committee on Data Protection, 1978). The proposals of the Committee led to legislation in July 1984 in the form of the Data Protection Act 1984. The fundamental intention of the Act is expressed as limiting the possibility of misuse of personal information that is held on computer, and also as complying with the Council of Europe Convention. The Act, however, applies only to personal data (that which relates to living people and from which they may be identified) and which can be automatically processed, either by computer or word-processor. The Act requires that all those who use personal data, the data itself and the purpose for which it may be used, should be registered with the Data Protection Registrar and that personal data may not be used, disclosed or sent abroad except in accordance with the terms under which the data is registered. Those people on whom data is held are entitled, under the Act, to be told what the data is. The implications of the Act for social research have yet to be worked through, but it seems likely that they will have little effect for the bulk of researchers, who take great care to record questionnaire material accurately and who would be perfectly happy to return to a respondent a copy of the information that had been given.

Because the Act applies only to data which is *personal* (where a living individual can be identified), it is generally accepted that most data used by secondary analysts does not come under the aegis of the Data Protection Act. It is normal practice for data made available for secondary analysis not only to have the name and address of the respondent removed, but also to have any other material that would assist identification removed or altered. Usually, this means grouping data on geographical location into broad regional categories (broad-banding). While the Act will enhance the rights of citizens in relation to data that is collected and stored in a personal form, it does not, of course, legislate for the ultimate use of survey data. As we have seen from the discussion above, the purposes for which such data may be used by secondary analysts is impossible to foresee; however, the ready availability of the data should ensure that the meaning and interpretations that can be derived from it are the subject of rigorous and continuing debate.

Notes

1 Martin and Roberts (1984a, pp.119–20) give a useful discussion of age, period and cohort effects.

2 In fact, in the case of the British Social Attitudes Survey, a panel element has been introduced, with a follow-up of half the 1983 respondents in the following year (Jowell and Witherspoon, 1985).

4

The potential of hierarchical surveys for secondary analysis

One of the most exciting developments during the last decade has been the availability for secondary analysis of surveys that have an hierarchical structure. The majority of datasets are based on individuals as the unit of analysis. They are flat (single level) files, which take the form of a rectangular table in which each row (or set of rows) is the data for one respondent and each column (or set of columns) represents a single variable. Household surveys often have a different structure – they are hierarchical consisting of data held at two or more different levels. The highest level is the household, which may contain a variable number of families (though usually just one). A family includes a variable number of persons, each will be asked a detailed series of questions. Therefore, the data record for households will vary in length depending on the number of families and number of persons in the household.

Most hierarchically organized surveys are government-sponsored and are therefore large and nationally representative. They are extremely powerful data sources, allowing the researcher to address many theoretical questions that were not envisaged by the designer of the original survey. Although hierarchical surveys are generally complex to analyse in their original form, they are increasingly available from the Data Archive modified to a rectangular file structure for easier management. They may be available as SPSS^x files, which include variable and value labels and may contain variables derived from more than one level of the hierarchy. These rectangular data files are relatively simple to use, even for the secondary analyst who has little knowledge of computing. In addition, surveys with a hierarchical structure are now easier to exploit than in the past, because of advances in software capable of handling complex data structures (see Chapter 7).

The Labour Force Survey (LFS) is an example of a survey with two levels of hierarchy – the household and the individual. Information about the labour market activity of each adult aged 16 and over in sample households is collected (OPCS, 1986). The Labour Force Survey is distributed by the Data Archive as a rectangular file based on persons, in which household information is included on *each* person's record. However, most British hierarchical surveys are available from the Data Archive either in their original hierarchical form or as rectangular files. Other examples of hierarchical government surveys include the General Household Survey, which annually interviews all adults in a sample of about 10,000 households, and the Family Expenditure Survey, which is an annual survey of more than 7,000 households, in which information about income and expenditure is collected from each household member aged 16 and over. Hakim (1982) provides an excellent description of the contents and survey design of the LFS, GHS and FES. The hierarchical structure of the GHS and its potential for secondary analysis will be discussed in more detail in this chapter. A hierarchical survey based on work establishments is the Workplace Industrial Relations Survey, which was first conducted in 1980; a second survey was conducted in 1984 (Millward and Stevens, 1986). In 1980, WIRS sampled about 2,000 establishments, with data on these establishments collected through interviews with a personnel and a works manager and a non-manual and a manual employee representative (Airey and Potts, 1981; Daniel and Millward, 1983). These individuals were interviewed as public role-holders who provided information about the work organization and patterns of industrial relations. Thus, the primary level of analysis is the work establishment.

An example of a non-government survey with a hierarchical structure, which is available for secondary analysis, is the ESRC-funded 1984 Time Budget Survey. This study asked all members over the age of 14 in sample households to complete a time-budget for a period of one week, which indicated the length of time the individual spent on various activities and the social context of each activity (Gershuny *et al.*, 1986). The Time Budget Survey was financed by the ESRC primarily to provide a research resource for the academic community.

There are a number of national household surveys in other countries. For example, in the United States the majority of household surveys are available as both rectangular and hierarchical files (ICPSR, 1986). The US Census Public Use Microdata Samples (PUMS) are hierarchical in structure, with each person's record having a logical relationship to the household record that precedes it. The Current Population Survey is a monthly survey of households which collects data on the labour force participation and other characteristics of persons aged 14 and over. It is available either as a hierarchical file or a rectangular file based on persons. Other hierarchical government surveys include the Survey of

Income and Education, the Survey of Income and Program Participation, and the Health Interview Surveys. The last has a hierarchical structure, but for ease of analysis has been converted into five separate rectangular files, based on households, persons, doctor visits, health conditions and hospital contacts. Some person data is included in each file.

Hierarchical surveys have three main advantages over single level surveys. First, the secondary analyst can choose the *level and unit of analysis*. Where there are multiple interviews in a firm or school, the analysis might be concerned with the organization as the main unit of analysis, with sub-units, groups, dyadic relationships and individuals within it as additional units of analysis (Hakim, 1987b). In the ESRC Time Budget study, the individual has been used as the unit of analysis for most analyses conducted to date, but it is also possible to analyse the data at the household level: for example, comparing the activity patterns and use of time by different types of household. In some cases the researcher might choose to analyse only certain *units within a particular level* of analysis. For example, the primary use of the WIRS by DE has been for studying establishments, based on the establishment as the level of analysis (Millward, 1983; Hakim, 1985). Within this level, analysts may choose to study only certain types of units (for example, retail establishments). However, a secondary analyst could also choose to analyse WIRS at the lower, individual level, to study the responses of particular types of individuals, e.g. managers or manual representatives. Thus, the unit of analysis might be managers for a particular study and in another study the unit of analysis might be manual workers.

A second advantage of hierarchical surveys is that they allow the possibility of *contextual analysis*. The individual is analysed within the context of the larger group or organization of which she is a member. The focus is on the individual, but the individual's role or behaviour is analysed with reference to characteristics of the group. Contextual analysis recognizes that the attitudes and behaviour of people are affected by the context in which they live (Blau, 1960; Davis, 1961). One major area of contextual analysis is in educational research, where the effects of schools on children's educational attainment and aspirations have been examined (Coleman, 1961; Hauser, 1970, 1974; McDill and Rigsby, 1973; Barton, 1970; Farkas, 1974; Alexander and Eckland, 1975; Rutter *et al.*, 1979). Hakim (1987b, p.56) notes that 'the effects of schools on their pupils has attracted a greater volume of research than the effects of other social institutions on their members, largely owing to the policy relevance of the subject'. Another area has been concerned with the effect of membership of a particular trade union branch on the attitudes and behaviour of individual employees (Lipset *et al.*, 1956). More recently, demographers have studied the effects of contextual variables on fertility and family planning in developing countries (Casterline, 1985; Entwisle and Mason, 1985). Contextual variables which measure the social or economic characteristics of the community (village or district), such as the degree of modernization, level of women's education, and location of family planning services, can be used to analyse the determinants of the number of children ever born to women. Contextual analysis of the Workplace Industrial Relations Survey allows analysis of the influence of the characteristics of factory or workplace on employee opinions about the effects of the introduction of microtechnology. Household surveys allow the researcher to examine how housing, assets and other household (contextual) characteristics are related to the attitudes and behaviour of individuals.

A third advantage of the hierarchical survey is that it allows analysis of the *interrelationships* between the characteristics of individuals within the same context. Sociologists are increasingly studying individuals within social contexts: for example, to understand the labour market behaviour of one household member it is necessary to relate it both to the labour market behaviour of other household members and to the family structure (Pahl, 1984; Harris, Lee and Morris, 1985). A household survey such as the GHS or the ESRC Time Budget Survey allows comparison of the husband's and wife's use of time or a comparison of their employment participation and earnings. The WIR survey can be analysed to show the congruence of responses between managers and employees within the same establishment, when they are asked the same questions about procedures for consultation between unions and management – for example, for handling disputes and about the introduction of new technology. To analyse the interrelationships between the behaviour or attitudes of different household members or between different employees within an establishment usually involves the derivation of individual-level variables, which rely on knowledge of the identity and characteristics of individuals in the same household or establishment. They require use of the hierarchical property of the survey and are contingent (conditional) on the identity of different individuals within that context. These *contingent* variables will be described in detail in Chapter 9.

Single level surveys

Before discussing hierarchical surveys, we shall review briefly single level surveys in order to clarify how they differ from a hierarchical survey. The survey researcher who is designing her own survey will specify the characteristics of the universe (or population) from which a sample will be drawn – for example, women aged 16 to 59, or the elderly above a specified age. The specification of the population to be surveyed and therefore the choice of unit of analysis will be made on theoretical grounds. It may be the household, in which case the respondent who provides information is not the unit of analysis, but is reporting information on behalf of that unit. The choice of informant will be based on who can provide the required information reliably and who is accessible; for example, in a study of poverty the unit of analysis might be defined as the household, and either the head of household or his/her spouse might be chosen as the informant.

During an interview in a single level survey based on a sample of individuals, four different types of information might be collected. These are:

1 the individual's characteristics: for example, educational qualifications, employment status and attitudes (individual level variables);
2 information about the individual's household: for example, housing tenure, possession of consumer goods, total household income, household composition (household level or contextual variables);
3 information about specified members of the individual's household: for example, the ages of the respondent's children, the occupation and educational qualifications of the respondent's spouse, the employment status of all other household members, the health status of the respondent's children (intra-household or contingent variables);
4 information about specified individuals outside the household: for example, the occupations of the respondent's four best friends (cf. Stewart, Prandy and Blackburn, 1980).

In surveys where all the information is collected from one respondent, the data for analysis will be organized as a rectangular (or flat) data file with a fixed and standard number of variables for each case in the file, that is, a case by variable data matrix (de Vaus, 1986). A case by variable matrix is a rectangular table of numbers, in which each row is called an observation, case or individual, and each column is called a variable (in fact, there may be several rows of data for each respondent and variables may occupy two or more columns). The following example illustrates a file containing one row for each individual. The first four columns contain a four-digit identifier; the next two columns might be the respondent's age last birthday (two digits); then the variable employment status occupies a single column (category 1 – employed; 2 – unemployed; 3 – housewife; 4 – retired; 5 – other), and finally two columns indicate the number of hours worked per week (for respondents who are not employed this is coded -9). The first few rows are shown, with spaces inserted between each variable for clarity.

0001	37	3	-9
0002	22	1	35
0003	58	4	-9
0004	41	1	20
0005	52	1	38
0006	25	1	35

Thus, each case (or unit of analysis) is an individual and the same variables or characteristics are obtained for each individual (case).

Secondary analysis of single level survey data is relatively straightforward. For example, a survey concerned with women's labour force participation would probably collect all the relevant information from the woman herself; this would include information on the number and age of her children, the occupation and employment status of her husband, and the woman's own characteristics, such as her education and previous occupational history. New variables may be derived from the data held as a rectangular case by variable data matrix. Thus, secondary analysis does not present any technical problems of data management because all the relevant information about other household members is included on the woman's record.

Hierarchical surveys

A hierarchical household survey may collect the same data as in the example above, that is, the number and ages of a woman's children, and the occupation and employment status of her husband, but it is held separately for each individual in the household and is therefore more complex to analyse. The following example shows a simplified hierarchical data file containing two levels (with only one row of data per household and one row per adult within the household).

Household Number 1	0001 04 2 2
Individual Number 1	0001 01 3 7 3 -9
Individual Number 2	0001 02 2 2 1 3 5
Household Number 2	0002 01 1 1
Individual Number 1	0002 01 5 8 4 -9
Household Number 3	0003 05 1 2
Individual Number 1	0003 01 4 1 1 2 0
Individual Number 2	0003 02 5 2 1 3 8
Individual Number 3	0003 03 2 5 1 3 5

There are three households in this example. Each household record starts with a four-digit identifier, followed by the number of persons (adults and children) in the household (a two-digit number); then a measure of housing tenure (category 1 – owner-occupier; 2 – rented) and, finally, whether the household has a telephone (category 1 – yes; 2 – no). The lower level of hierarchy is individuals. In the first household, two adults were interviewed, in the second, one adult was interviewed and, in the third household, three. The individual records begin with the four-digit household identifier, then the person identifier (two digits), followed by the same three variables as in the earlier example of a rectangular data file – age (two digits), employment status (one digit) and number of hours worked (two digits).

The secondary analyst, using such a hierarchical dataset to analyse the labour force participation of married women in terms of the characteristics of other members of her household, has a number of problems to confront before starting analysis. First, she must decide on the appropriate level and unit of analysis; secondly, she should assess the validity of the variables available in the dataset as indicators of the theoretical concepts to be analysed; thirdly, she may need to specify and derive variables that relate to different individuals within the household, which will require using more than one level of the hierarchy. The analyst will often use the hierarchical dataset to construct a workfile that contains all the relevant original and derived variables in a form that can be easily analysed, usually as a rectangular case by variable data matrix. The primary researcher has already addressed these issues in the design of the research, although she may not have been aware of making these decisions. For the secondary analyst, using data from a hierarchical survey, these decisions must be considered carefully and must be made explicit.

The General Household Survey

Because of its considerable potential for secondary analysis the General Household Survey will be used as an example of a hierarchical survey (Gilbert, Dale and Arber, 1983), although the issues raised are equally applicable if the analyst is using any other hierarchically organized dataset. First, the structure of the GHS will be described briefly.

The GHS is a national sample survey, which has been conducted continuously since 1971 (OPCS, 1985). It is based on interviews with about 10,000 households (25,000 individuals) per year. Prior to 1982 the achieved sample size was somewhat larger, about 12,000 households. The GHS data is collected from two interview schedules. The Household Schedule covers topics such as housing tenure, consumer durables and migration, and is answered by one adult member of the household, usually the head of household or his spouse (the definition of head of household used by the GHS means that heads of household are generally men). Each household member aged 16 and over answers an Individual Schedule about their employment, job satisfaction, educational attainment, health and use of health services, and income. Women aged 16 to 59 are also asked about their marital and fertility history and, since 1986, men under 60 have been asked their marital history. In addition, topics such as leisure, smoking, drinking, family planning and the circumstances of the elderly are included in some years. Since 1977, the GHS Annual Reports have contained a list of the topics covered each year from 1971 onwards, and the appendix of each Annual Report contains a copy of that year's interview schedules. A response rate of about 82 per cent is obtained (OPCS, 1985).

The GHS contains data at four different levels of hierarchy – the household, family unit, individual, and items of each individual's behaviour, such as doctor consultations and leisure activities (see Figure 4.1). Each household contains one or more families, which in turn contain a varying number of persons. Each person is asked whether he or she has consulted a general practitioner in the previous two weeks and, if they have, they are asked a series of questions about *each* such visit. Doctor consultations form a different level of analysis because each time an individual has consulted a doctor, this opens a path to a series of specific questions about that consultation. People who have not consulted a doctor will therefore have no variables about doctor consultations, while those who have consulted four times will have four separate sets of doctor consultation variables, one set relating to each of the four consultations.

Figure 4.1 *The main levels of hierarchy in the GHS*

Household	
Family Unit	(each household contains one or more family units)
Individual	(each family unit contains one or more individuals)
Doctor consultations	(an individual may have had no doctor consultations in the last two weeks, or may have had any number – the maximum number in 1980 was 12 consultations in the two-week reference period)

An illustration of the variable record lengths in a GHS data file is shown in Figure 4.2. Household 1 contains four persons in Family 1 and two persons in Family 2. Household 2 contains only one person. Most people have no doctor visit records, but in Household 1, person 1 has two doctor visits and person 3 has three visits.

Figure 4.2 *Example of hierarchical organization of data in the GHS*

- Household 1
  - Family 1 within Household 1
    - Person 1 within Family 1 in Household 1
      - Doctor visit 1 of Person 1
      - Doctor visit 2 of Person 1
    - Person 2 in Family 1
    - Person 3 in Family 1
      - Doctor visit 1 of Person 3
      - Doctor visit 2 of Person 3
      - Doctor visit 3 of Person 3
    - Person 4 in Family 1
  - Family 2 in Household 1
    - Person 1 in Family 2 in Household 1
    - Person 2 in Family 2 in Household 1

- Household 2
  - Family 1 in Household 2
    - Person 1 in Family 1 in Household 2

- Household 3
  - Family 1 in Household 3
    - Person 1 in Family 1 in Household 3
      - Doctor visit 1 of Person 1
    - Person 2 in Family 1 in Household 3
    - Person 3 in Family 1 in Household 3

Because the GHS involves four levels of hierarchy it is more complex to analyse than hierarchical surveys that contain data at only two levels. However, a greater number of levels also gives more potential for the analyst to create complex linkages – for example between the characteristics of individuals in different family units within a household. In educational research, there are often three or more levels in the hierarchy – for example, schools, classes and school children.

The GHS is available for secondary analysis either as an hierarchical or as a rectangular dataset. The University of Surrey has facilitated the secondary analysis of the GHS by preparing rectangular SPSS files for 1973 – 1982 and SIR files for 1977 – 1982 (Gilbert, Dale, Arber, 1983; Arber, Dale, Gilbert, O'Byrne, 1984). The Surrey GHS files contain a number of derived variables, which are based on information obtained from two or more levels of the hierarchy. From 1983 onwards, the GHS has been supplied by OPCS to the ESRC Data Archive as a SIR data file containing a number of variables, which have been derived from two or more levels of the hierarchy. The alternative formats in which GHS data can be supplied by the Data Archive for secondary analysis are discussed in Chapter 5.

Examples of secondary analysis using the GHS

The potential of hierarchical surveys for secondary analysis will be illustrated by three examples of research originally conducted by using a specialized survey. Each will be discussed in terms of the issues that would have to be considered if the same research questions were addressed using secondary analysis of a household survey, such as the General Household Survey. This will provide an illustration of the ways in which secondary analysis can be used to answer sociological questions, and will give examples of: (i) the choice of the appropriate level and unit of analysis, (ii) the conceptualization of variables to measure validly the concepts under study, and (iii) issues relating to the derivation of variables, which in a hierarchical dataset may involve two or more levels of the hierarchy.

The analysis of social mobility provides an illustration in which the individual is the unit of analysis and all relevant variables are held on the individual's record. The second example, the analysis of women's labour force participation, takes the woman as the unit of analysis and derives a number of variables from information about specified other household members. The third example, research into poverty, uses the household as the level of analysis and illustrates the derivation of household level variables, which use information held on the individual records of each household member.

Social mobility

A key issue within sociology is the degree to which there is open access to occupational positions that provide high rewards in terms of income, prestige and power. The classic studies of social mobility by Glass in 1949 (Glass, 1954) and the Oxford Social Mobility Study in 1972 (Goldthorpe, 1980) interviewed representative samples of men aged 20 – 64. A focus of attention has been the relationship between father's occupation, the respondent's educational attainment, his first job and his current occupation. Figure 4.3 shows this part of the model of social mobility.

Figure 4.3 *Model of social mobility*

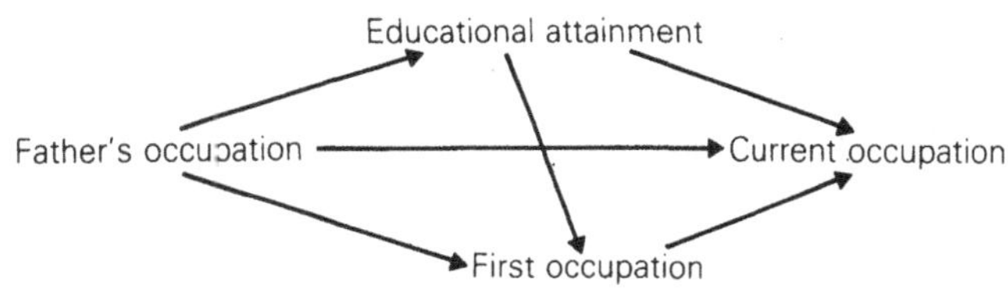

The GHS was not designed to research social mobility, but nevertheless has been used for this purpose (Heath, 1981; Hornsby-Smith and Dale, 1988; Jones, 1986). In fact, it offers a major advantage over other studies of social mobility in that it can be used to study women's inter-generational mobility, unlike the classic studies that collected data only on men. Heath (1981) used the 1975 GHS to demonstrate the inferior social mobility of women and Jones (1986, 1987) used the 1979–80 GHS to analyse gender differences in the social mobility of young people, focusing on the way in which patterns of social mobility are associated with the age of childbearing and household formation. Although the GHS has the advantage of including data on women, it does not contain all the variables necessary for the analysis of the model in Figure 4.3, because no information is available on the individual's first occupation. Thus the GHS cannot be used to study intra-generational mobility. In addition, the questions on father's occupation are asked only for individuals under age 50, and refer to the father's usual occupation (or last occupation if the father is not currently employed). This provides less standardized information than the mobility surveys, which collected information on father's occupation at a specified point in the respondent's childhood (when the respondent was aged 14 in Glass (1954) and Goldthorpe (1980)).

In the Glass (1954) and Goldthorpe (1980) mobility surveys *and* in the GHS, the data used for analysis is available as a rectangular case by variable data matrix where the case is the individual. In the GHS, information about current occupation and educational attainment is collected from the individual and is included on the individual's schedule. Information about the father's occupation is also collected from the individual *except* where the father also lives in the same household, when the father's occupation is recorded on the father's own interview schedule. However, this slight complication is not a problem for the analyst, because the Surrey GHS files have been constructed with information about father's occupation included on each individual's record; since 1983, the GHS files supplied by the Data Archive contain a derived variable representing father's occupation. Therefore, if a researcher wishes to use the GHS to analyse social mobility there is no need to derive variables that describe the characteristics of other household members and then link them to the individual's data record.

Thus, secondary analysis based on a complex dataset such as the GHS is relatively straightforward for analyses involving only variables at a single level, in this case the individual. The variables are obtained from the same interview schedule and are immediately available for analysis as a rectangular case by variable data matrix. However, a drawback may be that all the variables that the secondary analyst would ideally include in her analysis may not have been collected; an important variable for studying social mobility is first occupation, which is not asked in the GHS.

Women's participation in paid employment

The Women and Employment Survey (WES) examined the factors which influenced women's participation in the labour force. It was based on a nationally representative survey of more than 5,000 women aged 16 to 59 in 1980 (Martin and Roberts, 1984a, 1984b). The main unit of analysis was the woman and the interviews obtained information about the respondent, her children and family circumstances, and for married women also the income and occupation of her husband. Thus, information about the husband was collected and analysed, but it was collected from the woman and included on her interview schedule, resulting in a rectangular case by variable data matrix. In addition, a separate subsample of about 800 husbands of women in the main sample were interviewed, mainly about sex role attitudes and the domestic division of labour. This aspect of the research design permits the analysis of patterns of consensus or disagreement *within* couples. The WES also collected work histories, which add a hierarchical dimension to the dataset because women record a variable number of periods in and out of work and also a variable number of jobs. The work history data in the WES will not be considered here; Dex (1984) provides an excellent example of the analysis of work history data.

If the GHS could be used for analyses of women's labour force participation comparable to those in the 1980 Women and Employment Survey, this would allow comparison over time between the situation in 1980 (based on the WES) and in the late 1980s (based on the GHS). It would also allow comparative analyses of the factors influencing men's compared to women's labour force participation. The model put forward by Joshi (1984) in her analysis of WES will serve as the theoretical model to be examined using the GHS (Figure 4.4).

Figure 4.4 *Joshi's model of women's employment participation*

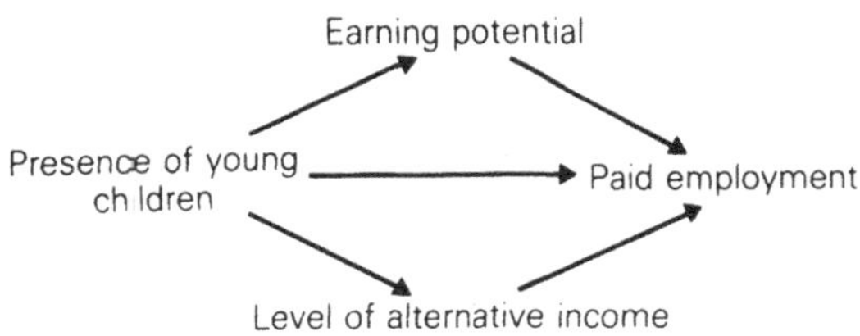

If the model in Figure 4.4 were to be analysed, using the GHS, a number of new variables would have to be derived, and decisions made about the most appropriate way to measure the relevant theoretical concepts. In the GHS the unit of analysis could be defined in the same way as in the WES and the relevant cases selected, women aged 16 to 59.

A key factor influencing women's employment participation is the number of children a woman has and the age of her youngest child (Martin and Roberts, 1984a). These are variables that are obvious candidates for collection in any primary research on women. This information is collected in the GHS as part of the section of questions on each woman's marital and fertility history. In addition, information about the age of each child in the household and their relationship to the head of household is collected in the Household Schedule. Number of dependent children has been derived and is available in the Surrey GHS files, and since 1983 all the GHS files supplied by the Data Archive contain derived variables which measure the number of dependent children and the age of the youngest dependent child. These variables have been derived by using more than one level of the hierarchy.

The variables 'participation in paid employment' and 'number of hours worked' are available on the individual's own data record in the GHS. They can be used to construct a variable that measures whether the woman works 'full-time', 'part-time' or is 'not in paid work'. 'Earning potential' is an individual level variable that was derived in Joshi's analysis of WES from the individual's characteristics. Joshi (1984) conceptualizes earning potential in terms of the individual's highest occupation during her lifetime and her total years of work experience, and from these variables constructs a measure of earning power. The same variables are not available in the GHS. However, a measure of earning potential could be derived from other individual level variables, such as the woman's highest educational qualifications and her current (or most recent) occupation. This GHS derived measure of earning potential is different from the indicator used in Joshi's analysis, but nevertheless has some validity as a measure of the concept. This derived variable is not available in either the Surrey GHS or the post-1983 GHS data files and, therefore, would have to be derived by the secondary analyst.

Joshi found that women in households where there were high levels of income from other household members were less likely to be in paid work. Joshi used the husband's total earnings as an indicator of 'level of alternative income'. In the GHS this variable could be defined in the same way, or could be conceptualized as the total earnings of *all other* members of the household. However, neither of these variables is available in any of the GHS files supplied by the Data Archive. Therefore, whichever definition is used, the derivation of a variable measuring 'level of alternative income' would involve the summation of income from one or more other household members, using at least two levels of the hierarchy. To derive a variable to measure husband's total earnings would require use of three levels of the hierarchy – the household, the family unit in order to identify the husband, and the individual.

The GHS could also be used in a similar way to study the factors influencing men's labour force participation, allowing an analysis of the ways in which family unit variables such as the age and number of dependent children have a different impact on men's compared to women's labour force participation.

Researching poverty

Poverty is usually considered to be a characteristic of households, or of income units (as defined by the DHSS in assessment of eligibility for supplementary benefit), rather than of individuals. Therefore, research studies of poverty have generally taken the household or the income unit as the unit of analysis. The most famous recent British research on poverty is the study of poverty by Townsend (1979), based on a sample of more than 2,000 households in 1968–69. Interviews were conducted with either the head of household or his/her spouse. The informant gave information about the circumstances of the household as a whole – for example, housing tenure, household expenditure, possession of consumer goods and housing amenities – and the characteristics and activities of specified household members, such as the employment status of each adult in the household. The informant in the survey, therefore, acted as a representative of the household. In addition, wherever possible each adult earner was interviewed about their own earnings and any of their occupational details which the main informant did not know. The resulting dataset was analysed by Townsend at three different levels: (i) the household, for analyses of household assets including housing deprivation; (ii) the income unit, for assessment of poverty based on eligibility for supplementary benefit; and (iii) the individual, for analyses of earnings and deprivation at work.

Townsend's study is complex and wide-ranging. It is impossible to characterize all but a small part here. As an illustration, we shall discuss part of his model of poverty, focusing on the extent to which the GHS could be used for a similar analysis. Dale (1985, 1987a) used the 1979 GHS to analyse poverty, and some of her analysis will be discussed in Chapter 11. Townsend's definition of poverty is based on relative deprivation, and cannot be measured by using the GHS because the relevant questions are not included in the interview schedule. However, it is possible to construct measures of poverty based on household income and on standard of living, in terms of the possession of consumer goods and household amenities. Part of Townsend's model of the relative risk of being in poverty (Townsend, 1979, p.916) is shown in Figure 4.5.

For simplicity of exposition, the household is used as the level of analysis and the five variables in the model are all at the household level. Information relating to these five concepts is available in the GHS, but in most cases it would be necessary to derive the relevant variables from a

Figure 4.5 *Model of relative risks of poverty*

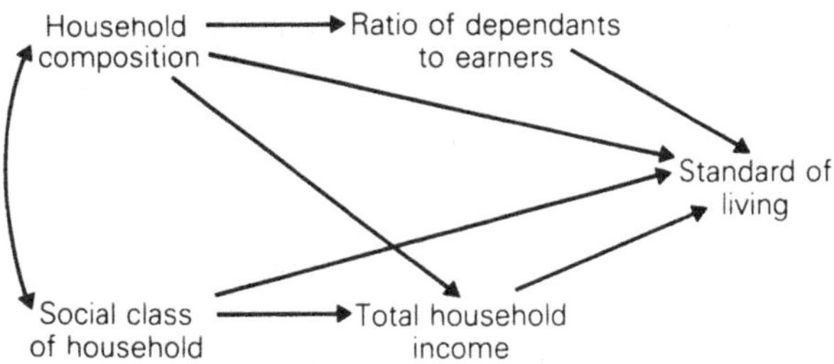

number of questions, some of which would involve more than one level of hierarchy (see Figure 4.1). A summary variable based on the number of consumer goods that are in the household could be used to measure the standard of living of the household. However, it is important to recognize that possession of consumer goods alone is a very poor indicator of the household's standard of living (this is discussed further in Chapter 11). A summary measure of possession of consumer goods, such as a telephone, freezer and central heating, would be derived from household level variables only and, therefore, would involve only one level of the hierarchy.

The ratio of dependants (i.e. non-earners) to earners in the household could be derived from individual level variables within each household and, therefore, involves two levels of hierarchy. Each individual in the household is asked if he or she is currently in paid employment, enabling an initial household level variable to be derived, which measures the number of earners in the household. The number of dependants in the household can be calculated simply from the difference between the total number of persons in the household and the number of earners. From this, a summary variable can be derived, which is the ratio of these two variables.

There are several derived variables that summarize the composition of the household, both in the GHS files prepared by Surrey and, since 1983, in the GHS supplied by OPCS and distributed by the Data Archive. However, if a different variable characterizing household composition is required – for example, one which distinguishes stage in the family life-cycle (Dale, 1987a) – this would have to be constructed from individual level variables within the household; an example is given in Chapter 11.

The social class of the household has usually been measured by the occupation of the head of household (Goldthorpe, 1983, 1984; Nissel, 1980). The GHS defines the head of household as the person responsible for the mortgage or rent of the accommodation, but, if this is a married woman, her husband is defined as the head of household (OPCS, 1985). Characterizing the household by the occupation of one household member is an example of a linked contextual variable (see Chapter 9), whereby information about one individual (the head of household) is used to characterize the entire household. Socio-economic group of the head of household is a variable available in most forms of the GHS supplied by the Data Archive. However, if the secondary analyst wants to measure social class of the household in some other way – for example, using the socio-economic group of the occupationally dominant household member (Erickson, 1984; Goldthorpe and Payne, 1986b) – she would have to derive the variable herself by using a hierarchically organized version of the GHS.

The final variable in the model in Figure 4.5, total household income, is a derived summary variable. It is derived from lower level units within the household, in this case from the summation of each individual's income from all sources. The GHS files prepared by Surrey and the post-1983 GHS files include this variable. However, if the analyst wishes to create a measure of poverty more similar to that used by Townsend, that is, income relative to the current DHSS supplementary benefit scale rates, she would have to derive this variable herself from data about all or some members of the household. The detailed example in Chapter 11 illustrates how this could be done.

Conclusion

This chapter has shown that a dataset such as the GHS contains many of the variables relevant for sociological analyses that have previously relied on specialized studies. Hierarchical datasets have been relatively under-exploited by the research community, but are very rich sources of data for theoretical and policy-relevant research. Before the secondary analyst embarks on analysing a hierarchical dataset she must consider (i) the appropriate level and unit of analysis, (ii) the conceptualization of variables in the dataset to measure validly the concepts under study, and (iii) the actual derivation of these variables, which in a dataset such as the GHS may involve using two or more levels of hierarchy. These issues will be discussed further when we return to the practicalities of the secondary analysis of household-based surveys in Chapters 9–11.

5

Choosing and ordering a dataset

Introduction

This chapter will start with the assumption that a research problem has been defined and secondary analysis identified as an appropriate means of investigating it. Using the ESRC Data Archive at the University of Essex as an example, we shall explain how to search for suitable data sources. Where the large UK government surveys are to be used, the differing forms in which they are available will be outlined and the basis on which to make a selection of a subset of variables and cases will be discussed. The final part of the chapter will focus on how to order the data once it has been identified.

Unless you are approaching secondary analysis with the specific intention of analysing one particular dataset of which you have special knowledge, then a first step will be to make a thorough search of the material held by the available Data Archives. The ESRC Archive at Essex is the major national repository of survey data in the UK; established by the ESRC (then SSRC) in 1967, it holds copies of almost all the large government surveys, all surveys financed by the ESRC and also a considerable number of other data sources, not all of which are survey-based. In the USA, there are numerous data archives throughout the country but the Inter-University Consortium for Political and Social Research (ICPSR), housed at the University of Michigan, acts as a central repository and dissemination service for machine-readable social science data, serving not just the American academic community, but social scientists throughout the world. UK users can obtain the annually updated ICPSR catalogue from the ESRC Data Archive. Lists of the main archives in the USA and other countries are given by Kiecolt and Nathan (1985), Hakim (1982) and Hyman (1972) and an up-to-date list of archives in various countries is also available from the ESRC Data Archive at Essex. A more detailed account of the role of data archives and the ESRC Data Archive in particular is given by Hakim (1982).

Searching the archive

The ICPSR *Guide to Resources and Services* is published annually and contains descriptions of all the studies held by the ICPSR at the time of going to press. Information on the holdings of the ESRC Data Archive may be obtained either by using the extensive two-volume catalogue (Taylor, 1986) or by using a computerized on-line retrieval system. Browsing through the published catalogue is probably the simplest way of getting an idea of the secondary sources that are available, and both the ICPSR and ESRC Archive Catalogues are organized on similar principles, based around a number of different indexes (title indexes, subject indexes, index of name of investigator) and both give short descriptions of each study linked to a study number. The detailed examples of making a data search that are given in this chapter are based upon the ESRC Data Archive at the University of Essex.

Not all the studies held by the Essex Archive are survey data. Although all studies are in machine-readable form, a substantial proportion represent data gleaned from administrative records, often relating to historical periods. For example, a study of *Slave Trade Movement Between Africa and the Americas, 1817-1843* is based upon records of all slave ships leaving Great Britain within this time period and sailing to the Americas. Other studies represent aggregate data, again collected from administrative records. The *World Handbook of Political and Social Indicators III, 1948-1977* consists of three files, the first containing aggregate political, economic and social data on 155 countries, and two other files recording daily and annual political events throughout the time period. Whether or not a study contains survey data is only apparent from reading the study description.

Each dataset deposited at the ESRC Data Archive is allocated a study number in sequence from 001 to 99001 or beyond. The study numbers themselves have no significance except that those beginning with 33 . . . indicate generic studies – defined as those repeated at regular intervals for which there is more than one study number. This mainly applies to the annual government surveys, for example, the Family Expenditure Survey is held for 1961–3, and 1968 onwards and each annual survey has its own study number. As the study numbers give little or no information about the data subsumed under them, the first volume of the Catalogue comprises five indexes, each organized around a different concept. First, there is a *Subject Category Index* organized under 25 broad headings, such as 'CHILD DEVELOPMENT AND CHILD REARING' and 'AGRICULTURE AND RURAL LIFE'. This gives an indication of the kind of material that is available within a chosen heading. To go back to our original example and assume that we are interested in finding what material is available on the child-care needs of young mothers, we would look under the subject heading 'CHILD DEVELOPMENT AND CHILD REARING'.

The *Name Index* may also be usefully searched, particularly if there are known researchers who have deposited relevant surveys in the Archive. The Name Index lists all those persons or bodies who are associated with a particular dataset — either as depositors, or collectors or sponsors. For instance, staying with the topic, we may look under 'Thomas Coram Research Unit', because this Unit is particularly concerned with research into families and children. The entry under 'Thomas Coram Research Unit' refers us to the 'University of London, Institute of Education' and, under this heading, several studies are listed. If, however, a further search seems worthwhile, we can move on to the *Title Index*, which lists, in alphabetical order, the titles of all studies available from the Archive. Again, we could scan the listing for a study starting with 'Child' or 'Mother'. If we are particularly concerned with a specific geographical area (perhaps we have some data on England and wish to draw some comparisons with Scotland or Northern Ireland), then the *Geographical Index* will list each study, hierarchically, under the country, region, town or village. For example, the Banbury Social Survey (Stacey *et al.*, 1975) would be listed under Banbury, Oxfordshire and England.

The *Population Index* is especially valuable where the population of interest forms a clearly identifiable group; in this example, 'mothers' forms the population and we can therefore go straight to this heading. It may be worth noting that the *subject* of the research would be defined as child-care needs, rather than mothers.

Having found perhaps two or three study numbers that look promising, Volume 2 of the Catalogue can be used to find the detailed description of each study. This volume is organized into two sections, reflecting the two sequences of study numbers. The first section contains all the single studies, where the study does not form part of a repeated series – for example, the 1972 Social Mobility Inquiry and the 1980 Women and Employment Survey. The second section contains generic studies such as the continuous government surveys – the GHS, LFS and FES – the MORI and NOP political polls, and longitudinal surveys such as the National Child Development Survey.

Appendix 5.1 (p.97) reproduces the description of the Women and Employment survey that is given in Volume 2 of the Catalogue. Under each study is a set of notes giving essential information for potential users. As well as the name of the principal investigator, data collection agency, depositor and sponsor, there is also a description of the study — what it is about, the population covered, the sampling procedure, the number of cases (both target and obtained), the number of variables, the method of data collection and the date of data collection. The study description also contains a short list of any publications based upon the data. It is well worth obtaining and reading these before making a decision about ordering a particular survey, as they can reveal a great deal about the scope and quality of the research material. It may also be useful to contact the depositor to find out about subsequent publications.

In addition, at the foot of each study description are three status codes – access code, class of data preparation, and size code – that provide a useful indication of the ease with which the data may be used. All users are required to sign an 'Undertaking Form' in which they agree to preserve the confidentiality of the data subjects and to refrain from distributing the data to any other user. Over and above this, there may be special conditions set by the depositor; the *access code* indicates what these conditions may be. Often there are none (Code A), but sometimes the depositor requires secondary analysts to send draft reports of research findings before publication (Code B or 2). With most of the continuous government surveys and a small number of other studies, the researcher needs to obtain written permission from the depositor before the Data Archive is able to release the data; there is often a requirement that an outline plan of the research must be sent with the request for use (Code C). Where government surveys come under this code, the staff of OPCS or the appropriate government department look over the proposed research to check that the design is appropriate to the data and that the researcher appears to have understood the limitations of the survey. Usually permission is readily given with only a short delay. The purpose of these restrictions, then, is not to restrict access but to ensure that the secondary analyst is using data that is suitable for the proposed analysis. The code S, used in the example in Appendix 5.1, indicates that there are 'special' conditions governing the release of the data. The actual request for access is made by the Data Archive on behalf of the researcher, who simply supplies the extra information with the application form.

The *Class* of data preparation code indicates the level of work (termed 'processing') done by the Archive after receipt of the study. (ICPSR uses a similar set of class codes to those described here.) A Class I study has complete documentation, often reproduced by the Archive from the material supplied by the originators and collated into a series of booklets. The data has also been 'cleaned'. This involves checking for wild and invalid codes, where values are outside the permissible range for a variable, and re-coding these to missing values. For some Class I datasets, set-up files are available for use with either SPSS, SPSS^x or SIR (choice of analysis package is discussed in Chapter 7). Particularly with the larger surveys, which contain many hundreds of variables, these set-up files can be immensely time-saving and helpful. Class II data is defined as that which is still undergoing processing in order to attain Class I standards; this means that it is being prepared for distribution and will shortly be available. Class III data is still awaiting processing. In both cases it is worthwhile for a potential user to express interest in the survey as the Data Archive acknowledges that demand for a particular dataset will help to move it to the top of the processing queue. Class IV data is that for which no processing will be done by the Archive. Only a very small proportion of studies fall into this category and they are usually those for which documentation or data are so incomplete as to make further processing by the Archive unpractical.

The other key piece of information forming part of the status code is the code indicating the *size* of the survey. There are three categories of size – Small (S), less than 1,500 card-images; Medium (M), 1,501 to 15,000 card-images; Large (L), more than 15,000 card-images. (The term 'card-image' derives from the time when computers used punched cards, each containing 80 columns of information, for both data and processing instructions; it is still customary to organize data into lines that are 80 columns in length. Thus, a card-image represents a line containing a maximum of 80 characters of information.) Although the size code gives some indication of the amount of computer space that the data will take up, its main purpose is to provide a basis for assessing handling charges. The Archive makes a fixed handling charge, dependent upon the size category assigned to the data, but it should be noted that postgraduate students within the UK and past depositors of data are not charged. Documentation supplied by the Archive is charged at the cost of reproduction.

Future editions of the ESRC Data Archive Catalogue will contain an additional code attached to those datasets that are considered to contain 'personal data' under the 1984 Data Protection Act. These are likely to fall into three groups:

1. Studies of named members of elite groups or institutions.
2. Studies that contain votes cast for named individual candidates.
3. Surveys containing opinions of anonymous respondents on named individuals (as in opinion polls).

UK researchers who obtain such data are likely to become a 'data user' as defined by the Act and will therefore be required to register as such.

The published Catalogue is not the only method by which Archive holdings may be searched. There is also free on-line access to an information retrieval system. Figure 5.1 summarizes the relationship between the published Catalogue and the on-line retrieval system. To use this system you simply complete and return a registration form (obtainable from the Archive), after which you receive a user number and password, which allow access to the retrieval system. Access may be either by modem (making a direct telephone link from your home computer to the University of Essex computer) or by the inter-university computer network JANET (Joint Academic Network) or British Telecom's PSS (Packet Switching System). The *On-line Information Retrieval System User Guide*, available from the Data Archive, gives the telephone number for use with a modem and the addresses for both JANET and PSS.

Figure 5.1 *Methods of searching the ESRC Data Archive Catalogue*

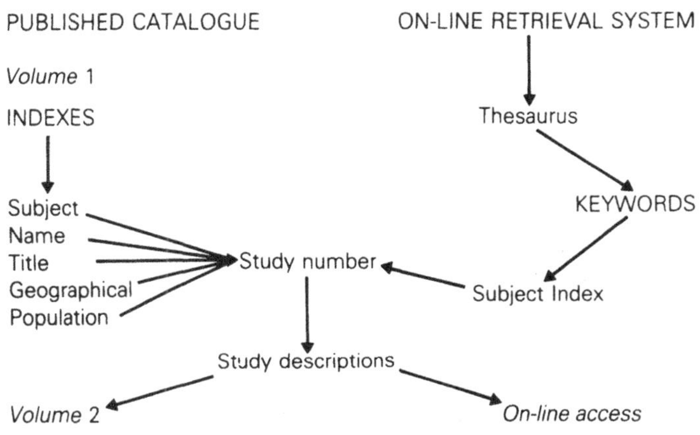

There are three databases that may be searched by using the Data Archive on-line retrieval system. First, a *thesaurus* is used to identify the keywords or classification codes by which to search the *Subject Index*. The thesaurus lists broader, narrower and related terms under each keyword. Secondly, there is the *Subject Index* itself, which links the keywords of the thesaurus to the Archive study numbers. Thirdly, the *Study description database* runs parallel with the thesaurus and Subject Index and is accessible through study numbers retrieved from the Subject Index. This database is used to generate the study descriptions in the second volume of the Catalogue, and therefore contains the same descriptions as the published Catalogue.

Recent additions to the holdings of both the ESRC Data Archive and the ICPSR Archive are announced in the quarterly *Data Archive Bulletin*, available free from the ESRC Archive.

Choosing a study

In Chapter 2 we outlined some general principles to use when considering secondary analysis of survey data. It is at the stage of selecting a data source that some of these principles need to be put into operation. Assuming that an Archive search has identified a number of potentially useful data sources, it is now necessary to use all available information to check whether the studies are appropriate for the needs of the secondary analyst, in terms of population sampled, content and quality. It should be pointed out that deposition at the Archive is not a hallmark of quality. The ESRC Data Archive does not, at present, use any selection procedures based upon an assessment of the reliability or validity of the data.

We list below a series of questions that the secondary analyst should try to answer when assessing the value of a particular study. Most of the answers will be contained within the study description published in the Archive Catalogue (Appendix 5.1), although it would also be wise to order all the available documentation before making a final decision to use the study.

1 What is the sampling procedure? What is the population sampled?
If you want to be able to make generalizations from your research then it is important to know whether the sample is representative and of what population. This applies to the geographical coverage – whether of England, Britain, Greater London, northern England – and also to the population sampled – whether all ages are covered, only adults from 20–59, only men, or both men and women. Appendix 5.1 tells us that the WES sampled women aged 16–59 living in private households. It also gives a detailed account of the way in which the stratified, multi-stage random sample was drawn.

2 What was the method of data collection?
It is important to know what methods were used to conduct the survey as this will influence the reponse rate and the kind of questions that can be asked. Was the survey conducted by postal questionnaire, or by

telephone, or were face-to-face interviews carried out with each respondent? Were proxy interviews used to gather information on other household members? The Women and Employment Survey was carried out by oral interview (Appendix 5.1).

3 What was the response rate? Is there any information available on the characteristics of non-respondents?

Many OPCS surveys manage to achieve a response rate of about 83 to 85 per cent, on a national basis (OPCS, 1981, 1983). This may be taken as a bench-mark by which to compare the response rate of other studies. In a survey of Greater London or any other large conurbation, response rates would be expected to be lower. Postal surveys also tend to obtain a lower response rate than interview surveys, although this will vary with the method of follow-up that is used. However, once the response rate begins to fall substantially, the representativeness of the respondents may be called into question unless there is evidence that the characteristics of non-respondents are unlikely to differ significantly along the main axes of the study. From the information in Appendix 5.1 we see that the target number of cases in the WES was 6,732 and the number of cases obtained was 5,588. We can therefore calculate a response rate of 83 per cent.

4 What documentation is available on the study?

The Data Archive will always be able to provide a copy of the questionnaire and a description of the sampling techniques used. However, if the data is to be used sensitively and accurately, it is also important to know the instructions that were given to the interviewers who carried out the field-work. If these were not codified it is possible that interviewers were not adequately briefed and may not have been consistent in their interviewing and recording. In any case, the secondary analyst may not feel confident about the training given to the interviewers and will certainly not be able to check the way in which responses that do not fit readily into a predetermined category have been dealt with. For example, the GHS asks respondents whether they did 'any paid work last week'. As people's definitions of work vary greatly, it is important that interviewers are told clearly the way in which work is to be defined – whether it should represent the respondent's own opinion or whether it is to be defined objectively. In the GHS, 'paid work' is defined objectively to include casual jobs such as baby-sitting, work on MSC schemes, and the work of wives who help in their husband's business, even though unpaid, provided they work at least 15 hours a week. Unless these sorts of details are specified, and the extent to which the interviewer may probe is made clear, then the same objective situation may be recorded in quite divergent ways. Similarly, it is important that the secondary analyst knows when the respondent's subjective view has been sought – for example, the GHS asks whether the respondent's health has, during the last twelve months, been 'good', 'fairly good' or 'not good'. This is recorded as the opinion of the respondent without any recourse to objective criteria.

Interviewer instructions are important because they should explain the underlying rationale behind the question, so that, if there is uncertainty over the appropriate coding of the response, the interviewer knows the principles around which the question hinges and is therefore better able to make an informed decision.

As well as interviewer instructions, it is also important to obtain a description of how the data has been coded. Most fundamentally, the column and 'card' location of each variable is required. This will invariably accompany any dataset dispatched by the Archive. Other information, however, is also important: for example, the coding frames used for open-ended questions and the way in which non-response has been coded; whether those to whom the question does not apply have been distinguished from those who did not answer; what codes, if any, have been used for missing values.

It is not always clear from the study description in the Archive catalogue exactly what documentation is available and, therefore, it is always a good idea to contact the Archive and ask for all that is available. Where interviewer instructions and coding notes do not form part of the documentation held by the Archive, it is well worth while contacting the originators to find out whether they are available.

5. Who conducted the survey?

This may seem like an invidious question to ask, but, where a secondary analyst needs to be able to rely upon the accuracy and integrity of the data source, she may well find it preferable to use a survey that has been carried out by an established organization that does its own quality control and methodological work, rather than by a postgraduate student who has been learning while working. Of course, the opposite side of the coin may apply – a postgraduate student may be putting into practice all the skills and techniques recently learned from a research methods course. The interview schedule and the quality of documentation available are likely to be good indicators of the quality of the data.

6 What publications have been produced?

The Archive asks depositors of data to supply references to any of their publications which make use of the data. These are then listed in the catalogue as part of the Study Description (Figure 5.1). Reading these publications will not only give a better insight into the study itself, but will also indicate the ground already covered and, perhaps, point to interesting questions still awaiting research. However, the most recent publications may not be listed and it is worthwhile contacting the depositor for a full list. In the example of the WES (Appendix 5.1) the publications give a very good idea of the scope of the survey and the analyses that have already been conducted; also, the technical report (Martin and Roberts, 1984b) contains invaluable background information for the secondary analyst.

7 What are the status codes of the study?

These have already been described earlier in this chapter (see pp.81–2). The most important code is the class number which indicates whether the data is available in a 'clean' and ready to use condition. Class I datasets meet both these criteria, while those in Class IV are likely to pose the greatest problems for the secondary analyst, usually because they have little if any documentation available and have not been through the cleaning process whereby stray codes are identified and re-coded to missing values.

The WES has been given a 'Special' Access category which indicates that the analyst should contact the Archive to find out the precise conditions which apply. It is in Class II because documenatation was still being prepared when the catalogue went to press. The fact that it is available as SIR files (see Chapter 7) is also indicated in the status code.

8 Which year should be used?

This question will apply only to the small proportion of repeated surveys – for example, the British Election Studies, the NORC General Social Survey, the British Social Attitudes Surveys, and the continuous government surveys. Often the year will form part of the research design – for example, in a study of voting behaviour, or in a comparison of attitudes in relation to social and political events. In other cases the most recent year available will be preferred – perhaps for a study of unemployment which used the Labour Force Survey. In some surveys, particular topics occur only in one year (for example, questions on homeworking were asked only in the Labour Force Survey of 1981) or in alternate years (e.g.the smoking data in the GHS) and then choice of topic may determine the year selected.

Once a study has been chosen for secondary analysis there are, for most datasets held at the Archive, no further selections to be made, except the mode of transport by which the data is to be sent. However, for a small proportion of surveys, which represent a large proprtion of users, the analyst must choose the form in which the data is to be used and select a subset of either cases or variables. The need to make these choices is confined almost exclusively to the large continuous government surveys – most notably the Labour Force Survey, the Family Expenditure Survey and the General Household Survey. In the following section, we shall consider the various forms in which these surveys are available and also the basis upon which to select a subset from the data.

Form of data and selection of subset

Both the General Household Survey and the Family Expenditure Survey are household-based surveys that are available from the ESRC Data Archive in several different forms. Chapter 4 described the hierarchical nature of the GHS and the various levels at which data are available. One of the key features of a hierarchical household-based survey such as the GHS is that it enables linkages to be made between different levels within the hierarchy (e.g.between the household and the individual) and between different members of the same household – for instance between husband and wife. While individual-based surveys may collect information about spouse or children, the analyst is not able to create new linkages over and above those asked of the respondent at the time of the survey. This places severe limitations on the scope of any analyses concerned with relationships between household members.

It is only in recent years that data management packages have been available to handle hierarchical data. With the advent of SIR, SAS, P-STAT and SPSS^x the analyst is now able to take full advantage of hierarchical data by creating whatever derived variables are needed at any level of the hierarchy. (Management and analysis packages will be discussed fully in Chapter 7.) It is, however, considerably more complex to analyse hierarchical data rather than rectangular data. As most standard *analysis* packages require a rectangular file with which to work, it is still necessary, once the linkages and derived variables have been made, to organize the data into a standard rectangular matrix before tabulations or statistical procedures can be used. The secondary analyst must therefore choose, in the case of the GHS, whether to order the data in a hierarchical or a rectangular (case by variable) form. This choice has profound implications both for the ease of analysis and also for the extent to which relationships can be established between and across levels of the hierarchy.

Forms in which the General Household Survey is available

RECTANGULAR VERSUS HIERARCHICAL

The ESRC Data Archive is able to supply the General Household Survey data as either flat or hierarchical files. Since the 1983 survey, OPCS have sent the GHS to the Data Archive in SIR format hierarchical files. These are available to users either in this original SIR format, retaining the hierarchical structure of the data, or, alternatively, flattened to the level of the individual and distributed as $SPSS^x$ or SAS files. For the years prior to 1983, the GHS is available in four different forms, two flat and two hierarchical. These various forms are summarized in Figure 5.2. The 'Surrey' files are so named because they were prepared at the University of Surrey with ESRC funding. The aim of the project was to produce datafiles that were readily usable by secondary analysts (Arber, Gilbert, Dale and O'Byrne, 1984). This is discussed more fully below.

Figure 5.2 *Alternative forms for the General Household Survey*

Year	*Rectangular*		*Hierarchical*	
1983 onwards	SPSS, $SPSS^x$ or SAS files		SIR export files	
1971–1982	(a) Rectangularized by the Data Archive	(b) Surrey SPSS files	(c) As originally supplied by OPCS	(d) Surrey SIR files
	1971–1982	1973–1982	1971–1982	1977–1982

The analyst needs to consider carefully whether the rectangular (flat) or hierarchical data will be the most appropriate for her needs. Although rectangular data is considerably easier to analyse, one of its main drawbacks is that individuals have lost their linkages to other household or family members. This problem is overcome to some extent by both the post-1982 GHS files and also the Surrey SPSS files for 1973–82 (Fig. 5.2(b)). The post-1982 files contain a number of derived variables linking items of information about the head of household (using the OPCS definition) to all household members; they include variables relating to head of household's socio-economic group, age, sex, country of birth and gross weekly earnings. There are also derived variables relating to the family unit – for example, giving the type of family, the number of dependent children, and the age of the youngest child.

The SPSS Surrey files contain about 80 intra-household linkages, which were considered to be of greatest analytic value for researchers.

These variables link information about the head of household to each individual in the household; variables include head of household's employment status, class, occupation and industry, as well as weekly and hourly earnings. Also, for families containing a married couple, the same variables, for *both* the husband and the wife, have been attached to *all* family unit members. This means that analyses that relate the health status of children to the class or highest educational qualification of either parent can be readily carried out. Such analyses cannot be done by using the rectangular GHS files for 1983 onwards, as the necessary derived variables are not present.[1]

If, however, the linkages provided in the Surrey SPSS files or the post-1982 flat files are likely to be inadequate, the alternative option is to use the data in its hierarchical form. From 1983 the Archive has received GHS datafiles from OPCS in a hierarchical SIR format, with variable and value labels and containing the derived variables referred to previously. For the years 1977–82 Surrey SIR files are available (Fig. 5.2(d)), fully labelled and with consistent missing values on all variables. (There is a considerable amount of continuity between the pre- and post-1982 files in terms of labelling and missing values.) The Surrey SIR files also contain a large number of derived summary variables described in more detail in the following section. For all years from 1971 to 1982 the GHS is also available in the original hierarchical form supplied by OPCS (Fig.5.2(c)), although this data is not organized into SIR files and is not labelled. Those who decide that they want to use the SIR files may find it worthwhile to obtain a Teaching Package (Dale), 1986c), aimed at facilitating use of SIR with the GHS and especially written for those with little computing experience. However, for the inexperienced secondary analyst, none of these forms of hierarchical data provides an easy option.

An alternative to using hierarchical data is to obtain the Surrey SPSS files and to derive new linked variables in addition to those already present. This can be done by using a further program, the 'Crosslinker', developed by Nigel Gilbert at the University of Surrey (Gilbert, 1982; Gilbert *et al.*, 1982) and available from the ESRC Data Archive. The Crosslinker is able to read the data for each household and compute whatever extra linkages are required by the analyst. Anyone intending to use it should note that it requires a datafile containing *all* household members (you cannot select only adults, for instance) and also certain key variables (e.g. FAMUNIT, PERNO).

Choice of files for 1973–82 GHS

Those using the GHS for 1973–82, whether in rectangular or hierarchical form, have an additional choice to make. For these years there are two flat versions available (Figure 5.2). The rectangularization of the GHS by the Data Archive (form (a) in Figure 5.2) creates a flat data file where the unit of analysis may be either the household, in which case the resultant data file contains only household level variables, or where the unit of analysis is the individual and household level information is attached to *each* individual in the household. In addition, where there are varying amounts of information about each individual, e.g. doctor visits in a two-week reference period, variables are created for up to the maximum number for any individual in that year's data. There may be as many as ten variables recording doctor visits for each individual, although for the vast majority of people these variables will be blank. Thus the rectangularized data is very much larger than the original hierarchical file. Using the GHS for 1971–82 in form (a) requires a considerable amount of preparatory work before analysis. The data files have no variable or value labels, missing value codes are not consistent and there are no derived variables – for example, measuring the highest educational qualification of an individual.

The Surrey SPSS files for these years ((b) in Figure 5.2) have been prepared by using version (a) from the Archive, and are also at the individual level. They differ from version (a) in having variable and value labels added to each variable, having consistent missing values, a range of derived variables and a codebook that documents each variable and provides a frequencies distribution for it. These features facilitate secondary analysis considerably. In addition to the intra-household linked variables contained in the Surrey SPSS files and described previously, both the Surrey SPSS and SIR files for 1973–82 contain two kinds of derived variables. First, there are variables derived from individual level variables (for example, highest educational qualifications and average hourly earnings) and, secondly, household and family unit variables derived from information about the individual members of the household and family unit respectively. Total household income provides an example of a summary household level variable, and the number of children in the family unit summarizes family level information. The Surrey files retain all the original variables used to construct these complex variables, making a total of about 800 variables in the 1980 Surrey SPSS files.

For 1977–82 the analyst may also choose whether to use the Surrey SIR files, ((d) in Figure 5.2) or the original hierarchical data supplied by OPCS. As with the flat files, the Surrey SIR files are fully labelled and documented and contain all the derived summary variables that are in the Surrey SPSS files.

Forms in which the Family Expenditure Survey is available

The Family Expenditure Survey also holds data at different levels of a hierarchy. It has an extensive Household Schedule and an Income Schedule for all spenders (defined as people aged 16 or over) within the household. When the Income Schedule has been completed by all 'spenders', a 7-day diary is left with each adult in which they are asked to record all expenditure during two consecutive 7-day periods. The structure of this survey, therefore, differs somewhat from that of the GHS.

The FES is available from the Data Archive in the following forms:

1.	Household level	Household variables only
2.	Household level	As (1) but with individual income and expenditure items aggregated for the household
3.	Household level	As (2) but with some individual items added without aggregation
4.	Individual level	With all income and expenditure items at the level of the individual
5.	Individual level with some household variables attached	As (4) but with some duplicated household level information attached to the individual
6.	Education only	This is data only for people in full-time education

The FES is distinctive in the very large number of derived variables supplied by OPCS. This means that most of the variables required by the secondary analyst are usually already available and do not need to be computed. However, it also means that the dataset is very large, with more than 1,200 variables in 1979. It is, therefore, virtually impossible for a researcher to use a complete dataset, and a choice of both level (individual, household, as above) and variables is necessary. The FES data for 1984 onwards is available in SIR format. Further information on the way in which this is distributed can be found in the ESRC Data Archive's Data Request Forms and Notes or from the Data Archive Bulletin.

Selecting a subset

The large continuous government surveys, in particular the GHS, FES and LFS, are of such a size that it is impracticable for most users to obtain the entire dataset for any one year. For example, the annual datafile for the 1984 LFS contains about 350 variables and 186,000 cases. The following section considers some guidelines for selecting a subset from these surveys.

Depending upon the form of the data, the user may be able to select either specific variables, or groups of variables held as card-images or record types. It may also be possible to select cases on the basis of a particular variable, such as age or sex. In the case of the Labour Force Survey there is a single form only – the data is available as individual level records and the user is asked to select variables. For both the FES and GHS, either variables or groups of variables may be selected and it is also possible to use selection criteria for extracting cases. For each of these three large and complex surveys the ESRC Data Archive produces a set of notes to guide the user through the intricacies of choosing and ordering the data. Whatever the precise method of selection, there are general principles that are important to consider before ordering the data, to ensure that all necessary variables have been selected. It is both expensive and time-consuming to find that you need to re-order another dataset because a key variable has been omitted from the original specification.

The first step is to think through in considerable detail the analyses that you wish to do. This, of course, is important for any secondary analysis, but particularly so when a selection of variables has to be made at the point of ordering the data. Making a detailed plan of the proposed analyses should ensure, first, that any limitations of the survey become apparent before ordering it and, secondly, that a key variable is not overlooked. This is particularly likely where several variables are needed in order to derive a new variable. For example, an analyst using the GHS may wish to distinguish full-time and part-time working on the basis of number of hours normally worked. Because standard definitions of part-time working use a different number of hours for teachers than for the rest of the work-force (under 26 hours and under 31 hours, respectively) it is also necessary to obtain the variable that indicates whether or not the respondent is a teacher before this definition of part-time working can be successfully operationalized. In Chapter 4 we discussed the way in which the secondary analyst can create derived variables to measure the concepts of interest. Generally, the derivation of variables needs to be thought through, with reference to all available documentation, before ordering the data.

Ordering the data

Having decided upon the survey to be used, obtained all available documentation, and, in some cases, specified the variables or cases required, you are now in a position to complete the Data Archive's order form. Again, the UK ESRC Data Archive is used as an example, but most of the points discussed apply equally to other Archives. Much of the required information is entirely straightforward – the title of the survey and the study number. However, you will also be asked to specify the medium by which you wish to receive the data. There are three main options, which will be outlined here:

The data may be sent to you, physically, through the post, either:
  on floppy disk (for use with a personal computer (PC)) or
  on magnetic tape (for use with a mainframe)

or you can obtain the data directly through a computer link using JANET (Joint Academic Network).

To supply data on *floppy disk* the Data Archive needs to know the make and model of the personal computer to be used, and its disk capacity. Although data can be written by using a wide range of floppy disk formats, this is not a suitable medium if the dataset is over 1 megabyte in size. High density floppy disks, for use on computers such as the IBM PC-AT (see Chapter 6), are now able to hold up to 1.2 megabytes of data, which represents about 60 2-column variables for 10,000 cases. However, in practice this is an over- estimate, as the entire disk cannot be used. None the less, for many purposes this will represent adequate capacity for a complete survey or a subset of data from a government survey. Whether you require your data on a floppy disk or a magnetic tape will largely depend upon whether you are using a mainframe or a personal computer for analysis. The relative merits of these two alternatives are fully considered in Chapter 6.

If you order your data on *magnetic tape* for use on a mainframe computer, a few further pieces of information will be needed on the order form. These are:

  the character code
  the number of bytes per record
  the blocking factor
  the density, expressed in bpi
  the number of tracks on the tape

Your computing advisory service will be able to give you the answers to all these questions as they are specific to the kind of computer that you are using. However, it may be useful here to explain briefly what each of these terms means.

Character code Data is recorded on tape in binary form (see Chapter 6) using a number of different coding systems. For representing numbers, characters and symbols, the most widely used code is ASCII (American Standard Code for Information Interchange). The other main alternative is EBCDIC, standing for Extended Binary Coded Decimal Interchange Code.

Bytes per record Data is organized into bytes (see Chapter 6 for a definition), with one character corresponding to one byte, and these in turn are organized into records. Typically, a record contains 80 bytes – that is, a record represents a card-image with 80 columns of data.

Blocking factor Records are in turn organized into blocks, where a block may, typically, contain anywhere between 1 and 80 records. The number of records in the block is given by the blocking factor.

Density An inch of tape will contain a different number of bits (pieces of information) depending upon how densely they are packed. A density of 1,600 bpi (bits per inch) packs 1,600 bits into one inch of tape (8 bits comprise 1 byte).

Number of tracks A tape has a number of tracks running along the length of it (usually either 7 or 9) with each track able to store data. Whether you require your tape written with 7 or 9 tracks depends entirely upon the computer that will be used to read the tape.

Data files may alternatively be transmitted by *network* by using the inter-university computer network, JANET. To obtain data in this way you will need to supply the Archive with your local computer's name and JANET address, as well as the password required to allow file transfer to take place. This information will be available from the Computing Advisory Service run by your institution, which will also be able to tell you of any other requirements that might be needed to obtain data in this way. You must also ensure that you have adequate disk space available in which to write the data. While this is one of the easiest ways of transporting data it is only a viable option for files that are less than 3–4 megabytes in size.

As well as specifying the format in which data is required, all users are also required to sign an undertaking to preserve the confidentiality of the data subjects, to acknowledge the depositors and the Archive in all publications which use the data, and also to refrain from distributing the data to any other user.

Having dispatched the order form, duly signed in the appropriate places, you are now able to await the arrival of your data confident in the knowledge that you are on course to a carefully planned and exciting research project.

In the next chapter we discuss the different kinds of hardware that can be used in the analysis of survey data and explain in more detail some of the technical terms that have been briefly mentioned here.

Note

1 However, Banks (1987) has described a method by which $SPSS^x$ may be used to create additional linkages using rectangular, individual-level data. See R. Banks (1987) '$SPSS^x$ v. SIR: some considerations re the GHS', The General Household Survey Newsletter (University of Essex: ESRC Data Archive).

Appendix 5.1
A study description from the ESRC Data Archive Catalogue

01746 Women and Employment
Project: SS ; 1143.

Principal Investigators Martin, J., United Kingdom, Office of Population Censuses and Surveys. Roberts, C., United Kingdom, Department of Employment.

Data Collector United Kingdom, Office of Population Censuses and Surveys.

Depositors Martin, J., United Kingdom, Office of Population Censuses and Surveys.

Sponsor United Kingdom, Department of Employment.

Purpose The overall objective was to establish the place of employment in women's lives. It aimed to establish both the extent of current unemployment among women and to understand what unemployment meant for women. It needed therefore to compare unemployed women both with those women who were employed and those who were economically inactive; it also needed to establish how important a paid job was for women and how much of their lives they spent in employment.

Variables Women's Questionnaire

(a) Patterns of movement in and out of the labour market

Whether women were working full-time, part-time or not working at different stages in their lives and at different points in time.

(b) Factors affecting participation in the labour market

Economic, social and psychological factors affecting decisions about whether or not to work. Reasons for working/not working.

(c) Recent and current employment activities

Description of type of work, conditions (pay, hours etc.) job satisfaction. Mobility between employers and type of work over the last five years.

(d) The consequences of not working and the process of job search

Attitudes to and consequences of not working. Investigation of different categories of 'not working', from 'registered unemployed' to 'not intending to work'. Economic, social and psychological consequences of not working for women wanting to work. How women look or intend to look for work. The reasons women give up seeking work.

(e) Factors affecting decisions about whether to work

Constraints of child care and other domestic responsibilities. Division of labour between husbands and wives. Attitude of husbands to wife working. Family financial situation. Availability of suitable work in terms of type of work, hours, pay, travel to work. Which factors would cause women to want to change their present situation (i.e. re working full-time, part-time, or not working).

(f) Careers and occupational mobility

Whether women see themselves as having careers. The future work intentions of women before they have children. Women's assessments of the level of their jobs before and after domestic absence. Whether women think their job utilises their skills, qualifications, training etc.

(g) General attitudes to women and work

The relative importance of work and family, male and female roles - views on whether men should take precedence over women for work if jobs are scarce. Attitudes to equal opportunities, general awareness of legislation and social trends.

Men's Questionnaire Information concerning education and qualifications. Current employment situation and occupation. Ways in which husband's situation affects wife's employment. Income and financial situation. Whether respondent's job could be/is done by women. General attitudes to women at work. Whether respondent can easily take time off work to care for children. Division of labour between husband and wife in the home. Whether respondent's mother worked outside the home. Assessment of recent legislation concerning equal opportunities.

Publications / Reports Martin, J. and Roberts, C., *Women and employment: a lifetime perspective*, (London: HMSO, 1984)

Martin, J. and Roberts, C., *Women and employment: technical report*, (London: OPCS, 1984)

Joshi, H., 'Women's participation in paid work', *DE Research Paper*, no.45, 1984

Dex, S., 'Women's work histories', *DE Research Paper* no.46, 1984

Cragg, A. and Dawson, T., 'Unemployed women: a study of attitudes and experiences', *DE Research Paper*, no.47, 1984

Martin, J. and Roberts, C., 'Women's employment in the 1980s: evidence from the Women and Employment Survey', *DE Employment Gazette*, May 1984

Martin, J. and Roberts, C., 'Non-working women: evidence from the 1980 Women and Employment Survey', *DE Employment Gazette*, June, 1984

Martin, J. and Roberts, C., 'Women working part-time: evidence from the 1980 Women and Employment Survey', *DE Employment Gazette*, August, 1984

Dex, S., 'Women's occupational profiles: evidence from the 1980 Women and Employment Survey', *DE Employment Gazette*, September, 1984

Joshi, H., 'The lifetime effects of child-bearing on women's paid work: evidence from the 1980 Women and Employment Survey', *DE Employment Gazette*, October, 1984.

Population Women aged 16 to 59 living in private households in Great Britain (In addition, the husbands of some of the women were also interviewed).

Sampling Procedures Stratified, multi-stage, random sample. (1) Random sample of 120 local authority districts, stratified by region, metropolitan/non-metropolitan and the proportion of the population in SEG 1-5 or 13. Districts were selected with probability proportional to the size of the electorate. (2) Random sample of 4 wards within each district with pps. (3) Random sample of approximately 20 addresses within each ward. (4) Doorstep sift to identify women aged 16 - 59.

Cases (target) 6732.

Cases (obtained) 5588 (sub-sample of husbands = 800) (approximate).

Method of Data Collection Oral interview.

Date of Data Collection April 1980 to June 1980.

Status Access S. Class II (SIR). Size L.

Source: Taylor (1986).

6

Elements of computing technology

The following two chapters are intended to give some practical guidance on how to get yourself set up for secondary analysis in terms first of computing equipment and then of programs. We discuss some of the criteria you might want to take into account in choosing hardware and software – the actual computer and the program that does the analysis. For many analysts there is no real choice, because only one set of facilities is available, but even if you are in this category you may still find it interesting to know something of the alternatives, so as to be able to have a say in any changes that may be proposed. Of course, computing science is a highly technical area. No user needs to know all of the details, but we start by providing a brief guide to the essential technical vocabulary, if only in order that you can defend yourself against a colleague determined to blind you with science. One caveat, which will be repeated: though the principles of what we say may be relied upon, the pace of technological change is such that many of the details (model numbers, specifications, etc.) change from one month to the next. A month after our typescript was sent to the publishers, IBM announced a new range of computers, which necessitated substantial revisions and additions to this chapter: who knows what will happen between now and publication day?[1]

Kinds of computer

We begin by looking at the physical equipment. Computers these days come in two principal varieties. First, there are the small machines that are used by one person at a time. The best known example of these is the IBM PC. Such a machine consists of a box the size of a briefcase that contains most of the works, a keyboard much like that of an electric typewriter, attached to the main box by a flexible cable, by means of which the user enters instructions, and a screen similar to that of a TV set, on which the computer displays its responses. In addition, there is almost always a device on which the results can be printed in order to make a permanent copy – most often something like a typewriter *without* its keyboard. For historical reasons these machines are often referred to as microcomputers, but we prefer to call them *personal computers*, or PCs (IBM have no copyright on those initials).

The second kind of computers are often called *mainframes*. The obvious difference from PCs is that mainframes are big: one will often occupy an entire air-conditioned room, and will look rather like a collection of hi-tech kitchen equipment – fridge-freezers, dishwashers, microwave ovens, and so on – arranged in rows and stacks. More important from the point of view of the user is how a mainframe is accessed. Attached to the machine by long cables (perhaps even telephone circuits leading to the other side of the world) are large numbers of *terminals*. Each terminal will usually look rather like a compact PC: at least, there will be a keyboard and a screen, though the rest of the works will be so compact that they need no separate box. Each user sits at a terminal and types instructions, to which the mainframe responds by displaying messages on the screen. Because it is so big (and therefore powerful), a number of users (sometimes hundreds) can use the mainframe essentially simultaneously. We say 'essentially' because what is really happening is that the computer attends to each user in turn, giving each perhaps one-hundredth of a second. To the user, it looks as if she is getting immediate attention, at least for small tasks. The mainframe will also have printers and other output devices attached to it.

Of course, computers come in intermediate sizes too, but for our purposes the above distinction is good enough. The importance of the distinction is that the programs that are needed for your analysis also come in two corresponding varieties. Later, we shall go into the differences between these varieties. In principle, therefore, someone setting out to use a computer for the first time has to decide whether she will be using a PC or a mainframe, and must choose the program accordingly. Sometimes it is the other way around – you choose the program first, and that determines the kind of machine. Often, of course, you are simply obliged to use what is available. But, for those who do have to make a choice, we can offer some advice.

Technical vocabulary

First, though, some more technical details. To begin with, what is a *program?* (And note the spelling – in the context of computers the US variant has become universal.) A program is simply a set of instructions, coded in a way that the computer is designed to follow, for carrying out some task or collection of tasks. It is rather like the totally explicit instructions you might write to enable someone with no background knowledge and no common sense to make a *sauce béarnaise.* Having once written down these instructions, all you would need to say in future is 'make half a litre of sauce', and your slave should be able to do it. Of course, making sure that the instructions were completely explicit and fool-proof could be quite time-consuming, and you might not get it right the first time, so it would probably make more sense to buy a tried and true recipe from a professional cookery writer. Similarly, if you want a set of explicit instructions to enable a computer to tabulate one column of figures by another, it makes more sense to buy someone else's recipe – or program – than to try to do it yourself. As an indication of the size of the task, the instructions in a typical general data analysis program might easily run to 100,000 lines. Programs are often referred to collectively as *software*, to distinguish them, of course, from the *hardware*, the physical equipment. Users are sometimes referred to, perhaps in jest, as *liveware.* (There is also *firmware*, which, as you might expect, is mysterious stuff intermediate between hardware and software. Software is normally stored in the form of magnetic imprints on tape or disk (more later), and read into the computer's memory whenever it is needed. Instructions that are needed all the time, such as how to display particular characters on screen, are sometimes encapsulated into a special, semi-permanent form of memory, and this is what is then called firmware. This is rather esoteric knowledge, though.) A collection of programs all intended to perform tasks within the same general area is sometimes referred to as a *package.* Strictly speaking, SPSS^x and the other software products we discuss (each of which does indeed carry out a variety of tasks within the general area of data analysis) are not packages because technically each consists not of a collection of programs but of a main program and a collection of subprograms. Nevertheless, to avoid confusion with the programs that the analyst writes to use the supplied software, we refer to these products as packages. This is actually quite common usage.

Programs are written in a variety of programming languages, but that doesn't affect the end user.

A few more technicalities are needed on the hardware. We shall start by describing a PC in more detail, and then say a bit about the distinctive characteristics of a mainframe. We repeat that the rate of technological development is so great that, by the time you read this, some of the details will probably be out of date, but the principles will still be applicable.

Personal computers

The main box of a PC contains three principal kinds of component. First, it contains the circuitry that actually 'does the computing' – adds numbers together, for instance. Most of this circuitry is contained within a single *integrated circuit* called a *microprocessor*, which most people know as the microchip. There are several different microprocessors in use in general-purpose PCs, most of the more widespread being made by the US company Intel.

Chips for everything

The original IBM PC used a chip called the 8088, and a lot of other machines have been produced using the same chip, which all work in roughly the same way, so that they can run the same programs. In particular, they all use the same *operating system*. The operating system is a special program that takes care of a lot of the finicky details of the relationship between an *application program* – the piece of software that does something of direct application, such as a program for data analysis or for word processing – and the hardware: not just the chip, but also the memory, the disk drives, and other gadgets (described below). A rough parallel is with the standardization of controls in cars. If you are used to driving a Ford Sierra, you can step into an Escort or a Granada and find that the same controls work in the same way – the lighting stalk is always in the same place, and rotating it forwards or pulling it back will always have essentially the same effect, although the components it controls may be quite different in detail – some Ford models will have dual headlights and some single, for instance. So, too, the standard operating system means that the same command will always list the files on a particular disk, whether it is a $5\frac{1}{4}$ inch unit, or a $3\frac{1}{2}$ inch, or even a Winchester (all explained below). Obviously, this is a big advantage for anyone who uses more than one machine. Less obviously, it is an even bigger advantage for the people who write programs, because it means that the detailed instructions that make up the program will have the same effect on different brands of computer. The usual operating system for 8088 machines was written by a company called Microsoft, who called it MS/DOS (Microsoft Disk Operating System). The very first version was written for the IBM PC, and is called PC/DOS. In most respects MS/DOS and PC/DOS are identical. Many machines that have an 8088 chip and run MS/DOS claim in their marketing literature to be IBM-compatible. This is really a matter of degree: some manufacturers have done their best to make their machine run just like an IBM PC in every way, while others have not gone quite so far. If you particularly want to run a piece of software designed for the IBM, and you are considering buying a machine of a different make (because it is cheaper, or because it has better facilities in other ways), insist on trying the program/computer combination before you put down your money, unless the publisher of the program specifically recommends it for your machine.

A whole family of chips has been designed by Intel to be compatible with the 8088, and thus to use MS/DOS. The Intel 8086 chip works in much the same way as the 8088, but it is in principle rather faster. It was used in the original Apricot, for instance, at one time the biggest selling British small business computer. The Apricot PC could be persuaded to run some IBM software without change, but it was not claimed to be truly IBM-compatible. It is an indication of the extent to which IBM have dominated this market that, in the summer of 1986, Apricot announced an IBM-compatible machine. A lot of other 'IBM-compatibles' use the 8086 rather than the 8088, because of its greater speed: in itself this causes no compatibility problems. When IBM themselves brought out their new range of personal computers, the Personal System/2, they chose the 8086 chip for the bottom-end machine, the Model 30. This will run almost all the software written for the old PC, though IBM claim it is typically about 2½ times as fast. A table of benchmark results in *PC User* magazine for July 1987 shows the PS/2 30's performance to be practically indistinguishable from that of the very cheap Amstrad PC1512. At the time of writing no manufacturers have announced PS/2-compatible machines; by the time you read this, such machines may well be commonplace, but the old, if obsolete, standard will still have some life in it.

The 80286 is a much more powerful chip, which again uses a version of MS/DOS. It is used in the IBM PC/AT (for Advanced Technology), and again there are many 'work-alikes', on which the same advice must be given – try before you buy. More powerful means not only that, for instance, the machine can do arithmetic faster, but also that it can have more *memory* attached to it, the advantages of which are explained later. Most software that was written for the 8088 or 8086 will run without change on the 80286, but not all: if in doubt, check before buying.

Again, there are two machines in IBM's PS/2 range that use the 80286 chip: the model 50 and the Model 60. These, too, are broadly compatible with the 'old' PC/AT – but not necessarily vice versa. A new, advanced operating system, OS/2, is appearing in various versions from early 1988 onwards, and programs written for this will work only on machines – including 'old' PC/ATs and compatibles – which have changed from MS/DOS to OS/2.

At the time of writing, the most powerful chip in this family is the 80386. This is again a more powerful version of the basic Intel design. Its most obvious advantage is that it can manage more memory (see below), though it will also do arithmetic and similar operations faster. It has a choice of operating systems, so that, provided compatibility with the basic IBM PC is not crucial, you can, for instance, opt for the power to run several different application programs simulaneously.

The other chip in common use is the Motorola 68000 and its variants. This is a powerful processor, but it seems to have lost out in the main PC market. A number of excellent machines use it, including on the one hand the Apple Macintosh and others of similar design, and on the other some powerful scientific computers, some of which will run versions of the software to be described below; but it seems clear that most software houses producing statistical programs are concentrating on the IBM-like market.

Before the 8088 was introduced, serious personal computing was dominated by the Zilog Z80 chip. PCs using this chip are often referred to as CP/M machines, because this is the name of the operating system that it uses. CP/M computers are still very useful, but they do not have the power needed for serious data analysis. The same can be said of computers that use the 6502 chip, of which the most common examples are the early Apples (before the Macintosh) and the BBC.

You will sometimes hear chips described as eight, sixteen or thirty-two bit processors. The main thing to say about this is that the differences between these are not as important as salespersons and technology freaks would sometimes have you believe. The number of bits makes some difference to how fast the computer works, and to how much memory it can cope with, but there are so many other factors that influence performance that the only sensible thing to do, if you want to know how a particular combination of hardware and software will perform, is to test it, or, more practicably, to read the report of a test carried out by one of the computing magazines that have come into existence.

In addition to the main, general-purpose, processor chip, many PCs have an extra chip called an *arithmetic coprocessor.* This is designed to do nothing but arithmetic (where the main chip, for instance, may also have to do the work of controlling the flow of data in and out of memory), and will considerably speed up any work that involves a lot of calculating. (Not all computing is calculating in the everday sense –

word processing is an obvious example of this. It is probably best to think of computers as devices for manipulating information – of which numerical data is a special case.) This extra chip will normally add between five and twenty per cent to the basic price of the machine, so it may well be cost-effective. Salespersons may refer to it as a maths chip. The suppliers of your chosen software will be able to tell you if you have to have one; sometimes it is optional, and again the software suppliers should be able to tell you how great the performance advantage of installing one would be.

Memory, bits and bytes

The second main component of a personal computer is the memory. This is often referred to as *random access memory*, or RAM. This is a rather mysterious term, but the idea behind it is that if you choose at random a particular location in memory in which to store an item of information, such as a number, then access will always be about equally fast. This is in contrast to a serial access medium, like a tape, on which access to some parts will be much slower than to others, because of the time spent spooling through it.

Manufacturers make a lot of fuss about the amount of RAM they provide. The basic storage unit is called a *byte*, which is in turn made up from eight *bits*. 'Bit' stands for *binary digit*.

The crucial importance of the bit is that, as you may know, computers work entirely with ones and zeros. This is because these numbers can be represented very simply by having a switch in its on or off state. One kind of transistor is really nothing more than a switch, and computer memory consists of large numbers of transistors, wired together in such a way that they can be quickly turned on or off (which is called writing to memory) or their on/off state observed (reading). These days, of course, transistors are not discrete components, as they were in the early transistor radios, but microscopic patches within an integrated circuit, or chip. So a computer contains a number of memory chips, each containing many thousands of transistors, as well as the main processor chip.

A digit chosen from this pair (on/off; 1/0) is called a binary digit, in the same way that a number chosen from our familiar ten can be called a decimal digit. As everyone knows (though we don't always think of it in these terms), the limited range of decimal digits, 0 to 9, can represent any number, however large or small, by positional notation – in the 'units' column a 1 means ten to the power zero, or one; in the 'tens' column it means ten to the power one, or ten; in the 'hundreds' column it means ten to the power two, or one hundred, and so on. (Working rightwards from the decimal point, each column represents a successively larger *negative* power of ten.) Similarly, if more long-windedly, the two binary digits, 0 and 1, can represent any number in terms of powers of two: in the first column (from the right) $1 = 2^0 = 1$; in the second column, $1 = 2^1 = 2$; in the third, $1 = 2^2 = 4$, and so on. (Zero always means zero.) So 13_{10} (thirteen base ten) can be represented in binary as 1101: $2^3 + 2^2 + 0 + 2^0 = 8 + 4 + 0 + 1 = 13$. Arithmetic in binary is perfectly straightforward – in some respects easier, because there are fewer tables to learn. In fact, you don't need to understand the details of this at all: the user never sees anything but decimal numbers, because the conversion to and from binary is always done automatically. Anyway, the one-zero code can be used to represent not only numbers but also letters and other characters, which is useful for applications such as word processing, and it turns out that eight bits are enough to represent 256 different characters ($2^8 = 256$), which is enough for most practical purposes.

So the basic unit of memory is the byte, and manufacturers usually say how many bytes of memory they provide. Most often, in fact, they report it in kilobytes. A kilobyte is actually 1024 bytes, not a thousand, because 1024 is 2 to the power 10 (back to binary). So a machine which is said to have 256K of memory (again, 256 is a whole power of 2) has about a quarter of a million bytes. (At the time of writing few serious machines would be sold with less than 512K: the pace of change is such that by the time you read this the standard amount may well be a megabyte – more than a million bytes.) The amount of memory a computer has will obviously influence the size of problem it can tackle. More important, perhaps, than the amount of data that can be held in RAM at any one time is the point that the program, too, has to be held in memory, so that a machine with too little RAM will either not be able to cope with a large program or will at best spend too much of its time swapping instructions between RAM and the disk. Other things being equal, it is best to get a machine with as much memory as possible. However, as usual it is advisable to consult the software suppliers, because some programs are not able to take advantage of large amounts of RAM. Also, it is usually perfectly straightforward to fit more memory later, if you should decide you need it, and memory is getting cheaper and cheaper.

Storage devices

The disks are the third sort of main component. A floppy disk, or *diskette*, is the usual semi-permanent storage medium for PCs. Usually the RAM loses its contents when the power is switched off, and in any case you will never have enough RAM for everything you need to store, so any information to which the processor does not need immediate access is recorded on an external medium. The nearest to common experience is a cassette tape drive, very similar to an audio-cassette player, and in which the information is recorded in much the same way, that is, by making a magnetic imprint. The main difference is that, where an audio tape contains a representation of smoothly changing sound waves, in the form of smoothly changing intensities of magnetization, a computer tape represents discrete bits (and octuples of bits – bytes) as discrete blobs of magnetization. (An aside: most national languages have bowed down to US intellectual and linguistic imperialism and adopted the English technical vocabulary. The French, characteristically, are resisting this tendency, and have formed a committee of the Académie Française to coin the necessary neologisms. Their word for byte is octet – actually much more descriptive.)

The main problem with cassettes, which is also true of the audio medium, is that, if you want access to a section of tape which doesn't happen to be near the head that records and plays back, you will have to wait seconds or minutes while the mechanism spools forwards or backwards. Cassettes, then, are used only in the most primitive home computers. (They are also used as a back-up medium, but not many PCs are supplied with this facility.) A diskette, on the other hand, looks a bit like a gramophone disk: it is a thin (therefore floppy) disk of plastic, protected by a sleeve of some sort, in which it is always kept, even when it is placed in the disk drive of a computer – there will be a window in the sleeve through which the drive can 'record' and 'play back'. (There may also be an outer sleeve, for extra protection when the disk is not in use.) The main difference is that, instead of being engraved with grooves which contain the information to be stored, it is coated with a magnetic material essentially identical to that on a tape. Recording is done in just the same way as on a cassette, by magnetizing or demagnetizing blobs of the coating. The advantage is that, just as a gramophone pick-up can be placed quickly on any track of a record that is on the turntable, so the read/write head can be moved to any part of the disk in a small fraction of a second. Thus, the disk is close to being a random access medium. It is on disks that data and programs are usually stored when they are not actually being used, and any serious computer will have one, or almost always two, disk drives. A user gradually builds up a library of diskettes, containing her data and programs. The cost of diskettes varies according to the kind of drives your PC uses: think of it as comparable to the price of an audio-cassette.

The disks on IBM PCs and the 'compatibles' all produce disks of identical physical and logical format – a disk written by one such machine can be read by another. The $5\frac{1}{4}$ inch disks used by this family are also used by other machines with different logical layouts, but it is sometimes possible to get around software incompatibility. The real problem arises, of course, when the disk is physically different. The other main variety in use with PCs is the $3\frac{1}{2}$ inch disk. These are used on most so-called lap-held computers, and on a few desk-top machines. If you want to transfer data between computers using these two formats you have two alternatives. If you have a one-off problem – a few disks to copy because you happen to have acquired them in the wrong format, or because you are changing machines – then you may find it easiest to have the copying done by a specialist firm, which will have a computer specially built with several different kinds of disk drive. (The ESRC Data Archive has such a computer, so it should be able to supply data in any format you ask for, but it is not in the business of providing a disk-copying service.) If, on the other hand, the problem is a recurrent one, you may choose the alternative solution, which is to have a cable made up with the appropriate plug or socket at either end, use this to connect up the two computers, and obtain communications software to allow them to talk to each other. Small PCs are beginning to be used in the field to record survey responses in the course of the interview, and some such approach is needed to transfer the day's data into the machine back at base. The computers need not be side by side: you can carry out the file transfer via the telephone system or a network.

The capacity of a diskette on an IBM PC is 360K: that is, you can store about 360,000 characters on it. This is simplest to interpret in the context of word processing, where a character is what is seems to be. If a word of text is on average six characters long, including the space that follows it, you can get about 60,000 words on to one diskette. In practice, the way that word processors work means that you would not attempt to store more than between a third and a half of that: the word processor will want to keep a back-up copy of your text, and perhaps also a working copy, as well as the master copy. But you can use as many diskettes as you like, within reason, and put them into the drives as you need them, much as you can get the whole of an opera through your audio system by putting on one cassette or disk after another.

Numbers can be stored in two different modes. First, they can be regarded as just another set of characters, with properties no different in kind from letters. Secondly, they can be regarded as the basis of our system of arithmetic, with very special properties. (To make this distinction clear, we sometimes refer to the first mode as numerals rather than as numbers.) In the second mode, numbers are stored rather differently. You can usually reckon that any number, however many digits it may have, will occupy four bytes (the numbers 7 and 2,569,076 take up the same amount of space). That means that 360K will hold about 90,000 numbers – say ninety values for each of a thousand respondents. By comparison with the size of a typical survey, that isn't very much. Again, in principle, you can get around this problem by storing your data set on several disks, but in practice this is not likely to work well. For instance, you may well want to access items of information from different disks in quick succession. The only real solution is to use disks with a larger capacity. Surprisingly, the $3\frac{1}{2}$ inch disks mentioned earlier have a capacity of over 700K, and 1.2 Megabyte drives are now available, but clearly this doesn't go far enough. The solution is *hard disks.*

Hard disks – and the future

Hard disks (sometimes called Winchesters, after the town in Hampshire where IBM developed this technology) work rather differently. Instead of a removable floppy disk, they use a rigid permanently mounted disk, in a hermetically sealed box, which allows finer tolerances, higher rotation speeds and greater capacities. A 20 Megabyte drive is now common in a PC; in the current number of *Byte* magazine a 190 MB drive is advertised for $2,769; no doubt they will get bigger and cheaper. Perhaps 5 Mbytes would be used for storing software, but if you have 15 Mbytes left you could store a dataset with nearly four million entries – four hundred entries for each of ten thousand respondents, for instance. Again, in practice, you would probably restrict yourself to half of this, in order to be able to make changes to the data and store the new version, but even so this is clearly enough storage for the usual run of surveys. Of course, it would still be quite inadequate for something like the entire General Household Survey, though it might well be enough for a subset, such as all the health-related variables. One snag is that the 15 Mbytes is a fixed upper limit: hard disks are intrinsically not interchangeable. (Actually there are drives with interchangeable cartridges, but they are rarely if ever fitted as standard equipment – you would have to plug it in as an extra.) This also means that whereas with diskettes you can easily send data through the post, with a hard disk you cannot. Mainly to get round this second problem, hard disk machines practically always have an exchangeable diskette drive as well. This also means that the size of your data library can be unlimited: when you want to use a particular dataset, which may extend over several diskettes, you copy it on to the hard disk, deleting existing files (which also presumably exist on diskette, so that they can subsequently be restored) to make room. Then the files are read into the program from the hard disk.

The newest storage medium is the *laser disk.* At the time of writing these are not widely used, but have great promise for certain purposes. One variety can use a commercial compact disk (CD) player, which you may have attached to your stereo system, with a special interface to the PC. A dataset that is to be widely distributed can be used to make a stamping master for CDs, which can hold a great deal of information and be produced at a low marginal cost. Of course, a CD player can only play back, or read, not write. A device that can write (permanently, by 'burning' the disk) and also read has recently become available: the acronym to look out for is WORM – Write Once; Read Many times. Non-erasability may look very wasteful: it works because (a) the method is in principle very cheap and (b) in practice people are in any case very bad at erasing old files.

Mix 'n' match

Although different processors, memories and disk drives can in principle be combined in any way, in practice people usually have access to one of three broad configurations. A basic PC will have an 8088 or 8086 processor, 256 Kbytes (or up to 640K – this is a limit imposed by MS/DOS) of memory, and two floppy disk drives, each with 360 or 720 Kbytes of storage. An advanced one will have an 80286 chip and an arithmetic coprocessor, 512K or a Megabyte of memory, a 20 Megabyte hard disk, and also a 1.2 or 1.44 Mbyte floppy drive. At the time of writing the first 80386 machines are just appearing: they look like having more memory and disk space, and a higher resolution screen for better graphics.

All of the programs we discuss in Chapter 7 can be obtained in a version that will run on an advanced PC; most will not run on a basic machine. None of them has been modified for the Macintosh or any of its relatives; several were converted for the 'professional' 68000 machines before the 80286 became available, but the software producers all now seen to be concentrating on the PC/AT market. In addition, of course, these programs will all run on most makes of mainframe, though often in a rather different form.

The other main components of a PC are the keyboard and display. Although in principle you can buy 'improved' keyboards for a PC, in practice there is not much to choose between them. Your keyboard will look like one from a typewriter, with two exceptions. First, it is nearly always detached from the rest of the machine, and linked to it by a flexible cable, so that you have more choice in your working position. (We know people who quite like working in bed, with the processor box and screen on a low table and the keyboard propped comfortably on their knees.) Secondly, it will have, in addition to the usual typing keys, as many again which, instead of corresponding to letters, numerals and punctuation marks, send special control signals to the computer. You will learn how to use these extra keys as you need to.

The display will always be a screen superficially like that on a TV receiver. You may have to choose between monochrome and colour. Colour can be very attractive: software writers use it to pick out important parts of the computer's messages to you, for instance. More important, many programs can produce graphical displays, which you can first inspect on screen and then print on a colour printer. The results from this can produce very effective presentations. The trade-off for colour is that the image on the screen, which is built up from a large number of dots, will usually not be so fine-grained as a monochrome image, and thus may be more tiring to look at. This is likely to matter most if you spend hours at a time staring at the fine details of the display. – if, for instance, you use the machine a lot for word processing.

Getting hard copy

Printers are not strictly speaking part of the computer, but you will certainly need access to one. Most common for the kind of application discussed here is the *dot matrix* printer. The print head of such a printer consists of a column of small, blunt needles which hit the ribbon and drive it on to the paper in a pattern that gives the shape of the letter. Usually, you can switch the printer between fast, coarse printing and slower, finer 'near letter quality' mode. Such a machine can also draw graphs and pictures by building up the image from dots. A *daisy wheel* printer works much more like an electric typewriter, with its letters arranged around the 'petals' of a rotating wheel. This sort of printer will give very high quality output, but is rather slow and cannot normally handle graphics. Of increasing importance are *laser* printers. Here the basic technology is that of a photocopier, except that the image to be printed is registered on the print drum by a low-powered laser. A basic laser printer will output a page of text in perhaps ten seconds, and the quality will be indistinguishable from typescript; in addition, slightly more elaborate ones will, with the right software, produce a wide range of fonts as well as graphics, and are being used for 'desk-top publishing'. Of course, you get what you pay for: such a machine would cost ten or twenty times as much as a basic dot matrix printer.

Heavy metal

Mainframes have much the same components as PCs, but the user never gets as close to them, so you do not need to know much about the details. The main practical difference is that the principal medium for transporting data is magnetic tape – this is what national data archives have mainly used, though they now use floppy disks and networks as well. Apart from that, you will normally sit in front of a screen and communicate via a keyboard – indeed, many people nowadays have a program that enables their PC to behave like (emulate, as they say in the trade) a visual display unit (VDU) terminal. (In North America, VDUs are called CRTs – cathode ray tubes.) This is often the same program that is used for file transfer.

How to choose

What are the main criteria for choosing between a mainframe and a PC? First, of course, many people have no choice in the matter: if you work for a large organization such as a university you will probably have access to a mainframe, and there will be no question of spending perhaps £5,000 to get your own PC (including software and some sort of printer). (Even at the time of writing, £5,000 is on the high side in Britain. Equipment in the USA is generally cheaper, so that North American readers may assume parity in the dollar–pound exchange rate.) On the other hand, if you work for an organization that has no computer, then the only possibility may be to get a grant for the purchase of a PC – and £5,000 may then not look too bad as a proportion of total costs. But, nevertheless, it is worth considering the pros and cons – a small organization may have the option of buying time on a mainframe, and a large one may regard social scientists as a nuisance and prefer to fob them off with their own small machine rather than have to provide them with time, disk storage space and special software on the mainframe.

The first advice, though, is to use what is available. There is little point in going to unnecessary expense and trouble if there is already a working system. It is also a great comfort to be joining an existing community of users, who can provide help and encouragement.

Secondly, consider accessibility. Your own PC is on your desk, for you to use at any time. You may well be able to take it home to work without interruption. The terminals for your mainframe may be in the computing centre itself, or perhaps there is a lab in every building, or you may, again, have a VDU on your desk. If you have a modem (a device which allows you to plug your terminal into a telephone socket), you may be able to use your mainframe from home, too, by dialling direct to the mainframe (which will have its own bank of modems) or by accessing a network. But not all mainframe facilities are available twenty-four hours a day or at weekends: if you like to work after the pubs shut on Saturday night, check whether you will be able to do so. Find out, too, how much time the mainframe is unavailable for mysterious reasons labelled 'systems time' – when the operators probably need the machine to play 'Dungeons and Dragons'.

Thirdly, there is the matter of reliability. Modern computers are all pretty reliable, in the sense that they break down comparatively infrequently, but on the whole PCs are better than mainframes. Check with other users of the mainframe you will be accessing: the main problem may not be that you often cannot get on to it, but rather that you run a real risk of the machine crashing when you are in the middle of a job, so that you lose the work you have done that session. On the other hand, a mainframe will usually have good engineering back-up, so that if it does 'go down' it usually comes up again pretty quickly. If your own PC goes down, you will be dependent on the responsiveness of your dealer or repairer. If the trouble is difficult to sort out, you may be completely without a machine for a week. And, of course, the cost of repairs will have to come out of your budget.

Fourthly, consider the security of your data. We mean this in two senses. First, there is the question of unauthorized access. In academic research this may not matter much (unless you are worried about the crook in the next office stealing your work), but in commercial settings it may be relevant. Most PCs have no real security in this sense; if someone steals one of your floppies she will be able to read its contents. (You can get a program to encrypt and decrypt your data, but it would be a lot of trouble to do this consistently.) Data protection laws mean that it should still be impossible to identify individuals, but even the aggregated data may be valuable. On a mainframe it is usually possible to make your files (the name given to an organized collection of information) reasonably secure in this sense.

The second sense in which you need to consider security is the risk of your data's being accidentally destroyed. Floppy disks are quite vulnerable in this way: put one down near a telephone, and when the phone rings the magnetic patterns will be disrupted; or try pouring coffee over it. Hard disks can get damaged by a mechanical failure, which causes the read/write head to dig into the magnetic coating – the dreaded 'head crash'. More subtly, the software may 'corrupt' the data. Or, hard to believe, you may make a mistake and delete an essential file. Now your computer's manual will tell you to guard against this sort of problem by making frequent security copies. If you back up your hard disk at the end of each day's work, then whatever disaster strikes you can always go back to the situation of a day before – provided you haven't had a fire that has destroyed your back-ups too. But, in practice, very few people are sufficiently self-disciplined to carry out these security procedures, so that you will probably live dangerously. On the other hand, any respectable large mainframe installation will have a routine of backing up every file on the system once a day. (Actually what usually happens in practice is that every file that has been created or modified in the last twenty-four hours is backed up.) There is a great feeling of comfort in the knowledge that, whatever stupidity you may perpetrate, you will have lost at most a day's work. Not everyone would agree with this opinion: some experienced computer users trust themselves to make security copies and to keep all their copies under lock and key more than they will trust the disinterested systems of their central facility. In this connection, we should mention yet another storage device: the 'tape streamer' – a cassette drive on to which you can dump the contents of a hard disk far more easily than you could by feeding in a succession of diskettes.

The superior support of a mainframe is more general than this. (This is about the fifth point, according to how you count them.) Most large installations will employ several people whose job it is to help users. Also, you will probably not be the first to be using the particular piece of software, and most people are quite happy to pass on the fruits of their experience. With a PC, of course, you are likely to be literally on your own. On the other hand, most PC software houses, recognizing this problem, provide some sort of telephone consultancy service, which is often very effective. In passing, it is worth pointing out that this service is normally available only to those who have actually purchased the software and registered their purchase: if you copy (i.e steal) the program from a friend then (a) you should be too embarrassed to call for help and (b) such a call may well be refused. Another development, which is improving the situation of PC users, is that large organizations are now quite often buying a large batch of PCs, and installing the same software on each. In these circumstances, advice and engineering back-up may well be as good as on a mainframe. At best, the PCs are all connected to a central machine via a network, and even security dumping may be handled centrally.

The sixth criterion is cost. Here, no universally valid advice can be given. At educational institutions in the UK computing is not normally charged for, although it may be rationed; in most countries a charge is made. If you have to pay for the use of a mainframe with real money (as opposed to internal accounting), then the costs will depend on whether you pay a full or subsidized rate. The user liaison person in the computing centre should be able to estimate the costs for a straightforward project – but if you are inexperienced you may have little idea of how much computing you are likely to have to do. With a PC, of course, the costs are negligible once the machine and the software have been paid for. This is really a great advantage: it can be extemely frustrating to have to report an incomplete analysis when you are convinced that a few hours' more work would have given more elegant results. On the other hand, if you are on a really tight budget the hardware and software costs may simply be beyond you. We cannot provide any firm guidance on this, because prices are changing so fast – almost always downwards. In particular, PC software suppliers seem to be recognizing that they are now addressing a mass market: the unit cost is coming down, and so is the very basis for costing. For instance, many programs are now available on a *site licence* basis: the institution pays a single fee, and is permitted to make a large number of copies for distribution to its members. Other software (though not, at present, any large statistical programs) is available either free (because it was written by an enthusiast who is only too pleased for his (most hackers are men) genius to be recognized), or as *shareware*, an arrangement under which users are encouraged to 'borrow' other people's copies of a program, on the understanding that they will pay to become a registered user, with entitlement to updates and advice, if they decide they like it. It may be worth your while to join the user group for your PC, in order to have easy access to cheap software.

The last criterion is power, though for some people it will come first. Again, this must be subdivided. Processing speed looks at first sight to be a big advantage of a mainframe, but in practice it may not matter much. Your PC may only have a fraction of the speed of a mainframe, but it is all yours, whereas you will usually be sharing a mainframe with a lot of other people. The only circumstances where it really makes a difference is when you are doing a seriously big analysis. On a mainframe, you will often be discouraged from trying to grab too big a share of the machine at a time when other people are trying to use it, often by being charged at a high rate during normal working hours. If you work late at night (perhaps by submitting a job with instructions to the scheduler program to run it after 22.00 hours) you will get a much bigger share of the machine. If you are running the sort of jobs that take hours of a mainframe's undivided attention, then it is probably not sensible to try to make do with a PC. But, here, we are talking about analyses using tens of thousands of cases: if your dataset is a thousand or two then a PC/AT can probably handle it. It is true that the actual processing may take an hour or two, but there are two other considerations. The first is that nobody ought to arrange their work in such a way that they never do anything except sit at a computer – this is a real health hazard, if only in extra risk of back pain. The second is that many PC programs are so much easier to use than the corresponding mainframe software that your total productivity is likely to be greater on a PC even if the actual processing is slower: we spend far more of our time thinking about how to do an analysis and trying to work out what that means in terms of instructions to the computer than we do in actually waiting for the answers to come back.

But there are other aspects to power, of which the most important is storage capacity. In practice, not many PCs have more than 20 Mbytes of disk space, which implies limitations to the size of dataset that can be accommodated, as already discussed. You can get bigger hard disks, but they get expensive, and have their own problems – the time needed to do a security dump, for instance. On a mainframe, however, the storage capacity is essentially unlimited. Not only are the disks far larger, but behind them stand the tape drives. A magnetic tape (more like a reel-to-reel tape than a cassette) has a capacity of more than 100,000,000 characters. It costs less than £10. You can have as many of them as you like. If you have a lot of data you can keep it on tape between runs and either read it direct into the computer or store it temporarily on disk when you actually want to use it. This is all rather cumbersome by comparison with the way you use a PC, but if you have really big datasets this is the way to do it.

The pace of change

The last thing to be said about the choice between mainframe and PC is that the balance of advantage is changing. In 1984 hardly anyone thought seriously about the possibility of doing survey analysis on a PC. Today, it is a very serious option, at least for small or medium sized tasks. In the early 1990s mainframes will probably be the exception rather than the rule. And most forecasts about development in computing technology overestimate the time factor.

Note

1 For a more extensive discussion of the potential of personal computers for social scientists, see Madron, Tate and Brookshire, 1985. Note, however, that many of its details are of necessity even more out of date than our own material.

7
Software for data analysis

The previous chapter concentrated on the computers and ancillary equipment needed for secondary analysis. All the ingenious hardware is of no use without programs to run: the boxes of flashing lights may look impressive, but what really makes a difference to the data analyst's life is the software she has access to. There are literally hundreds of packages available for analysing data. What are the differences between such packages, and how should you choose? What, too, are the essential differences, and what are the minor ones? As with hardware, change in software is taking place so quickly that it would not be practicable for us to offer a recommendation for a best buy. Rather, what we provide is an indication of the kinds of facilities that you may need, so that you can shop around with a helpful checklist. A general point: practically every widely used data analysis package exists in mainframe and PC versions. The two versions are always either essentially identical or at least very similar in the facilities they provide, though you should always check this with the supplier, especially if you are contemplating changing from one to the other. Where they are more likely to differ is in what the jargon calls the *user interface:* the details of how you put in your instructions and see the results. We discuss this point in detail later.

Appendix 7.1 (pp. 132–3) lists addresses of software suppliers and in addition the various kinds of documentation that also appear in the main bibliography.

Some widely used packages

In order to make the discussion somewhat less abstract, we shall concentrate on discussing a few packages that are among the most widely used by social scientists, and which we have chosen because they represent the main varieties of such programs. If, however, your computing centre swears by something we do not discuss, you should probably take what they offer. To avoid a complete pig-in-a-poke, ask some hard questions based on our analysis.

The facilities in these packages can be divided for convenience into two areas: data management and statistics. Data management includes commands for storing and retrieving the data files, for selecting the variables and observations to be analysed, for modifying the data in various ways, and for attaching labels so that output will be easier to understand. Statistics includes the actual numerical procedures for tabulating, summarizing, calculating measures of association, etc. Almost certainly your choice of a package is likely to be influenced by requirements in both these areas. Some packages claim to be all-rounders, to be at least reasonably good at both data management and statistics, and most analysts would hope to be able to get away with using just one package. But some analysts have such demanding requirements or such complex data that only a combination of packages will satisfy them.

A few preliminary words about each program should help you find your way through the discussion that follows.

> **Minitab** is a student-oriented program with good, though restricted, statistical procedures, reasonable facilities for simple data management, but poor labelling and no ability to handle complex file structures.
>
> **SPSS^x** is a widely used program with good all-round facilities except in advanced data file manipulation.
>
> **P-STAT** is another general-purpose package, biased more towards data management than towards statistics.
>
> **SAS** is a powerful set of programs, which does most things well – at a cost in complexity, especially for the learner.
>
> **SIR** is a specialized database management system, unrivalled in its special field but with no pretensions in statistical procedures.

Data structures

Methods of statistical analysis almost without exception regard a set of data as a rectangular table of numbers, of the kind described at the beginning of Chapter 4. Data laid out like this is the most straightforward to manage and, indeed, to conceptualize. Unfortunately, by no means all data sets have this simple structure. The General Household Survey, for instance, is most naturally regarded as hierarchical in structure. As we explained in Chapter 4, the primary unit of data collection is the household, and each household contains one or more family units, which in turn contain a varying number of persons. Each person is asked whether they have been to see the GP recently, which for most respondents will draw a blank, but for which some will have several incidents to describe.

There are several difficulties about managing and analysing data with a structure like this. Many of these difficulties are discussed in Chapter 4, and much of Chapter 10 will be devoted to a discussion of the practical procedures needed. Here, it is enough to say that some programs can cope with hierarchical data more easily than others – indeed, for some it is quite impracticable.

Other data management facilities

The ability to manage complex file structures is perhaps the most profound difference among these packages. Almost all packages marketed for survey analysis are adequate in other aspects of data management, so there is no need for detailed discussion. Most of these other facilities begin with data definition. Briefly (for now), the first step in any major analysis is to take the trouble to write what is sometimes called a data dictionary. The details of this are discussed in Chapter 8.

Data manipulation

Having stored your data, with its dictionary and other documentation, you are unlikely to do much analysis with the data in its original form. The most common way in which you are likely to want to manipulate it is probably recoding a variable. This is the term generally used to describe the operation of modifying the set of categories used to record a variable, usually by collapsing several adjacent categories into one. For instance, respondents' age may be recorded in years, or even as date of birth, but for many analyses this is simply an unmanageable amount of detail, and you will want to collapse it into ten-year intervals, or even a dichotomy. Different packages do this with greater or less economy of effort. One widely used program would need the following sequence:

```
if (20 <= age <= 29) then newage = 2
   else if (30 <= age <= 39) then newage = 3
   else if (40 <= age <= 49) then newage = 4
   else if (50 <= age <= 59) then newage = 5
   else if (60 <= age <= 69) then newage = 6
```

```
else if (70 <= age <= 79) then newage = 7
else if (80 <= age <= 89) then newage = 8
else if (90 <= age <= 99) then newage = 9
```

This is clear (once you know the conventions) but cumbersome. In another program you would write:

```
recode age (20 thru 29 = 2)(30 thru 39 = 3)
    (40 thru 49 = 4)(50 thru 59 = 5)(60 thru 69 = 6)
    (70 thru 79 = 7)(80 thru 89 = 8)(90 thru 99 = 9)
    into newage
```

This is rather better. But (a) this does not mean that all manipulations would be easier in the second package than in the first (which is why we leave them anonymous for now); and (b) an experienced user would realize that in this instance, with regular recode intervals, the same result could be achieved in either package by something like:

```
compute newage = truncated (age / 10).
```

The next most common kind of manipulation is selecting a subset of cases. Some packages do this by allowing you to set a condition which is checked against every case before processing, e.g.

```
select if sex = 'f'
```

This condition remains in force for the remainder of the run, unless you have specified that it is to be temporary, in which case you could subsequently select for males and repeat the analysis. Other packages, as an alternative, allow you to first sort the file into females followed by males, and then to automatically repeat every analysis for the two groups. This looks attractive, but the sorting can be very time-consuming – it can take much longer than the tabulations or factor analysis that follow. Other packages again allow you to specify repeated analysis by sub-groups without prior sorting.

As well as manipulations involving individual variables or groups of variables (of which the above are only two examples – for an extended example, see Chapter 11) you may want to carry out operations involving entire files. Two simple examples are adding variables and adding cases to the file. Updating a panel, by adding the latest wave of information as it becomes available from the archive, is usually seen as adding variables: voting preference for respondent number 1,083 in

1987 is regarded as a different variable from her voting preference in 1986: the case is the same. On the other hand, adding a new year of the GHS is seen as adding cases: marital status for respondents in the 1986 survey is the same variable as marital status for 1987 respondents – but this time we have different cases. Thinking back to the rectangular dataset described earlier, you can see that these two sorts of updating can be seen as adding either complete columns (variables) or complete rows (cases) to the rectangular file. Notice that this simple idea depends on the columns or rows being complete: in other words, we assume that the panel has lost no members, and that the GHS interview is unchanged. When, as almost always happens in practice, this simple condition does not hold, we have to 'fill in the gaps', usually by using the missing value facility.

Adding variables or cases can be done either by adding raw data in the form of a further set of card images, or else by setting up a system file for the new data, and merging this with the original system file to create an enlarged one. (System files are explained in Chapter 8: they use a special, more efficient format specific to the package.) Most packages allow you to do either of these. Merging system files often allows greater flexibility, by matching the variables to be associated by means of a key variable. For instance, one way to cope with the problem of a hierarchical file structure, like the GHS, is to create separate files for the variables measured at the different levels. Then, provided your package allows it (as most of these packages do) you can create a merged file in which household data is added to the case for each person in a given household, or else, for instance, you can calculate the total income of the members of a household, and add it to the household case.

Statistical facilities

For most people, perhaps surprisingly, the statistical facilities provided by a package are of secondary importance. For a jobbing survey analyst who is not a statistical expert the facilities common to almost all packages will be more than sufficient. A 'real statistician', on the other hand, will often work by deriving a mathematical model of an aspect of social behaviour and comparing the data with the model. If the model is at all novel the statistician will certainly need to go beyond the facilities of any 'packaged' approach. For her, the important thing is that it should be easy to use the main package for data management, and to output the data in suitable format for entry into a specialized statistical routine.

Standard facilities

Most survey analysis concentrates on the production and manipulation of tables showing the relationship between two or more categorical variables. Many analysts feel their expertise is concentrated in the substantive area of the research rather than in statistical methodology. They are wise never to go beyond the calculation and comparison of percentages, though when it comes to writing for publication they usually conform to the ritual of reporting chi-squared values. Cross-tabulation facilities are, on the whole, so similar that we shall confine ourselves to discussing one particular design feature that seems a genuinely useful advance. The traditional approach to the analysis of contingency tables, which emerged from Columbia University in the 1940s, entails first forming a table to show the relationship between the two variables initially hypothesized to be involved in a causal relationship, and then successively 'controlling' for other variables suspected of being able to 'explain' the initial relationship, by their position as intervening or causally antecedent variables. (For a good introduction to this approach, see De Vaus, 1986.)

The process of trying the various 'test' variables involves generating numerous multi-way tables, and this can be very time-consuming, especially with a large dataset. (Because the data is normally stored case by case this is the way it has to be read, too: to get three entries from each case the package has to read the entire case.) One way to get round this is to foresee all the alternative tables, and instruct the package to produce them all in one pass. With most packages it is almost as quick to produce several tables in a single pass as it is to produce one. The snag is, of course, that you cannot usually foresee all the alternatives in this way.

A more elegant approach is at the time of writing available in P-STAT. The idea is to think of all the variables that look likely candidates for the analysis, and to create one giant, multi-way table based on all of them. Probably the variables will be recoded from their raw values, but usually into relatively fine categories. The original super-table may contain thousands of cells, and you never attempt to understand it in this form. Instead, you tell the package to display different cross-sections and perspectives of it.

To take a very simple example, you could start by tabulating Respondent's occupation by Father's occupation by Respondent's education, with the two occupation variables in six categories and education in four. The super-table thus has six times six times four cells = 144. You could then display one view – R-job by Pa-job, with all the R-educ categories collapsed into one. This table would have thirty-six cells, rather a lot for a simple analysis, so you might decide to collapse some of the occupational categories in order to just distinguish between manual and non-manual workers. Having had a look at this two-by-two table you decide to look at the effects of R-educ, and display the two-by-two-by-four table. Then you collapse two of the education categories, and so on. While all these collapsed tables are being displayed, the original super-table remains available, so that you can always ask for a different view. Of course, collapsing categories means essentially adding a few cell frequencies together – very much faster than regenerating tables from the raw data.

If your preferred style of analysis involves exploring lots of multi-way relationships, especially with reasonably large datasets, it could well be worth your while to look for a package that allows the super-table approach: this sort of efficiency of design could be a bigger advantage than any amount of hardware turbo-charging.

There are other solutions to the same problem, at the heart of which is the wastefulness of reading an entire dataset from disk every time you want to look at a different two or three variables. One approach is that used by Minitab. This package is designed to analyse a relatively small dataset – small enough to be held in random access memory in its entirety. This means that every table is generated from what is already in RAM, so that disk access only takes place at the beginning of a run. Packages that work in this way are very quick, but are ultimately limited by the amount of RAM available; this really means that such a package is not likely to be worth considering for analysing full-scale surveys.

Another approach is referred to as the use of inverted files. This is really a misnomer, since the relationship between these files and conventional ones is closer to matrix transposition than to inversion. The term is also ambiguous, because it is used to refer to two quite different approaches. The more promising of these, which is at present available only in the QUANTIME suite of programs used mainly by commercial researchers, works in the following way. Each *variable* is stored in a separate file. To generate a table, the two or three or more files containing the desired variables are read and the table assembled. Obviously, this is very efficient compared with the conventional way of working. Another advantage is that whenever you create a new variable you just write it to a new file of its own, instead of having to create a new version of the entire dataset.

Other statistics

With the exception of SIR, which is almost a pure data management system (though it does have good tabulation facilities), all the packages mentioned have reasonable statistical capabilities, including, for instance, multiple regression with analysis of residuals. SAS is probably the best of them (especially if we include its separately priced extra products, like the Econometric Time Series program). SPSS^x is much better than the old SPSS, and includes some unique procedures such as a powerful multidimensional scaling procedure. P-STAT, at the time of writing, has a rather primitive factor analysis routine, but does incorporate the fashionable Exploratory Data Analysis methods introduced by Tukey (1977), as does Minitab, which also has good facilities for generating artificial data, to be used in sampling experiments, etc. Where differences in data manipulation are often rather subtle, differences in statistical routines are usually fairly obvious, and you should have no great difficulty in browsing through the various manuals to see whether you will be able to use your favourite test. As we have already suggested, you always have the option of using your main package for data management and outputting a suitably processed version of the data into a file that can then be read by an exotic statistical program.

The user interface

The most powerful data management and statistical procedures are of little value if they are difficult to use, and software designers are paying more and more attention to this aspect of their work. There are three main ways to use a program of any kind, which we shall refer to as batch, interactive and combined. A batch program is one that expects to receive all of the instructions for an entire run in one batch. It works systematically through them, and produces the results in one batch, too. This is the way all computing was done at one time. In the 1960s, the instructions were prepared on punched cards, which were handed to an operator for feeding into the computer, which replied with a pile of printout. That was if you were lucky: often you got back only a page or two of printout, with a message explaining (or not – the message was often rather obscure) that you had misplaced a comma on your seventy-third card. Nowadays, you prepare the instructions for a batch program by sitting at a VDU terminal and typing them into a file, using a program called an editor, which is often like a simple word processor. Having created the instruction file, you tell the computer's operating system to pass the instructions to the analysis package. The package then does its best to obey them, and puts the results in another file, which you can either display on the screen or else send to the fast printer. As in the olden days, the 'results' file may contain only error messages (though today they are on the whole relatively understandable). When this happens, you use the editor to make the necessary corrections to the instruction file, and resubmit it. When your file contains a long sequence of data-modification instructions the 'de-bugging' process can take several days. Even with a simple error-free job, turn-round will be at least a minute or two. This can be a bit frustrating when you are working through the data in an exploratory way, trying one approach and wanting immediately to try something different when the preliminary results suggest it.

(It would, perhaps, be as well to spell out at this point what we mean by errors. The conventions used to write instructions to a computer differ a good deal, but they can all be regarded as closely analogous to natural language. In particular, there will be rules of grammar (usually referred to as syntax, though they include what a 'human' linguist would call semantics), which you have to observe. The errors that a program will notice and complain to you about are syntax errors – spelling a command name incorrectly, or not providing the appropriate items of extra information, for instance. Providing you get the syntax right, the program will be happy to obey – even if it means doing something quite different from what you intended. To give a homely example, if a drill sergeant instructs his squad to 'right sniff', they will ignore him, because 'sniff' is not a permitted element of the drill command language. If, on the other hand, he wants them to turn right, but bellows 'left turn', they will mechanically do so.)

Using an interactive program is quite different. You sit at a terminal and type instructions directly to the analysis package (no files, no editor). It responds immediately to each instruction, and displays each set of results on the screen. (Normally, it will put the results in a file as well, so that you can later get a printed log of your terminal session.) When (not if!) you make errors (of the 'right sniff' kind), it tells you at once, and you can immediately repeat the instruction, correctly phrased. There is usually a facility where you can type 'help', and get at least a statement of the correct general syntax for the command, so that you don't even need to get out the manual. When one step in the analysis suggests a recasting of the data, you can do it at once.

The advantages of this are obvious. The main snags are these. First, 'immediate' is relative: even the simplest tabulation of two variables based on one year's GHS data involves processing hundreds of thousands of numbers, and on the fastest practical computer that will take several minutes. (Remember that if you are using a super-powerful mainframe you will be sharing the machine with a good many other users.) If you have a really large dataset to work on, you may have to forgo the luxury of instant response and organize your work around substantial batches of analysis, which can run at low priority or even overnight while you get on with other things.

Secondly, complex data manipulations do not really lend themselves to this approach. If, for instance, you wish to create a fancy household-level index, which involves linking several files, recoding some variables, adding together others, and finally aggregating up from visits to the doctor, through persons, to the household, you will have to spend a long time thinking through the task. Then it will be convenient to type the entire sequence of instructions into a file, where subsequently they can be easily amended. Finally, you will want the package to obey the entire sequence, tell you of any syntax errors, and print out a sample of the modified data, so that you can check through the manipulations on a few cases 'by hand', in order to make sure you haven't accidentally said 'left' when you meant 'right'. This checking is much easier to do on printout than on the screen.

Not surprisingly, efforts have been made to design packages that combine the advantages of batch and interactive use, and this is our 'combined' type. With a package of this kind (P-STAT was probably the first, but several others have now followed) you may begin to use it either in batch or in interactive mode. In batch mode it works conventionally. If you are using it interactively, all will continue normally until you make a syntax error. At this point, you will find that all your instructions so far, which the package has been happily obeying, have also gone into a file, and you are now invited to edit that file, using an editor which is part of the analysis package. There will probably be a 'help' facility to guide you. When you think you have got it right you can either tell the package to start again from the first instruction in the file or, if you are sure all was well up to a given point, to restart from that point. This sort of approach can even work with a long sequence of data modification commands on a giant file: you may start the run by selecting a small subset of cases, and try out successive commands on that subset. When you are satisfied that all is well, you tell the package to repeat the sequence on the entire dataset, perhaps running overnight so as to avoid peak-time charges.

A refinement of this package design involves the use of screen windows. This means that the package divides the screen up and displays, for instance, your instructions in one window, the results (or error messages) in a second, and the raw data in a third. You can change the contents of each window without necessarily interfering with the others. This can be very convenient: it means, for instance, that you don't have to write down all the error messages before editing the instruction file. The main problem with this kind of facility is that it makes heavy demands on the compatibility of the link between screen and computer. PCs can generally handle this, because the screen is usually a standard fitting, but there are dozens of different VDU terminals in common use, so that it is much harder to write a mainframe program that does clever things with the screen. At the time of writing, the only mainframe package to offer this kind of user interface is SAS; even with SAS you have to have one of the terminals on the approved list (though it may be possible to persuade someone in your computing centre to write an interface program for a different terminal). We are promised a new interactive mainframe version of SPSS^x for 1988.

We have been assuming so far that packages are driven by a series of commands that the user types in, but some work in a rather different way, by the use of 'menus'. This means that the package offers you a series of fixed options (a menu) and that your choice from one menu will lead to the package offering you the next one in the hierarchy. It is rather as if the menu in a restaurant were so organized that you had first to choose from a list of courses, from which you might choose 'starter', and that the waiter then went away and brought back the starter menu, from which you chose 'fish', whereupon he went off for the fish starter menu, from which you could then choose your smoked trout pâté. On this analogy, the command driven approach corresponds to the experience of going into your favourite restaurant, whose repertoire you know more or less by heart, so that you can simply reel off a list of your requirements without even asking the owner/chef what's on. The analogy is quite a good one: if you know what you are doing, a command driven program is much quicker to use, but a menu approach is easier for a novice. To take the parallel a little further, a menu offers you only a fixed set of choices (though it may be quite a wide one), whereas in your favourite restaurant you can ask for variations that nobody would have been likely to foresee, provided the constituent elements are available – oysters with chocolate sauce, perhaps. Of course, there's no guarantee that it's a sensible choice.

These questions of user interface design are by no means minor matters. The total amount of work you get out of your system will almost certainly depend far more on how easy it is to use than on whether your processor chip runs at 8 or 4.77 MHz – despite the attempts of advertisers to concentrate on blinding with science. So, when shopping for a package, you should certainly try to get evidence on these matters, preferably from experienced users. At the same time, you should try to assess the quality of the documentation, the availability of on-line help (i.e. can you press the appropriate button and get at least a summary of the syntax of the current command), and the provision of other learning aids, such as a built-in tutorial program, or a manual with worked examples as well as comprehensive definitions, or the availability of courses that you can afford. Find out, too, what kinds of personal support are available. If you are a lone PC user you will want to know that there is an expert available at the other end of the telephone – most PC software suppliers offer such a service. Mainframe software suppliers often insist on each site nominating one person as the 'consultant' through whom all requests for help are channelled.

Possible packages

While repeating our caveat that software is developing so fast that any specific advice is likely to be obsolete before you read it, it may be helpful to describe in a little more detail the small number of packages that we have chosen as representative of the field, so as to give an idea of the nature of the choice open to you.

Minitab was originally written as a teaching package. Because of this, it was for a long time ahead of the field in terms of ease of use, though other packages have been catching up. It is conversational, with quite good 'help' facilities. Its statistical facilities are very good in certain directions, especially regression and exploratory data analysis. It has no factor analysis built in; however, it has quite a good internal programming language, including matrix operations, so that people have written routines for some of the simpler multivariate methods, and published them in the User Group Newsletter. Its tabulation is quite good, but there is no way to attach labels to values, which makes tables hard to read. Its graphics are fine as part of the analysis process, but not really good enough for presentation purposes. It is entirely restricted to flat files; there is no way to merge system files, though you can add variables and cases in a rather primitive way. The entire dataset has to be held in RAM. How much of a problem this is depends on what your local computing centre will allow: at Surrey at one time, the 'worksheet' was configured to hold 1,000,000 elements – enough for 300 variables by 3,000-odd cases, which is enough for most datasets short of the GHS – but this is unusually large. Mainframe and PC versions are essentially identical; it is available for CP/M personal computers, as well as for more recent ones. It is fine for the analysis of aggregate data, but not so well suited for surveys. Documentation is clear: a manual and a Student Handbook, which is really a supplementary statistics textbook.

SPSS^x is probably the most widely used data analysis package in academic and other non-commercial social research (at one time the University of Edinburgh reported that SPSS was its most widely used software of any kind – it was called more often than the FORTRAN compiler). It has been said that its best feature is its documentation: rather intimidating because of its size, but comprehensive and clearly written. It has generally good data management facilities, though complex file management is sometimes rather convoluted; the 1986 edition of the manual gives little help on this. Its statistical facilities will satisfy most non-statisticians, and continue to be extended. New procedures can (in principle) be added by users. With a little effort and the purchase of an extra module you can get the package to produce tables well enough laid out and labelled to go straight into a report. The (optional) graphics subsystem produces good results, though it is expensive and quite hard to use. Communications with other programs are satisfactory. The mainframe version should be regarded as a batch system; although on some computers it can be run interactively it is very clumsy. The PC version is very similar in its facilities, and has an excellent, modern user interface. There is a very large user community, so that it is relatively easy to get advice and help. Data archives often provide SPSS^x data definition files with the raw data. SPSS^x is the successor to SPSS (versions 1–9). It is similar to use, but not entirely compatible. Most important, however, SPSS^x can read old-style SPSS system files (and so, for that matter, can the other programs described here, except Minitab).

SAS was for many years available only on IBM mainframes, and even today, when versions exist for most important brands, it is less widely distributed than SPSS^x. It is the most comprehensive package of its kind: within the 'base product' its data management facilities are a complete programming language, and its statistical procedures are highly thought of. It is possible to write almost any non-standard procedure in the programming language and store it as a *macro*. SAS is a complex system, and takes a long time to learn thoroughly, though the beginner can start more modestly. Its user interface includes a screen editor: excellent if you have a suitable terminal. Extras include graphics, econometrics, data entry... you name it! The PC version has a very good user interface, and is otherwise essentially identical to the mainframe version; it needs a powerful machine if it is not to appear sluggish. Documentation is comprehensive. Computer-aided learning is available (as well as the conventional courses offered for most of these programs).

P-STAT has excellent data management facilities, using PPL (the P-STAT Programming Language). Its statistical facilities are less complete than some of the opposition, but include a very well-designed cross-tabulation procedure, as well as regression and principal components analysis and a good general linear model facility. (For statistics not available within the program you are recommended to use BMDP, a collection of excellent statistical procedures with relatively weak data management, which can be seen as complementary, though independent.) The mainframe interface includes a built-in editor, which works on any terminal and permits rapid de-bugging. At the time of writing, the PC version is said to be about to get a menu-driven interface, which should make initial learning easier. The current reference manual is well-organized; a set of worked examples provides a good introduction.

SIR (Scientific Information Retrieval) differs from the other packages mentioned in not claiming to be a general survey analysis program; instead, it specializes in data management: though marketed as a relational database system it includes powerful facilities for hierarchical and network data. The first task, when using SIR with a new dataset, is to write a *schema* that describes the structure. (Many datasets are supplied by the Data Archive complete with the schema definition.) This done, it is relatively easy to move variables up and down a tree structure. Its statistical facilities are limited to basic descriptive statistics and cross-tabulation. The usual way around this limitation, when more advanced statistics are required, is to use SIR to produce a flat file, which is then exported in the form of an (old style at present) SPSS system file. The natural next step is to continue the analysis with SPSS^x, or with any other program that can accept SPSS files. The SIR control language was designed to look broadly similar to old SPSS. SIR is not in itself particularly difficult to use, but it is normally used for conceptually complex data management tasks; you should not consider using it unless you have such a task, in which case you may have no real alternative.

Compatibility of packages and files

Every one of these packages has chosen a different format for its system files. At one time, this was a serious limitation on the analyst's flexibility, but the problem has now largely been solved: most of the major packages can now read a system file written by one of the others, and often files written by PC spreadsheets and database programs. The main exception among the packages described is Minitab. However, with the important exception of SIR's lack of advanced statistical capabilities, you should not often need to worry about this. The control languages are, unfortunately, completely different from each other. Even SIR and SPSS, superficially similar, have very different vocabularies. For this reason it is best, if you can, to limit yourself to learning just one package.

Which package for me?

Minitab and SIR probably choose themselves. Minitab is easy to learn, well-designed within its limitations, and very useful for a variety of small everyday jobs, as well as for teaching statistics, but not the right choice for anyone with a large survey to analyse. SIR is very powerful and flexible if you have a complex data structure, but not necessary otherwise.

Among the other three packages, your choice may well be dictated by availability, for many computing centres will provide only one general-purpose survey package. If you have a choice, SAS has power and versatility, P-STAT has an elegant data management language, and SPSS^x is most widely used.

Appendix 7.1

Software sources and documentation

This appendix contains addresses from which further information on each of the packages can be sought, in the USA and UK. If you are in another part of the world, contact the US address, since all the packages originated there. We also list one or two manuals for each package. For SPSS^x and SAS in particular there are many other more specialized documents that we do not list.

Minitab

Addresses:

Minitab Inc., 3081 Enterprise Drive, State College, Pa, 16801, USA.
CLE.COM Ltd, Kings Court, 92 High Street, Kings Heath, Birmingham B14 7JZ, UK.

Documentation:

Reference Manual, Minitab Inc. (1985).
Minitab Student Handbook, Duxbury Press: Boston, Mass. (1985).

P-STAT

Addresses:

P-STAT Inc., PO Box AH, Princeton, NJ, USA.
Timberlake Clark, 40B Royal Hill, Greenwich, London SE10, UK.

Documentation:

P-STAT User's Manual, Princeton, NJ: P-STAT Inc.

SAS

Addresses:

SAS Institute Inc., Box 8000, Cary, NC, 27511-8000, USA.
SAS Institute, Whittington House, Henley Road, Medmenham, Marlow, Bucks, SL7 2EB, UK.

Documentation:

SAS User's Guide: Basics. Version 5 Edition, SAS Institute Inc. (1985).

SIR

Addresses:

SIR Inc., PO Box 1404, Evanston, Ill., USA.
SIA Ltd, Ebury Gate, 23 Lower Belgrave St, London SW1W 0NW, UK.

Documentation:

Robinson, B.N. *et al. SIR Scientific Information Retrieval User's Manual Version 2.* Evanston, Ill.: SIR Inc., (1980).

Schulzinger Fox, J. *The Sir/DBMS Primer.* Madison, Wis.: University of Wisconsin at Madison Academic Computing Center (1984).

Dale, A. *A Teaching Package for the Database Management System SIR*, University of Surrey, (1986).

SPSS[x]

Addresses:

SPSS Inc., Suite 3000, 444 North Michigan Avenue, Chicago, Ill., 60611, USA.

SPSS UK Ltd, Mark House, The Green, 9–11 Queens Rd, Walton-on Thames, Surrey, KT12 5NA, UK.

Documentation:

SPSS-X User's Guide, 2nd edn, SPSS Inc. (1986).

8

Getting started: preliminary analysis

Earlier chapters have discussed selecting and ordering an appropriate dataset and the kinds of hardware and software available for analysis. In this chapter we shall be concerned with the next step in the process of secondary analysis – what to do with the data, having obtained it. We shall assume that the analysis package used is SPSS^x, although in Chapter 10, which is specifically concerned with hierarchical data, examples will use SIR. Generally, the principles outlined will apply equally whatever package is used, although the syntax of the commands will, of course, vary somewhat.

For those using a mainframe computer, data may either be transmitted from the supplying Archive by a network link or physically sent on a magnetic tape. Those using PCs will usually obtain their data on a floppy disk. If a network link such as JANET has been used, then the relevant files will be transmitted directly ('downloaded') to the user's computer and may be used immediately. If they have been sent through the post, either on floppy disk or magnetic tape, the first step is to read them on to the computer. Where a magnetic tape is used, it will be important to supply to your home computer site the format specifications that were on the data order form, so that the tape can be read correctly.

Reading data from tapes: possible problems

Although no problems should be encountered at this stage, reading data from a magnetic tape occurs at very high speed (a typical speed would be 75 inches of tape per second) and requires immense precision. Checks built into the reading mechanism mean that any misalignment is immediately picked up and the reading halted. Because of the precision involved, tapes should be stored at the same temperature and humidity conditions that are needed by the computer on to which they will be read. It is important not to leave them lying around in a dusty or very warm environment.

Any damage to the data while in transit may mean that a section of the tape becomes unreadable. Usually this will be picked up by the software used to read the tapes, but it is always a wise precaution to check the data files as soon as they have been read on to the computer to ensure that the data is complete. Obviously it is not possible to physically inspect the data file, so an easy alternative is to generate a frequency distribution of all the variables held. Loss of a portion of data is one of the most likely problems to be encountered, although if it occurs it is readily apparent from the frequency distributions. This is because the portion lost is unlikely to be a complete number of cases; much more probable is that a few characters would be lost from one case, or a larger chunk spanning several cases. Any partial loss of a data record will result in items of data appearing in the wrong location; for example, the columns in which the variable NCHILD (number of children) should be held may appear to contain data for AGE. If the frequencies on NCHILD show a distribution from 0–99 then it is immediately obvious that something is wrong! A frequency distribution will also give the total number of cases in the dataset, and this can be compared with the original documentation to ensure that the number is correct. If any problems occur, the first step will be to consult your institution's Computing Advisory Service and, if that does not resolve the problem, consult the Archive that supplied the data.

Standard checks on data

Whatever the method used to transport data from the Data Archive, it is a sensible precaution to run a series of checks, for example, by generating a frequency distribution for each variable that can be checked against available documentation to ensure that all the data are present and in a correct form before embarking upon analysis. To do this it will be necessary to use a program that reads the data and applies descriptive labels. In some cases an SPSS^x program or set-up file may be supplied with the data, but, if not, it will be necessary to write one.

As well as giving the computer the variable names and the card and column locations from which to read each variable (the DATA LIST), the SPSS^x set-up file should also include variable labels and, except for continuous variables such as age and income, value labels for each category of the variable. It is helpful if variable names are mnemonics which reflect the meaning of the variable (REGION, AGE, SEX,

MARITAL, SEG, INCOME) rather than sequential characters (VAR1, VAR2), which convey no meaning. To illustrate the way in which variables may be named and labelled, Figure 8.1 shows the labelling used with the variable which represents the 19 categories of the Registrar General's socio-economic groupings. The variable is given the mnemonic name SEG and, as a shorthand description, it may be labelled 'Registrar General's Socio-Economic Group'. Each of the 19 categories is then given a value label that describes them as accurately as possible within the constraints of SPSS^{x}. These constraints mean that a variable name may be no longer than eight characters and only the first 16 characters of a value label will be displayed in cross-tabulations – although the maximum number allowed is 60. In Figure 8.1 the aim has been to incorporate the maximum amount of useful information into the number of characters available. Labelling the variables and the values of each variable not only makes future use easier and faster but also ensures that the secondary analyst has thought carefully about the meaning of each category of each variable.

Figure 8.1 *Constructing variable and value labels in SPSS^{x}*

VARIABLE LABEL SEG 'Registrar General's Socio-Economic Group'

VALUE LABELS SEG
1 'Employers, size 25+'
2 'Managers, size 25+'
3 'Employers, size <25'
4 'Managers, size <25'
5 'Prof.worker:self-emp'
6 'Prof.worker:employee'
7 'Ancillary, artists'
8 'Supervisor:non-man.'
9 'Junior non-manual'
10 'Personal service'
11 'Foreman: manual'
12 'Skilled manual'
13 'Semiskilled manual'
14 'Unskilled manual'
15 'Non-prof:own account'
16 'Farmer:empl/manager'
17 'Farmer: own account'
18 'Agricultural worker'
19 'Armed Forces'/

Missing values should also be supplied for those categories that represent 'not applicable' or 'no response'; sometimes, also, 'don't know' will be declared missing. Most packages allow up to three categories to be declared 'missing'; by using this facility the analyst is able to ensure that these categories are routinely left out of analyses. The value of this becomes apparent if we consider responses to a question on income from paid work. Those who do not have any paid work may be coded as -9, and these may represent 20 per cent of all responses. If the mean value of income from paid work is computed, all responses, *except* those defined as missing, will be included. It is obvious that if the value '-9' is not defined as missing the result will be quite erroneous. The missing value categories may also be labelled, so that the distinction between different kinds of missing values is readily apparent.

Figure 8.2 gives a skeleton set-up file for use with $SPSS^x$. Either upper or lower case may be used interchangeably in $SPSS^x$ commands and definitions; to emphasize this point a mixture has been used in this example. All labelling is preserved in the case in which it is entered, although other names and keywords are converted to upper case by $SPSS^x$. This means that a variable originally declared in the data list as 'age' can subsequently be referred to as 'AGE'. The $SPSS^x$ *Basics Manual* (SPSS Inc., 1984) and the $SPSS^x$ *User's Guide* (SPSS Inc., 1986) give a fuller discussion of the various components of a set-up file.

This process of naming, labelling and defining missing values for each variable may result in a very long set-up file, perhaps containing several hundred lines. Unless you can use a keyboard quickly and accurately it may be easier to write out all the commands and labels on to coding sheets, to be entered directly on to the computer by skilled keyboard operators.

It is helpful to use the error checking facilities built into most packages to check for syntax and typing errors before sending the job to be executed by the computer. $SPSS^x$ allows a command, 'EDIT', to be inserted into the set-up file in order to check for errors without actually reading the data and carrying out all the commands in the file. Most computing on a mainframe will be done in batch mode (see Chapter 7), whereby a file containing all the required commands is sent to the computer, which then carries them out as and when it has time. It is very valuable, therefore, to be able to ensure that as many errors as possible have been eliminated before dispatching the program file.

When the $SPSS^x$ set-up file has been written, any errors corrected and the commands executed by the computer, a frequencies listing will be produced for each variable named (or implied) in the frequencies command. Figure 8.3 shows the listing for one variable, SEG. It is important to look through these frequencies carefully, checking each variable against whatever documentation is available. This may mean checking against the questionnaire to see whether the proportions of

Figure 8.2 *Outline set-up file to read data using SPSS[x]*

```
FILE HANDLE SURVEY/NAME=SURVEYDATA.D
DATA LIST FILE=SURVEY FIXED RECORDS=1
   /1 CASEID 1-8
      REGION 9-10
      AGE 11-12
      SEX 13
      MARITAL 14
      SEG 15-16
      INCOME 17-21

VARIABLE LABELS
    CASEID 'Identification number'
    REGION 'Geographical region of Britain'
    age 'AGE OF RESPONDENT'
    SEX 'SEX OF RESPONDENT'
    marital 'Marital status of respondent'
    SEG 'Socio-economic Group'
    INCOME 'Weekly income from employment'

VALUE LABELS
    region 1 'South' 2 'North' 3 'Wales' 4 'Scotland' -1 'No response'/
    age 99 '99 and over' -1 'No response'/
    sex 1 'Male' 2 'Female' -1 'No response'/
    marital 1 'Married' 2 'Single' 3 'Widowed' 4 'Divorced' 5 'Separated'
    -1 'No response'/
    SEG 1 'Employers,size 25+' 2 'Managers,size 25+'
    3 'Employers,size <25' 4 'Managers,size <25' 5 'Prof.workers:self-emp'
    6 'Prof.worker:employee' 7 'Ancillary,artists'
    8 'Supervisor:non-man.' 9 'Junior non-manual' 10 'Personal service'
    11 'Foreman:manual' 12 'Skilled manual' 13 'Semiskilled manual'
    14 'Unskilled manual' 15 'Non-prof:own account'
    16 'Farmer:empl/manager' 17 'Farmer:own account'
    18 'Agricultural worker' 19 'Armed Forces' -1 'No response'
    -9 'Not applicable/income' -1 'No response' -9 'Not applicable'

MISSING VALUES
   REGION, AGE, SEX, MARITAL (-1)
   SEG, INCOME (-1, -9)
frequencies general=REGION TO INCOME/
```

respondents in each category look plausible, or against a code-book or other available published material. At this stage, it is possible that some variables will contain codes for which there is no apparent category in the documentation. These may either represent mis-punching ('wild' codes) or, alternatively, an extra category may have been added to the variable after the documentation was printed. If this appears likely, it may be necessary to contact either the Archive that supplied the data or the depositors, to obtain extra information. At this stage it is also worth while to re-read any coding notes or interviewer instructions in order to get a clearer understanding of the way in which the data has been produced.

Figure 8.3 *Frequency distribution forming part of the output from the set-up file shown in Figure 8.2*

SEG *Registrar General's Socio-Economic Groups*

Value Label	*Value*	*Frequency*	*Per cent*	*Valid Per cent*	*CUM Per cent*
Employers,size 25+	1	2	.1	.1	.1
Managers,size 25+	2	185	6.1	6.3	6.4
Employers, size <25	3	81	2.7	2.8	9.2
Managers,size <25	4	136	4.5	4.7	13.9
Prof.worker:self-emp	5	33	1.1	1.1	15.0
Prof.worker:employee	6	99	3.3	3.4	18.4
Ancillary,artists	7	195	6.4	6.7	25.1
Supervisor:non-man.	8	31	1.0	1.1	26.1
Junior non-manual	9	364	12.0	12.5	38.6
Personal service	10	116	3.8	4.0	42.6
Foreman: manual	11	137	4.5	4.7	47.3
Skilled manual	12	686	22.7	23.5	70.9
Semiskilled manual	13	469	15.5	16.1	87.0
Unskilled manual	14	190	6.3	6.5	93.5
Non-prof:own account	15	104	3.4	3.6	97.0
Farmer:empl/manager	16	24	.8	.8	97.9
Farmer: own account	17	17	.6	.6	98.5
Agricultural worker	18	31	1.0	1.1	99.5
Armed forces	19	14	.5	.5	100.0
No response	−1	14	.5	missing	
Not applicable	−9	100	3.3	missing	
	TOTAL	3,028	100.0	100.0	

VALID CASES 2,914 MISSING CASES 114

Having labelled the data, established that it is complete and corresponds to available documentation, the next step will usually be to save it in the form of an SPSS^x system file. If you are using a large dataset it may be useful to retain in your system file only those variables that are likely to be needed in analyses. This is discussed in the following section.

System files

An SPSS^x system file contains both the data and the data definitions (the labelling and missing values), stored in binary form (Chapter 6 gives an explanation of binary codes). The advantage of holding data in this form is that it is immediately readable by the computer, which does not therefore have to undergo the usual process of converting the data from character format into binary before use. This means that analyses using system files are considerably faster than where the computer reads the 'raw', character format data. (In a similar way to an SPSS^x system file, a SIR database holds both data and definitions in binary form.) This usually results in a considerable expansion in the size of the data, because all variables are given the same amount of storage space irrespective of whether or not they need it. To counteract this, SPSS^x system files may be made in compressed form, which, in effect, packs the data much more tightly. Compressed system files will be obtained automatically if this option has been selected by your computer centre; if not, a subcommand in the set-up file may be used. With a large dataset this is a very valuable facility as it means that a system file need take up no more space than the original data file (and about one-third of the space of an uncompressed system file) and yet is still a great deal quicker to use. None the less, a price is paid for compression – it means that access is not quite so fast as with uncompressed files, even though the amount of central processor time (cpu seconds) needed to read a compressed system file is about one-third of the time taken to read the original data file.

The system file represents the file that you will be using for further analysis – for this reason it may be termed a *workfile.* This file need only hold those variables that are actually going to be used in planned analyses. Particularly if the original dataset is large, it may be useful to use the SPSS^x command KEEP VARS, placed immediately before the SAVE command, to nominate those variables that should be retained in the system file.

The contents of a system file can be documented to ensure that the analysts can always recall basic information about the dataset held: for example, the date of the survey and any selection of cases or variables that has been made. Later in this chapter we shall describe in more detail ways of documenting system files.

It is a wise precaution to run a frequencies procedure using the newly created system file to check whether the results correspond to those produced using the original datafile. In some circumstances, it is possible for a system file to be incomplete and yet appear to have been successfully made – for example, if the time allocation for the job was slightly too short and the job terminated before completion. In batch mode, a log file is usually produced automatically, to record the course of a job from the time it is submitted to the computer until its completion. It is good practice to check systematically the contents of the log file after each run to ensure that it has been successfully completed.

Gaining familiarity with secondary analysis

Having created a system file containing the dataset supplied by your Data Archive (or a subset of variables from it), you are now able to prepare the analyses that you wish to carry out. Those with little experience of secondary analysis may find it useful to obtain a social science teaching package, *Exploring British Society* (Arber, Gilbert, Dale and Rajan, 1984), which provides four small subsets of data drawn from the General Household Survey, with workbooks to accompany each dataset. The data comes with ready prepared set-up files and instructions for creating a system file, while the workbooks explain the basics of analysis in the context of four different substantive areas: class, gender, poverty and ageing. The packages provide an opportunity to become familiar with computing by using a small and easily managed dataset and they also give a feel for the kinds of analyses that the General Household Survey will support.

The teaching package described above provides all the variables required for the examples given in the workbooks. However, in most research projects the variables available in the dataset will not adequately meet all requirements and it is often necessary to derive additional variables, perhaps to combine the information from two or more different variables – for example, summing together all forms of income, or computing an attitude scale from a number of separate variables. In more complex cases the secondary analyst may derive a variable to measure a concept not readily available in the dataset but which can be pieced together by combining a number of different items of information. The following section gives some guidance on the practicalities of deriving variables. We make the assumption that the dataset used is a simple case by variable matrix, with either the individual or the household as the unit of analysis. Figure 8.4 outlines the types of variables that will be covered in this chapter. A fuller discussion of these types of variables is provided in Chapter 9. These variables may be either at the individual or household level (or, indeed, at any other level) but are derived from flat data files and do not, therefore, make linkages between different levels of a hierarchy.

Figure 8.4 *Types of variables that may be used with rectangular data*

Type of variable	*Example of variable*	*Description*
ABSOLUTE	age; sex; region; marital status; housing tenure	Absolute variables do not need to be derived; they exist as direct answers to survey questions
SUMMARY	average hourly pay; attitude score derived from a number of individual items; quality of housing score	Summarizes the information from a number of existing variables by means of an arithmetic operation
CONSTRUCTED	typology of labour market status; typology of housing tenure	Combines information on a number of variables to represent a concept not in the original dataset
COMPARATIVE	income quartile by comparison with all in sample, either individual or household	Uses information from one variable to establish a comparative ranking on that variable for each case

Derived variables

Once the secondary analyst has worked out which variables must be derived in order to operationalize the concepts of interest, a set of procedures may be used for creating them. After the derived variables have been checked for accuracy and documented, they may then be incorporated into a new system file and thereby permanently saved.

A basic procedure for deriving variables

We first describe the creation of a very simple variable in order to illustrate the basic procedures needed, and then discuss the derivation of some rather more complex variables. We shall assume that the dataset being used is a case by variable matrix at the level of the individual and that we wish to compute a variable to give the hourly earnings of those in paid work, using data on total weekly earnings and total number of hours worked. This is a *summary* variable (Figure 8.4), combining information from two existing variables by means of an arithmetical operation. The basic steps in the procedure are set out below:

1 DEFINE A TARGET VARIABLE

Define a name for the new variable which will measure average hourly earnings (PAYHOUR), termed the 'target' variable.

2 DEFINE THE COMPONENT VARIABLES

Locate the variables to be used in the derivation and check that they contain the appropriate information. These are termed the component variables and, in this example, are named TOTPAY (total weekly earnings from employment) and TOTHRS (total weekly hours in paid work). Check the exact meaning of the component variables and whether the units used are appropriate. In this case, TOTPAY is expressed in pounds and pence, while TOTHRS represents the total number of hours worked in the week. It is important to note that TOTHRS includes overtime working. Also, the analyst must check that the two component variables refer to the same week. If not, the variable will be quite meaningless!

It is also important to be clear about what the derived variable represents. For example, where the respondent holds more than one job, do both the component variables refer to ALL employment, or just the 'main' job held? How have the self-employed been treated (it is often difficult to attribute a regular weekly income to them)? Thus, good documentation is *essential* if secondary analysis is to be successful. It is also important to be clear that the derived variable will NOT represent the hourly rate of pay, but will give the average hourly earnings, inclusive of overtime. These are quite different, but often confused!

3 COMPUTE THE NEW VARIABLE

Using SPSS^x, this is shown below:

```
COMPUTE PAYHOUR = TOTPAY/TOTHRS
```

This statement divides total earnings by the number of hours worked, to give hourly earnings. However, step 2 would have ascertained that the variables TOTPAY and TOTHRS are only recorded for those in employment; other respondents will have been coded as missing on these variables. There will also be a number of respondents who choose not to answer questions relating to income from employment or who cannot recall the number of hours that they worked. These, too, will have missing values on either TOTPAY, TOTHRS or both. For all these cases, when SPSS^x encounters the COMPUTE command shown above, it will return a 'system-missing' value. This is a value assigned by SPSS^x when it is unable to carry out a computation because the answer would be indeterminate. In this example, it will occur where either of the component variables (TOTPAY or TOTHRS) is missing or where TOTHRS is coded as zero. (Division by zero is not possible as it produces a mathematically undefined number – infinity.) In all these situations a system-missing value will be assigned. However, it is often useful to distinguish those to whom the derived variable does not apply, because they are not in paid employment, from those who have missing data for some other reason – perhaps a refusal to answer the questions. The way this may be achieved is shown below:

```
COMPUTE PAYHOUR=TOTPAY/TOTHRS
RECODE PAYHOURS(SYSMIS = -1)
IF (EMPLOYED NE 1) PAYHOUR = -9
```

Using these commands, all those who were initially allocated a system-missing value by the COMPUTE command will firstly be recoded to −1; then, those who were not in paid employment at the time of the survey and who would not, therefore, have been asked about income from employment, are given the value −9. This will ensure that those who retain the value −1 are people who have been asked the relevant question (they were coded 1 on EMPLOYED) but who have missing values for some other reason.

Because these commands are carried out sequentially, it is necessary for the command lines to take the order shown above. If the ordering was reversed, then those not in paid work would initially be allocated the value −9 on PAYHOUR, but would lose it again and be given a system-missing value when COMPUTE command was executed.

4 LABELLING AND ASSIGNING MISSING VALUES

When you have created the variable PAYHOUR, it is useful to label it and assign missing values as appropriate. For example:

```
VAR LABEL PAYHOUR 'AVERAGE HOURLY EARNINGS
VALUE LABEL PAYHOUR -9 'NOT IN PAID
      EMPLOYMENT' -1 'NO RESPONSE'
MISSING VALUES PAYHOUR (-1, -9)
```

5 CHECKING THE DERIVED VARIABLE

The next and perhaps most vital step in the computation of any derived variable is to check it exhaustively. The first and easiest method is to obtain a frequency distribution of the new variable and each of the component variables. Although this will generate a long list of values, which will probably not be worth printing as hard copy, a quick glance at the values, particularly at the top and bottom of the ranges, will indicate whether the derived variable looks plausible.

A second, more detailed method is to list for a small number of cases each of the component variables and the new derived variable. In SPSS^x, the procedure LIST VARIABLES is used. The SPSS^x command and a few lines of the output that it generates is shown in Figure 8.5. This line by line output is produced for each case, starting from the first and going through to the hundredth.

Figure 8.5 *Use of LIST VARIABLES Command in SPSS^x*

```
COMPUTE PAYHOUR=TOTPAY/TOTHRS
RECODE PAYHOUR(SYSMIS= -1)
IF (EMPLOYED NE 1) PAYHOUR= -9

LIST VARIABLES=PAYHOUR, TOTPAY, TOTHRS, EMPLOYED/
  CASES FROM 1 TO 100
```

PAYHOUR	TOTPAY	TOTHRS	EMPLOYED
5.00	200.00	40	1
-9.00	-9.00	-9	4
3.50	150.50	43	1
4.25	157.25	37	1
2.00	40.00	20	1
-1.00	-9.00	39	1
-1.00	143.55	-9	1

Using this method it is possible to check that the calculation has been correctly carried out and that cases with missing values on the component variables (shown as −9 here) are assigned a missing value and not included in the calculation of the derived variable. Obviously this is not practicable for all cases; however, by use of the CASES subcommand it is easy to select a small number of cases, either taking a few at the beginning of the dataset (for example, cases 1 to 100) or, better, to take readings all through the data at specified intervals of, perhaps, 50 cases. For this the subcommand would simply read:

```
CASES BY 50
```

A third type of check, not appropriate for continuous variables but useful with categorical variables, is to cross-tabulate the derived or target variable by each of its component variables. Any cases that are in the 'wrong' cell can be easily spotted. This is discussed more fully later in this chapter.

6 DOCUMENT THE DERIVED VARIABLE

The final step is to document the derivation of this new variable. It is very easy to forget to do this, as it brings no immediate pay-off and often seems unnecessary. However, if the derived variable is to be saved in a new system file, the method of its construction then becomes one step removed – the user of the system file may not know or remember the basis upon which the variables held in it have been derived and, if the file containing the commands to create the derived variable is accidentally erased, this information may be permanently lost. Thus a researcher using the system file could not check whether PAYHOUR contained all types of income or only some, or the way in which missing values had been treated. It may not even be clear what units had been used to measure the variable. It is often very difficult when in the thick of work to believe it possible to forget all the details that have become so firmly embedded in one's mind. However, research on a project does not end when the final analyses have been completed; inevitably, work on preparing publications and reports carries on beyond this. Often referees' comments on publications submitted to journals mean that further analysis is necessary, perhaps a year or more after the project has formally finished. In these circumstances, it is almost impossible to retain in one's mind the details of earlier work. Therefore, it must be carefully and systematically recorded.

Different people develop different methods of recording, and so a number of suggestions will be made here. First, a project log-book might be kept. This is often valuable, apart from merely recording derived variables. The kind of information that may be logged under the appropriate date includes: when the data was ordered; when the data arrived; any problems with reading it; the name of the set-up file used to hold all the labelling, missing values, etc; the creation of the first system file and any selection of cases or variables made; the method of derivation of subsequent variables and the name given to the second system file. All this information can be recorded against the date when it took place. Should a file accidentally be erased (it often happens!), knowledge of the date when it was created will be a great help in ensuring that it can be retrieved from the back-up tapes held by most computing units.

A second way of recording is to use the document facility available in most packages. Using SPSS^x as an example, the DOCUMENT command will record an unlimited amount of text and can be inserted into the set-up file used to create the derived variable. It will then be stored in the system-file and can be recalled at will. An example of what might be used to document the example above is:

DOCUMENT The variable PAYHOUR has been made by dividing the total weekly income from employment (TOTPAY) by the number of hours spent in paid work (TOTHRS), for the reference week of the survey. Values are expressed as pounds and pence. People with missing information on either TOTPAY or TOTHRS have been assigned the value of −1. Those who are not in paid work are given the value −9

Alternatively, the commands used to create PAYHOUR (shown in Figure 8.5) could be copied into a DOCUMENT command. To recall the documented information from a system file, the only command needed is:

DISPLAY DOCUMENTS

Deriving a summary variable

Having covered the basic steps in variable derivation, we shall now move to another rather more complex *summary* variable. Again, we assume that the data is a case by variable matrix, where the case is the individual. We wish to sum all forms of income for each individual into a single variable that can represent the total income from all sources for that person. Again, the steps involved in deriving this variable are outlined using the procedures of SPSS^x.

1 Define a name for the target variable to be created – we will use TOTINCID.

2 Find the names of the variables to be summed – INCOME1, INCOME2, INCOME3 and INCOME4. Check that each of these component income variables (INCOME1, INCOME2, etc.) is measured in the same monetary units (in this example, pounds and pence) and covers the same unit of time. If they do not, then an initial step will be to convert them to the same units. For example, if INCOME1 refers to a 4-week time period and all other variables refer to

a week, then INCOME1 could be converted to a time unit of one week as follows:

COMPUTE INCOME1=INCOME1/4

3 Compute the new variable, TOTINCID.

There are two methods by which values may be summed across variables using SPSS[x]. These are shown below:

```
COMPUTE TOTINCID=INCOME1 + INCOME2 +
  INCOME3 + INCOME4

COMPUTE TOTINCID= SUM (INCOME1 TO INCOME4)
```

Where all respondents hold valid information on all the variables, these two methods will give exactly the same results and the second has the advantage that it does not require a long list of names to be written out, provided the variables to be summed are all held consecutively within the dataset. The methods, however, differ in the way in which they treat missing values. The first method adds together valid values where all the component variables have a valid value. If *any* component variable has a missing value, then TOTINCID will be system-missing for that respondent. Clearly, if information is not available for one income source, then a total based on only three may seriously misrepresent the true total and it may be preferable for the target variable to be set to missing.

The second method computes the sum of *valid* values on the component variables. Using this method, if only one variable contains valid information, then TOTINCID will take that value. However, the SUM function may be given extra flexibility by using a suffix to specify the number of variables that must be valid before TOTINCID may be computed. This is shown below, using the suffix .4 to denote that all four variables must contain valid information:

```
COMPUTE TOTINCID = SUM.4 (INCOME1 TO INCOME4)
```

In this form the command will produce exactly the same results as:

```
COMPUTE TOTINCID=INCOME1 + INCOME2 +
  INCOME3 + INCOME4
```

Both methods now return the target value as system missing if there is missing data for any of the component variables.

However, survey data is not always so straightforward. It often happens that a component variable is missing, not because the respondent has failed to answer the question but because, at an earlier filter question, she declared having no income from that source and so no subsidiary question on the amount of income was asked. To illustrate this, we shall assume that the survey contains a preliminary, filter question (HASINC1) asking whether or not the respondent receives any of INCOME1. If the answer is 'Yes' (coded 1), then the amount is asked; if the answer is 'No' (coded 2), INCOME1 will be categorized as 'not applicable' and given a missing value (−9). In this situation it is usually desirable to set up a zero category on each of the INCOME variables for those who say that they do not have any of this kind of income, before doing the computation for total income (TOTINCID) (Figure 8.6). This enables those with no income to be distinguished from non-respondents. Once this has been carried out, then either of the summations shown before can be used. Figure 8.6 gives the command lines needed for this and also an illustration of output from a LIST VARIABLES command using this method of summation.

4 Labelling and assigning missing values

A descriptive variable label should be given to TOTINCID. In the example in Figure 8.6, TOTINCID will be system missing for those with missing data on *any* of the four income variables. It may be useful to recode the system missing value to a numeric value, perhaps −1, which can then be labelled and set to missing, as shown in Figure 8.6.

5 Checking

The LIST VARIABLES command shown in this example enables a check to be made on the computation of the variable. Further checks follow the procedures outlined for the previous example.

6 Documentation

An illustration of the way in which the derivation of this variable may be documented is also contained in Figure 8.6.

Deriving a constructed variable

Rather than using arithmetic operations to derive a variable, we may wish to combine variables by using a series of logical statements in order to measure a concept that is not included in the original dataset. For

Figure 8.6 *Deriving and checking a summary variable using SPSS^x (i)*

```
IF (HASINC1 EQ 2) INCOME1=0
IF (HASINC2 EQ 2) INCOME2=0
IF (HASINC3 EQ 2) INCOME3=0
IF (HASINC4 EQ 2) INCOME4=0

COMPUTE TOTINCID=INCOME1+INCOME2+INCOME3+INCOME4
or
COMPUTE TOTINCID = SUM.4 (INCOME1 TO INCOME4)

VARIABLE LABEL TOTINCID 'Total income from all sources'

DOCUMENT This variable sums all sources of income; the component
   variables are INCOME1, INCOME2, INCOME3, INCOME4. Where any
   component variable is missing, a system missing variable is assigned.

LIST VARIABLES=TOTINCID,INCOME1,INCOME2,INCOME3,
   INCOME4/
                CASES FROM 1 TO 100 BY 5
```

TOTINCID	INCOME1	INCOME2	INCOME3	INCOME4
100.0	10.0	10.0	50.0	30.0
50.0	10.0	10.0	10.0	20.0
.	500.0	50.0	−9.0	−9.0
.	120.0	−9.0	10.0	100.0
60.0	0.0	0.0	40.0	20.0
.	−9.0	−9.0	−9.0	−9.0

· indicates a system-missing value

It may be helpful to recode the system-missing value to a numeric value, perhaps −1, and then set this to missing as below:

```
RECODE TOTINCID (SYSMIS= -1)

VALUE LABEL TOTINCID 'Missing data'/
MISSING VALUES TOTINCID (-1)
```

example, the Labour Force Survey may be used to establish a distinction between 'core' and 'peripheral' workers (Dale and Bamford, 1987). Three separate variables can be combined to construct a 7-fold categorization of labour market status. The workers in each of the 7 categories may be expected to vary in the extent to which they resemble 'core' or 'peripheral' workers. The three variables are: JOBPERM (job permanent or temporary), FTPT (job full or part-time), and EMPSTAT (whether an employee, self-employed with employees, or self-employed without employees).

Recent research into employment and labour markets has been

concerned with developing a distinction between the 'core' and the 'peripheral' work-force. It is hypothesized that, with the impact of economic recession and uncertain markets, firms have increasingly sought flexibility in the number of workers whom they employ (Atkinson, 1984). This may be achieved by establishing a peripheral workforce of part-time and temporary employees, whose work hours may be varied without incurring either the costs of overtime or of workers remaining idle because of lack of demand. Another way of off-loading the costs of fluctuating demand is to purchase goods or services from self-employed workers. In order to explore whether those workers who are categorized in the literature as 'peripheral' do, in fact, show the expected characteristics of variable working hours but without paid overtime and with little protection from employment legislation, an initial typology of employment status may be set up that reflects the expected major lines of demarcation. This typology is made by deriving a constructed variable that combines the three employment status variables listed above into seven different categories. In order to work out the commands needed to derive this typology, it is useful to draw a table of the intersections of the component variables and to assign each cell in the table to a value on the target variable. This is shown in Figure 8.7.

Figure 8.7 *Setting up categories for a constructed variable, WORKSTAT*

		FTPT (1) Full-time	FTPT (2) Part-time
EMPSTAT	JOBPERM		
(1) Employee	(1) Permanent	1	2
	(2) Temporary/ contract	3	4
(2) Self-employed no employees		5	6
(3) Self-employed with employees		7	7

The labels for each of these three component variables are given below:

JOBPERM 1 'Permanent job' 2 'Temporary job'/
FTPT 1 'Full-time 2 'Part-time'/
EMPSTAT 1 'Employee' 2 'Self-emp. no employees'
3 'Self-emp.+employees'/

The values in the body of Figure 8.7 refer to the values on the constructed variable, WORKSTAT. As the concept of permanent or temporary work applies mainly to employees the self-employed are not categorized on this basis. We have chosen to make no distinction on the basis of full- or part-time working between the self-employed with employees. This has been done on theoretical grounds as the ability to buy the labour power of another person is seen to be of fundamentally greater importance than the distinction between working full-time or part-time. Therefore, all employers with employees are assigned the value of '7' on WORKSTAT. By contrast, the distinction between full- and part-time work *is* made for the own-account self-employed (without employees) – coded 2 on EMPSTAT. There is evidence that at least some own-account self-employed resemble employees in that they sell their labour to an employer and, particularly if they are female, are likely to be home-workers (Dale, 1986a). In this case, the distinction between full- and part-time working may be important in differentiating two forms of self-employment.

Figure 8.8 shows the way in which SPSS^x may be used to derive the variable WORKSTAT, with the appropriate labelling and missing values included. These seven categories may then be grouped into 'core' and 'periphery' on the basis of the characteristics that they exhibit.

There are a number of points to be made about Figure 8.8. Firstly, it is often useful to set the variable to zero before beginning. This is done in the first line, using the command:

COMPUTE WORKSTAT = 0

This ensures that all respondents who do not meet the conditions stipulated in the subsequent commands can be readily identified. Using SPSS^x, such respondents would, by default, be given a system-missing value. The second line states the conditions that have to be fulfilled before a value of '1' is allocated to WORKSTAT. The use of the logical operator 'AND' ensures that each of these three conditions, (employee status *and* a permanent job *and* a full-time job) must be fulfilled. Subsequent lines set out the conditions to create categories 2–7 on WORKSTAT. Those who are not in paid work (EMPLOYED NE 1) will be coded as −9 on WORKSTAT. All those who do not fall within one of these categories will retain the value '0', given them by the original COMPUTE command. This residual category will be set to missing by the MISSING VALUES command. The checking stage will reveal whether or not there are any respondents in the residual '0' category.

Earlier sections mentioned that variables constructed from

Figure 8.8 *The derivation of a constructed variable, WORKSTAT, using SPSSx*

```
COMPUTE WORKSTAT = 0
IF (EMPSTAT EQ 1 AND JOBPERM EQ 1 AND FTPT EQ 1) WORKSTAT=1
IF (EMPSTAT EQ 1 AND JOBPERM EQ 1 AND FTPT EQ 2) WORKSTAT=2
IF (EMPSTAT EQ 1 AND JOBPERM EQ 2 AND FTPT EQ 1) WORKSTAT=3
IF (EMPSTAT EQ 1 AND JOBPERM EQ 2 AND FTPT EQ 2) WORKSTAT=4
IF (EMPSTAT EQ 2 AND FTPT EQ 1) WORKSTAT=5
IF (EMPSTAT EQ 2 AND FTPT EQ 2) WORKSTAT=6
IF (EMPSTAT EQ 3) WORKSTAT=7
IF (EMPLOYED NE 1) WORKSTAT= -9

VALUE LABEL  WORKSTAT
             1  'Permanent, FT employee'
             2  'Permanent, PT employee'
             3  'Temporary, FT employee'
             4  'Temporary, PT employee'
             5  'FT self-emp. no empl.'
             6  'PT self-emp. no empl.'
             7  'Self-emp.+ employees'/

MISSING VALUES WORKSTAT (0, -9)/

DOCUMENT  The variable WORKSTAT has been derived from
     JOBSTAT, FTPT, and EMPSTAT. It applies to all those in paid
     work. Those not in paid work are coded -9. Those with missing
     values on EMPSTAT or who fail to fulfil one of the other criteria
     above will take the value 0.

CROSSTABS        workstat by jobperm/
                 workstat by ftpt/
                 workstat by empstat

OPTIONS 1

LIST CASES VARIABLES=WORKSTAT,JOBPERM,FTPT,EMPSTAT/
              CASES BY 50/
```

Note The IF statements shown above may be more concisely expressed by using DO IF and ELSE IF commands, fully described in the SPSSx Manual. However, this is not quite as easy for the beginner to understand. Similarly, the tables specified in the CROSSTABS could be written more concisely as: WORKSTAT BY JOBPERM, FTPT, EMPSTAT.

categorical variables could be checked by a series of cross-tabulations, with the derived variable cross-tabulated against each of the component variables, as shown in Figure 8.8. When doing this it is important to insert an option to allow categories defined as missing to appear in the table. (This is OPTION 1 in the SPSSx cross-tabulation procedure.) These three tables will allow us to check not only that those coded '1' on

JOBPERM appear in either category '1' or '2' of WORKSTAT, but also to establish the characteristics of those coded '0' on WORKSTAT. It was suggested earlier that the code '0' would contain people with no job, but at this stage we likely to find that it also contains those who have a job but who did not say whether it was as an employee or self-employed, permanent or temporary, full- or part-time. If this proportion is very small, we shall probably be happy to allow them to remain '0' and therefore missing on WORKSTAT. None the less, by their inclusion in this initial set of cross-tabulations, we are able to satisfy ourselves that the characteristics of this group do not differ markedly from those of the other groups. If, however, we did find marked differences, then we would need to seriously reconsider the variable construction. It is also by this method of checking that we can ensure that the marginal totals for each variable are correct and that no respondents have been lost or misallocated.

Having successfully constructed this initial variable (WORKSTAT), we may choose to combine the categories into a further variable, which we shall call 'CORE'. We shall assume that the categories of WORKSTAT that correspond to core workers are '1' full-time permanent employees and '7' the self-employed with employees. All other valid categories are assigned to the peripheral work-force (in practice it is not this simple!). Using SPSS^x, one way in which this would be achieved is:

```
RECODE WORKSTAT (1,7 = 1)(2,3,4,5,6 = 2) (0=0) INTO
                                CORE

MISSING VALUES CORE (0)

VALUE LABELS CORE 1 'CORE WORKERS'
   2 'PERIPHERAL WORKERS'/
```

When the derived variables have been created and error checked a new system file can be made, which contains these variables as well as all the other relevant variables from the original file. At this stage, it is vital that the construction of the new variables is carefully documented so that, at any time in the future, it is possible to check exactly the way in which the variables were derived and, if necessary, recreate them. An example of the DOCUMENT command that may be used with the derivation of WORKSTAT is given in Figure 8.8.

Deriving a comparative variable

Figure 8.4 described a comparative variable as using information from one variable to establish a comparative ranking on that variable for each case in the sample. In the example shown here, we use a dataset at the level of the household, rather than the individual (although still a rectangular case by variable matrix). We set out to derive a variable (named 'QUINTILE') that categorizes households into quintiles on the basis of their total income. We can then use this new variable, QUINTILE, to examine the characteristics of households who fall into each of its five groups. This approach is often used in studies of inequality in order to obtain a measure of relative rather than absolute income. A very useful discussion of the methodological problems of measuring income inequality is given by Van Slooten and Coverdale (1977) who provide examples from the 1975 Family Expenditure Survey of analyses based upon income quintiles. The distribution of households at different lifecycle stages across income quintiles (O'Higgins and Bradshaw, 1984) provides another example of the way in which relative inequalities may be charted. A more basic discussion of the use of percentiles is given by Marsh (1988).

The target variable is named QUINTILE and is derived from the variable TOTINCHH (total household income). A frequency distribution of TOTINCHH which incorporates the subcommand NTILES will indicate where the cut-off points for each quintile should be. Figure 8.9 shows the SPSS^x commands needed to derive the variable QUINTILE. The value of £66.00 is given as the cut-off point for the first quintile, and similarly £79.00 for the second, and so on. In this example, income has been rounded to the nearest whole pound.

In this chapter we have dealt only with derived variables from one level, either individual or household. In a simple case by variable data matrix there is no possibility of creating more complex variables that combine information about other household members. It is only when data is held in a hierarchical form that it is possible to create linkages between different levels. Ways of conceptualizing and computing these more complex variables from the subject of Chapters 9 and 10.

Descriptive analysis

After we have derived the necessary new variables and set up an SPSS^x system file, the initial stage of a project will often involve some descriptive work that sets the context and establishes the parameters of

Figure 8.9 *Using SPSS^x to derive a comparative variable, QUINTILE*

```
FREQUENCIES VARIABLES=TOTINCHH/NTILES=5/

   TOTINCHH    TOTAL INCOME

 PERCENTILE  VALUE  PERCENTILE  VALUE  PERCENTILE  VALUE
    20.00    66.00     40.00    79.00     60.00    93.00
    80.00   115.00

COMPUTE   QUINTILE=9
IF  (TOTINCHH LT 66)QUINTILE=1
IF  (TOTINCHH GE 66 AND TOTINCHH LT 79) QUINTILE=2
IF  (TOTINCHH GE 79 AND TOTINCHH LT 93) QUINTILE=3
IF  (TOTINCHH GE 93 AND TOTINCHH LT 115) QUINTILE=4
IF  (TOTINCHH GE 115)QUINTILE = 5

VALUE LABELS QUINTILE 1 'lowest quintile' 2 'second quintile'
   3 'middle quintile' 4 'fourth quintile' 5 'highest quintile'/
MISSING VALUES QUINTILE (9)
```

the study. This is usually an important stage, which should not be passed over too lightly. There are a great many texts that deal in considerable detail with confirmatory and explanatory analysis (cf. Hellevik, 1984; Gilbert, 1981) and others that deal with exploratory data analysis (Tukey, 1977; Hartwig and Dearing, 1979; Erikson and Nosanchuk, 1979; Marsh, 1988). In the following section, we attempt only to outline some of the simplest kinds of descriptive analyses that can readily be applied to the kind of data discussed in this chapter and that may form a useful initial step, before embarking upon more sophisticated analyses.

While simple frequency distributions and cross-tabulations can give a basic description, graphical representations can often give a clearer understanding of the structure of the data. The use of bar charts, graphs and pie charts can make it a great deal easier to comprehend the relationships between categories and to draw comparisons. Figures 8.10a and 8.10b show the same set of data presented in both tabular form and as a graph.

By using a graph we can see at a glance that women's employment participation rates are at lower level than men's, and that women's have been fairly constant over time while men's have fallen. Although this information is also contained in a table, it takes considerably longer to work out from it the relationship between men's and women's employment rates. Further, if we wish to make international

Figure 8.10a *Percentage in paid employment, men and women, UK 1973–1983*

	% in paid employment	
Year	***Men***	***Women***
1973	88	53
1974	87	54
1975	86	54
1976	85	54
1977	84	54
1978	84	55
1979	84	56
1980	83	56
1981	79	54
1982	76	53
1983	75	53

Source: Labour Force Statistics 1963–1983, **OECD, 1985.**

Figure 8.10b *Percentage in paid employment, men and women, UK 1973–1983*

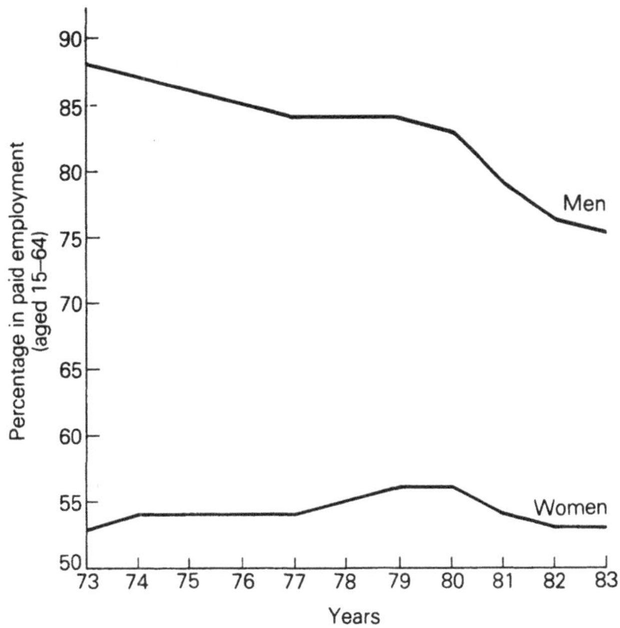

Figure 8.11a *Table of socio-economic groups (SEG) for men and women*

	Percentages		
	Men	*Women*	*Total*
Professional	7	1	4
Employers and managers	16	5	10
Intermed. and Jun.non-m	17	53	34
Skilled manual	39	7	22
Semiskilled manual	13	25	19
Unskilled manual	5	9	7
Farmers, ag.workers	2	2	2
Total	100%	100%	100%
	(963)	(985)	(1948)

Source: Arber, Rajan, Gilbert and Dale (1984).

comparisons, it becomes much easier to juxtapose a number of graphs in order to obtain a preliminary overview of the differences, than to work through a series of tables.

It is often more appropriate to use bar-charts instead of graphs, particularly where variables are not continuous and it is not valid to draw a line linking data points. For example, a bar-chart may be used to compare the occupational distribution of men and women, but it would not be appropriate to use a graph to make this comparison. Figures 8.11a and 8.11b present the occupational distribution of men and women, using both tabular form and bar-charts. The categories correspond to those of SEG (Socio-Economic Group) used in Figure 8.3, but have been collapsed by the use of the RECODE statement shown below.

```
RECODE SEG (5,6 = 1) (1,2,3,4 = 2) (7,8,9 = 3) (11,12,15 = 4)
           (10,13 = 5) (14 = 6) (16,17,18 = 7) (ELSE = 9)

VALUE LABELS SEG

           1  'Professional'
           2  'Employers and managers'
           3  'Intermed. and Jun.non-m'
           4  'Skilled manual'
           5  'Semiskilled manual'
           6  'Unskilled manual'
           7  'Farmers, ag.workers'
           9  'Missing value'
```

Figure 8.11b *Bar-charts of socio-economic groups (SEG) for men and women*

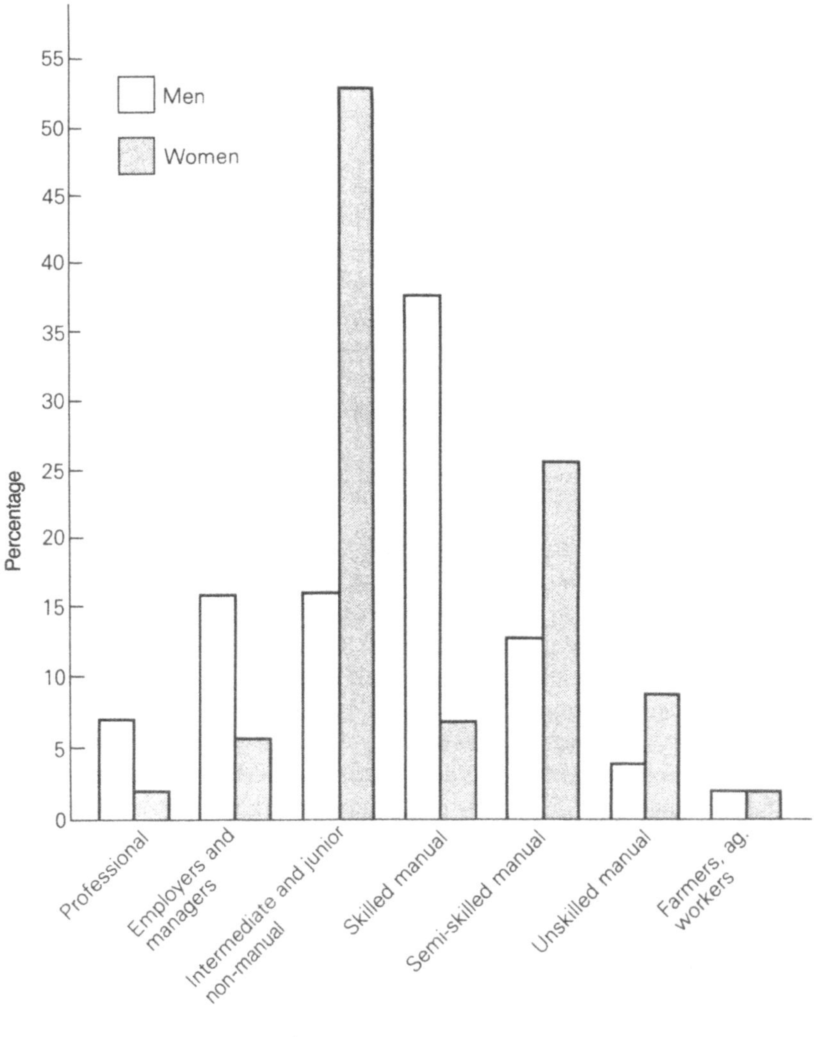

Source: Arber, Rajan, Gilbert and Dale (1984).

Pictorial ways of presenting data are also able to summarize a considerable amount of information. Pie charts are a useful way of displaying the distribution of an unordered variable. If segments are then shaded according to the degree to which they hold a particular characteristic, both sets of information can be combined within one drawing. For example, a pie chart may be drawn where the segments represent the employment categories defined in Figure 8.8 (see Figure

Figure 8.12 *Typology of employment status. All in employment*

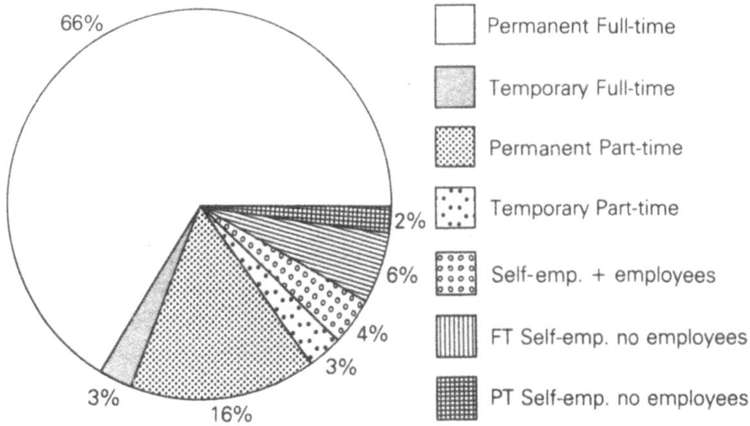

Source: LFS 1984

8.12). Further information may be incorporated by using shading or hatching to reflect mean values for each segment on a relevant characteristic, perhaps hourly rates of pay or variability in work hours. Although a single table is able to present both sets of data with more precision, the pie chart allows the reader to compare the two elements, size and intensity, more readily.

These figures need not be drawn by hand; all are available as part of the graphics module available with most analysis packages. This means that if, for instance, SPSS[x] is being used, then bar-charts, graphs and pie charts can all be drawn as an extension of the same process of analysis. Alternatively, data from any source can be entered directly from a terminal. To do this, however, does require the graphics module available on your computer and a graphics terminal on which to display and interact with the data. Many personal computers (see Chapter 6) have graphics software available at quite low prices and, if one also has a graphics printer attached, this can provide an easy and cheap alternative to a mainframe graphics package.

Although lacking the precision of numerical tabulation, both at an initial stage in an analysis and in the final report stage, visual presentation can be of great value in making immediate impact and in giving the reader an understanding of the relationships within the data. It is much harder to obtain this through the inspection of cross-tabulations.

9

Conceptualizing variables in household-based surveys

Although the potential of hierarchical surveys for sociological analysis is very great (as outlined in Chapter 4), the hierarchical structure has, as yet, been under-exploited. In order to realize this potential, most secondary analysts will need to derive new variables from information held at more than one level of the hierarchy. Often these derived variables will be output into a flat data file for analysis with conventional packages, such as SPSS^x. This chapter will consider the types of variables that can be derived from hierarchical surveys. We shall continue to use the General Household Survey as an example of a household-based survey.

The discussion of hierarchical datasets will be simplified by assuming that the GHS has only two possible levels of analysis. Thus, the researcher may choose either the *household* or the *individual* as the level of analysis. In Chapter 4 we discussed three examples that involved different levels and units of analysis: a study of social mobility with the individual as the level of analysis, a study of women's labour force participation in which the individual was the level of analysis and the unit of analysis was women aged 16–59, and a study of poverty in which the household was the level of analysis.

In a hierarchical survey, new variables can be derived either by using information from only a single level, or by using more than one level; the latter are termed multi-level variables.

Single level variables are derived from a *single level* of the hierarchy. In the two level example in this chapter, they could be derived either from individual level variables or from household level variables. The derivation of such variables is straightforward, because it relies solely on information available in the rectangular case by variable data matrix at the level either of the individual or of the household. They do not involve any information pertaining to another level of the hierarchy. Examples of variables derived only from household level variables are total number of consumer goods possessed by the household, and a measure of housing type derived from information on housing tenure and size of

FIGURE 9.1 *Derivation of variables from a two-level household survey*

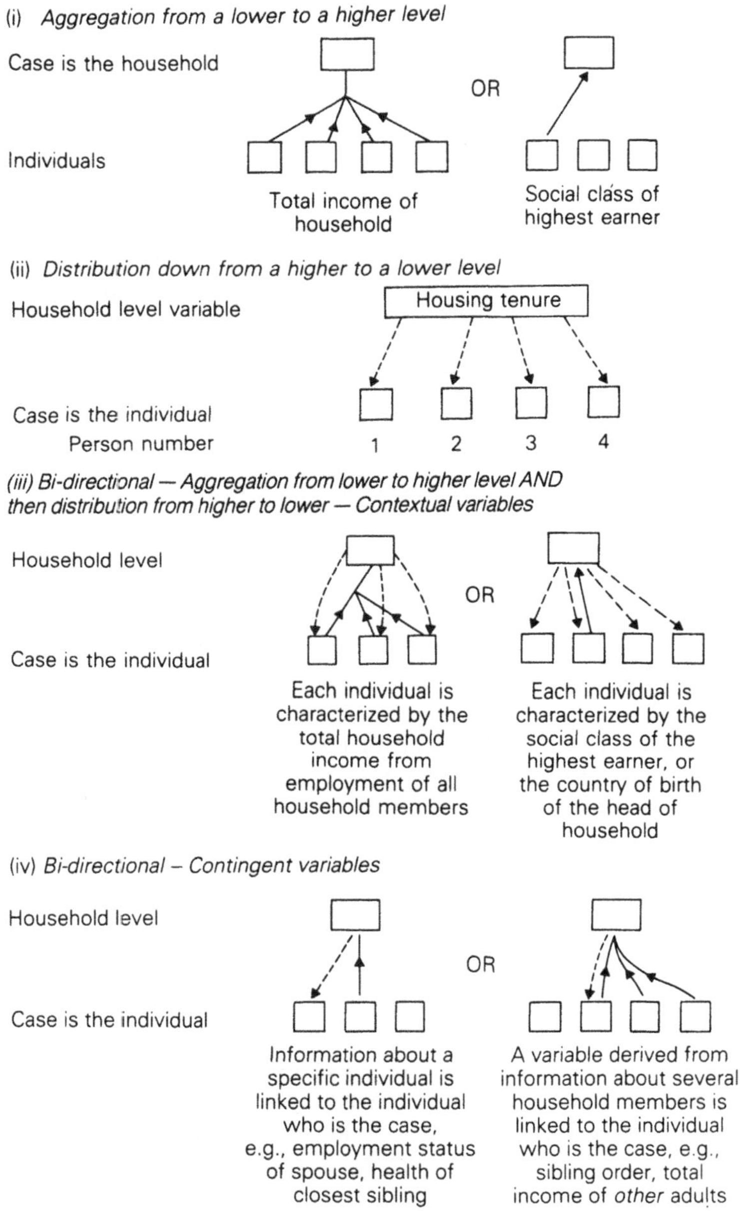

dwelling. Individual level variables derived only from individual level data include average hourly income, total income of the individual from all sources, and a categorization of individuals in terms of their labour market position. The derivation of the last three variables was discussed in Chapter 8.

Multi-level variables are derived by using information from more than one level of the hierarchy. They can be characterized as falling into the four types shown in Figure 9.1. If the household is the unit of analysis, additional household level variables may be derived from the records of all or some individuals within the household, that is, *aggregating* up, as in Figure 9.1(i). For example, the total household income is the sum of the income of each household member. A second type of multi-level variable is derived when data is *distributed* from a higher to a lower level, as in Figure 9.1(ii). Each individual within the household is assigned the same value on the household level variable. For example, housing tenure is a household level variable that can be 'attached' to each individual's record within the household. The terms 'attaching' and 'linking' variables to one another are used to refer to 'linking' the characteristics of the household (or of another household member) to the individual who is the unit of analysis. This terminology is correct if the researcher is creating a flat file in which multi-level variables are added to each individual's record, but the use of the terms 'attach' and 'link' are not correct in terms of using software designed to manage hierarchical files, such as SIR and P-STAT, which just reference the relevant variables when required.

Thirdly, there are bi-directional variables (see Figure 9.1(iii) and (iv)). Here the individual is the unit of analysis. Variables may be derived by first aggregating across all or some individuals within the household and *then* 'attaching' this derived variable to all or some individuals in the household.

Contextual and contingent analysis

Hierarchical surveys allow the possibility of contextual and contingent analysis (see Chapter 4). Contextual analysis may be defined as analysis which focuses on the individual's behaviour or attitudes with reference to a group context. Because the discussion in this chapter is limited to only two levels of hierarchy, the individual and the household, contextual variables will hold information about the household, which is used to characterize the individual. Thus, contextual variables are derived by characterizing an individual by some property of a higher level unit, the household. All individuals within the household have the same value on each contextual variable.

Individuals may be characterized by two kinds of contextual variables, classified according to the extent of use of the hierarchy. First, they may be formed by distributing household variables down to each individual in the household, as in Figure 9.1(ii); secondly, a contextual variable may be derived from information about several individuals in the household, and this derived variable is then distributed down to each household member (bi-directional variables), as in Figure 9.1(iii). These descriptions are, in fact, an over-simplification, since in a hierarchical survey, such as the GHS, distribution may traverse more than two levels and bi-directional variables may use three or more levels of the hierarchy.

The majority of studies of contextual analysis have focused on larger contexts than the household or family: for example, studies of the effects of schools on children's educational attainment (cf. Coleman, 1961; Hauser, 1974; McDill and Rigsby, 1973; Rutter *et al.*, 1979), as discussed in Chapter 4. Galtung (1967) distinguishes three types of context: (1) the *category*, a set of units with no structure, e.g., a geographically defined area; (2) the *social system*, a set of units (individuals) with some interaction (weak connections) between one another, e.g., a school class or work organization; (3) the *group*, a set of units with strong connections with one another, e.g., a family or household. Van den Eeden and Hüttner (1982) in a wide-ranging review of multi-level research conclude that sociological research to date has focused primarily on social systems as contexts and very seldom on primary groups. Thus, this chapter seeks to remedy the lack of attention to conceptual and methodological issues when the context is a small group, such as the household or family.

When deriving contextual variables it is important to be aware of the differences between using the household or family as the context and using larger social systems, such as schools or firms. Contextual variables derived from summing or averaging the characteristics of individuals may make more conceptual sense when the group is large and members of the context are relatively homogeneous. To facilitate the comparison of contexts, researchers often aim to achieve a similar size for all contexts studied (van den Eeden and Hüttner, 1982). Thus, because households vary in size and structure, from single person households to complex households of three generations and those containing unrelated persons, it is often more difficult to characterize the household by simply averaging the characteristics of all household members, than where a school or similar social system forms the context. Within households, the diversity of characteristics between household members often has a crucial impact on the *type* of contextual variables that can be derived. Examples will be given later in this chapter.

Contingent variables are often derived to analyse the interrelationship between the characteristics of various household members. These variables have largely been neglected in the literature on multi-level analysis, yet are profoundly important for sociological research. The key difference between contextual and contingent variables is that contingent variables usually have a *different* value for each individual in the context (household), whereas contextual variables have the same value for *all* household members. As a simple example of a contingent variable, a married person may be characterized by the age of his or her spouse. The age of spouse is likely to differ for each partner in a married couple. In an analysis of the GHS, Payne (1987) focused specifically on intra-family associations to demonstrate that having a parent or other family member unemployed increases the probability that a young person will be unemployed. In a study of the determinants of women's labour force participation, such as the analysis by Joshi (1984) of the Women and Employment Survey (discussed in Chapter 4), a contingent variable might be derived that measures the amount of 'alternative income'. A variable measuring the income of all *other* adults in the household could be appended to the woman's record.

Contingent variables are derived by 'linking' information about one or more household members to the individual (who is the unit of analysis) on the basis of theoretically defined relationships. When considering contingent variables in a household survey with only two levels of hierarchy, the individual will be the unit of analysis. Thus, contingent variables always involve the use of at least two levels of the hierarchy and are bi-directional (see Figure 9.1(iv)). They are more complex to derive than bi-directional contextual variables, because first, the appropriate relationship between individuals within the household is identified and a variable is derived based on this; secondly, this derived variable is attached to the individual who is the unit of analysis.

Types of variables

The conceptualization and construction of derived variables from hierarchical datasets will be illustrated with reference to the typology in

Figure 9.2. This typology is based on an adaptation and extension of typologies proposed by Lazarsfeld and Menzel (1961) and Galtung (1967). The variables have been classified according to the processes required for their derivation. The typology is a formal classification intended to have heuristic value for sociological research. It illustrates the *range* of types of variables that could be derived from a hierarchical dataset based on two levels of hierarchy: the household and the individual, and provides a framework for illuminating the potential and some of the problems of deriving different types of variables when the context is a small primary group, such as the household. An underlying theme is that all derived variables need to be assessed in terms of the validity of the resulting measures.

Column (a) in Figure 9.2 illustrates six types of variables that can be used where the unit of analysis is the individual. For simplicity of presentation only two levels of hierarchy have been assumed, but in practice these types of variables will often be derived by using more than two levels of hierarchy. Five of these types of variables are derived: all except 'absolute' variables. The typology includes both contextual and contingent variables. The individual as the unit of analysis may be characterized by five types of contextual variables (column b) and by four types of contingent variables (column c). All contextual and contingent variables involve the use of both the household and individual level. Contextual variables may be bi-directional or may only involve distribution down from the household to the individual level, but the derivation of contingent variables will always require movement up and down the levels of the hierarchy (bi-directional). The five types of contextual variables in Figure 9.2 (column b) could also be used as household level variables in an analysis where the household is the unit of analysis.

The various types of variables in Figure 9.2 will be discussed in turn, using examples from individual level (column a), contextual (column b) and contingent variables (column c). Some of these types have less potential value for sociological research and, therefore, will be discussed in less detail. Readers are referred to Sonquist and Dunkelberg (1977) for an excellent exposition of the logic and mechanics underlying variable generation and scale construction. Statistical techniques for the derivation and analysis of contextual variables are discussed in Boyd and Iverson (1979), however, the focus is on social system variables, such as schools, rather than primary groups, such as the household.

Figure 9.2 *Types of variables where the individual is the unit of analysis in a hierarchical dataset, such as the GHS. Assuming only two levels – the individual and the household level*

INDIVIDUAL LEVEL VARIABLES (a)	*CONTEXTUAL VARIABLES (or household-level variables)* (b)	*CONTINGENT VARIABLES (conditional on the identity of the unit of analysis)* (c)
ABSOLUTE e.g. age, sex, height	ABSOLUTE e.g. housing tenure, possession of a freezer	
SUMMARY e.g. pay per hour, alienation score derived from a series of attitude items	SUMMARY e.g. total household income, proportion of adults who smoke, number of persons per room	SUMMARY e.g. total income of *other* adults in the household, total cigarettes smoked by *other* adults in household
CONSTRUCTED e.g. typology of workers categorized as belonging to 'core' or 'periphery'	CONSTRUCTED e.g. household structure, typology of family class, smoking by married couples	CONSTRUCTED e.g. typology of relationship of age of *each* child to ages of other children in the household
COMPARATIVE e.g. percentile of individual's height compared with height of all individuals in the sample	COMPARATIVE e.g. percentile of household income compared to all households in sample	COMPARATIVE Comparison of the individual with other household members, e.g. sibling order
	LINKED e.g. education of head of household, class of 'economically dominant' adult, country of birth of head of household	LINKED e.g. age of oldest sibling, educational qualifications of spouse, age of youngest child
CONTEXTUAL All the types of variables in column (b)		
CONTINGENT All the types of variables in column (c)		

1 Absolute variables

Absolute variables characterize the unit of analysis and are *not* derived from any other variables: for example, age, sex, housing tenure. Contextual variables that are 'absolute' characteristics of the household are only attributable to the household, and are not derived from any information about the characteristics of lower level units or other cases (Figure 9.2, column b). In the GHS, these variables are collected on the Household Schedule: for example, housing tenure, age of house, possession of a freezer or a telephone.

2 Summary variables

Summary variables involve the creation of a new variable on the basis of *arithmetic operations* performed on the values of one or more variables. Any mathematical operation may be involved: for example, summation, averaging, proportions, standard deviations, correlations. These derived variables will usually have values at the interval or ratio level of measurement, and less frequently at the ordinal level. Some writers refer to 'summary' variables as 'aggregate' variables (Tsui, 1985; Boyd and Iversen, 1979). Readers familiar with the Lazarsfeld and Menzel (1961) typology will recognize that 'summary' variables are a sub-type of their 'analytical' variables.

Individual level summary variables (Figure 9.2, column a) may be derived by using mathematical operations on variables characterizing the individual: for example, total income of the individual from all sources, and pay per hour. Chapter 8 gave examples of the derivation of these two individual level summary variables, using SPSS^x.

Contextual summary variables (Figure 9.2, column b) may be derived either from household level variables only (for example, total number of consumer goods owned by the household) or from individual level variables within the household. The latter are derived from the same variable (or variables) for all (or some) individuals within the household: for example, total income of all household members, average number of cigarettes smoked by adults in the household. Contextual summary variables, derived from information about individuals within the household, are more complex to create because the researcher must go up and down the hierarchy – they are bi-directional variables.

Some of the arithmetic operations that can be used to create summary variables will be discussed in more detail, focusing primarily on contextual summary variables derived from individual level variables, which are 'attached' to each individual in the household (bi-directional).

Summations In the GHS, household level variables created through summations may relate to income, such as total household income and total income from state benefits. Very simple summations may form useful analytic variables: for example, the number of adults in the household who are in paid employment, and the number of elderly people in the household who are disabled.

The derivation of variables usually requires decisions about the handling of missing data, and this is particularly important when using summations. For example, data is frequently missing on income, either for one or more individuals in the household, or one or more of the component items of income may be missing, such as income from savings or investments. The researcher may deal with missing data in a number of ways: (i) by omitting all households with any missing data – although, depending on the proportion and characteristics of households with missing data, this may make the resulting sample unrepresentative; (ii) by performing some kind of estimation of the missing data prior to the summation; or (iii) by summing total income on the assumption that the missing income data has the value 'nil'. The latter could produce misleading results, because households with any missing income data would be analysed as having a lower income than their actual income. The researcher must justify which choice is the most appropriate in terms of the analyses to be performed and the amount and nature of missing data. These decisions about how to handle missing data must be made prior to the derivation of variables. Handling missing data when deriving single level and multi-level variables is discussed in Chapters 8 and 10 respectively.

Averages and proportions Contextual household variables based on averages (means or medians) might include average age, income, education, and average number of cigarettes smoked by household members. It is important to consider the meaning of contextual variables that are averages for all household members or for all adults in the household. The interpretation of averages is difficult if there are a wide range of values on variables: for example, age and number of cigarettes smoked. If variables are at the ordinal level of measurement, it may not be appropriate to derive variables based on means and medians. The theoretical interpretation of variables such as median self-assessed health status or average educational qualifications of all household members is far from clear! However, depending upon the researcher's analytic purpose, it may be meaningful to create variables to measure the median disability, mean income or average number of cigarettes smoked by all adults. Thus, the use and interpretation of contextual variables based on averages needs a good deal of care when households are the context.

The proportion of adults or household members with a particular characteristic is a contextual variable that is relatively simple to derive, and may be easier to interpret than averages: for example, the proportion who smoke, have a chronic illness, have higher educational qualifications. In addition, variables can be derived to represent the proportion of household members with a value above (or below) a specified level: for example, the proportion of adults with an income above £200 per week. However, proportions are particularly difficult to interpret where there is a range of different types of household: for example, an elderly person living alone, a lone mother with two children, a three-adult household. Thus, when contextual variables are based on proportions, the implications of a varying number of household members and varying household composition must be taken into consideration.

Summary contextual variables such as summations, averages and proportions have proved to be of value in studying social systems, such as schools, trade unions, and other large collectivities, but are perhaps less useful as a means of characterizing individuals within households. In contrast, typologies constructed to characterize individuals by the nature of their social context are more frequently derived where the household is the context than where the social context is a school or other large collectivity. These will be discussed in section 3.

Contingent summary variables (Figure 9.2, column c) are derived by using arithmetic operations from variables characterizing specified others in the household: for example, average number of cigarettes smoked by *other* adults in the household, total income of adults *other than* the respondent in the household. The health of an individual may be affected by the behaviour of other household members: a study of health may derive a contingent summary variable which measures the total number of cigarettes smoked by *other* adults in the household.

3 Constructed variables

Constructed variables are derived from two or more variables according to a theoretically defined logical process: for example, to form a typology of household structure. The result will be a categorical variable. At their simplest they are constructed from variables held at a single level in a case by variable matrix.

Sociologists frequently construct typologies: for example, whether a married couple have joint or segregated role relationships (Bott, 1971; Edgell, 1980), whether workers have instrumental or collective attitudes (Goldthorpe *et al.*, 1969). Britten and Heath (1983) constructed a measure of family social class based on the cross-classification of four variables: wife's and husband's occupational class, and wife's and husband's employment status. The resulting measure of social class had fifteen conceptually distinct categories, which were subsequently regrouped into five. The creation of a typology involves an examination of the interrelationship between two or more variables. The researcher's theoretical decisions will determine how a new variable should be constructed from the intersection of other variables. Once the relevant theoretical decisions have been made the new variable is constructed by using a series of logical statements (see Sonquist and Dunkelberg, 1977).

Individual level constructed variables (Figure 9.2, column a). An example of a variable constructed solely from individual level variables was given in Chapter 8, where workers were categorized as belonging to either the 'core' or the 'periphery'. This example also discussed methods of checking that the distribution of cases in the constructed variable was correct, and that any cases with missing values on any of the constituent variables were appropriately dealt with in the construction of the derived variable.

Contextual constructed variables (Figure 9.2, column b). A 'constructed' variable, which could be used either as a contextual variable or as a household level variable, is a typology of household structure. For various analytic purposes the researcher may wish to construct a number of different typologies of family or household.

In our research on statutory service provision for the elderly disabled (Evandrou *et al.*, 1986; Arber, Gilbert and Evandrou, 1988), we were interested in how receipt of services varied with the household structure in which the elderly person lived and, in particular, with the gender of the carer. A great deal of theoretical work was involved in defining distinctions between households containing elderly people. The result was a 25-category variable, which distinguished categories of households such as:

elderly person alone
married elderly couple only
two or more 'single' elderly men
two or more 'single' elderly women
one or more 'single' elderly person and one or more 'single' adult men
one or more 'single' elderly person and one or more 'single' adult women
one or more 'single' elderly person with non-elderly married couple only
one or more 'single' elderly person with non-elderly married couple and children under 5

(*Note* The term 'single' was used for those not currently married.)

This constructed variable contained all the key features required in subsequent analyses. It was very rarely used as a 25-category variable, but was recombined in various ways for different analytic purposes (Evandrou *et al.*, 1986; Dale, Evandrou and Arber, 1987; Arber, Gilbert and Evandrou, 1988). Thus, it is possible to construct extremely complex household variables based on hierarchical data, but the value of such variables must be weighed against the time taken in their construction and in checking that they are correct. A detailed example is given in Chapter 11 of a household level variable constructed to distinguish different types of household in a study on inequality.

Contingent constructed variables (Figure 9.2, column c) may be derived from information relating to two or more specified household members. For example, a constructed variable may characterize the relationship between the individual, who is the unit of analysis, and one or more other household members. A researcher studying children may want to characterize each child by whether other children in the household are older or younger. The number of children in the household (or family unit) together with the age of each household member could be used to construct a contingent variable which had the following values:

sole child in household (or family unit)
one older child
one younger child
two or more older children
two or more younger children
both older and younger children

If the secondary analyst wanted to include the gender of other children in the constructed variable, this would result in a constructed contingent variable with more categories which would be more complex to derive.

Where there are two or more children in a household, their value on such a constructed contingent variable will usually differ. This would not be the case for a constructed contextual variable, where all household members have the same value.

4 Comparative variables

Comparative variables characterize the unit of analysis in terms of the relationship between the value of one (or more) variables for that case and the value of the same variable for all (or some) other cases in the sample.

Individual level comparative variables (Figure 9.2, column a). The individual's value on a particular variable can be compared with the values for other cases in the sample: for example, a variable can be derived which measures relative height – whether the individual is in the top 10 per cent of height, next 10 per cent, etc. Comparative variables may also involve the comparison of derived summary variables between cases: for example, relative level of respondent's total income from all sources by comparison with all individuals in the sample. The derivation of this comparative variable using SPSS^x is illustrated in Chapter 8.

Contextual comparative variables (Figure 9.2, column b) can be derived from a comparison of the values of a household level or contextual variable with the value for all (or some) other households in the dataset. For example, a variable could be derived to measure the relative income level of households in the sample by creating a variable that compares the total income of each household with the total income for all households in the dataset expressed in quartiles or deciles. A comparative contextual variable would mean that each individual in the household is characterized by the relative level of income of their household compared with other households in the sample.

Contingent comparative variables (Figure 9.2, column c) compare an individual's value on a variable with that for all (or some) other household members; that is, the comparison is *within* the household, not between households as in contextual variables. For example, each child in a household could be characterized by sibling order; *each* elderly person in a household could be characterized in terms of their relative degree of disability – using a rank order from the most to least disabled; adults in a household may be compared in terms of their relative level of earnings. Comparative variables within households generally have the values 1, 2, 3, etc. Thus on the variable 'sibling order' the third child would have the value 3, and on a variable comparing the disability levels of the elderly in a household, the most disabled elderly person would have the value 1.

5 Linked variables

A linked variable is a derived variable in which the unit of analysis is characterized by information about one individual in the household: for example, information about the social class of the head of household is 'linked' to the unit of analysis. (As noted earlier in this chapter, the term 'linking' is not correct when using SIR, which just references the variables when required.)

Contextual linked variables (Figure 9.2, column b) characterize the household by an attribute of *one* specified household member. They are bi-directional variables, because variables pertaining to the link-member are 'attached' to *each* individual in the household, see Figure 9.1(iii). This procedure is explained using SIR in Chapter 10. It is crucial to justify theoretically what it means to characterize the household by the attributes of one household member and, if it is meaningful, to justify *which* individual should be used as the indicator for the whole household.

Often properties of the head of household are used to characterize the whole household and are used, therefore, as contextual variables for all individuals in the household: for example, the social class, educational attainment, or country of birth of the head of household. The assumptions underlying the definition of who is the head of household may need to be considered. There have been many critics of the conventional use of the (male) head of household (Nissel, 1980; Hunt, 1980; Stanworth, 1984) and also defenders (Goldthorpe, 1983, 1984). Alternatives that have been suggested include characterizing the household by attributes of the individual who is 'economically dominant' (Erickson, 1984; Goldthorpe and Payne, 1986b).

In some cases it may be most appropriate to characterize the household by the attributes of an individual chosen on some other criterion: for example, the most disabled elderly person in the household, or the oldest person. Functions that determine the *maximum* or *minimum* values across all individuals within the household may be used to determine which individual should provide the linked variable. These functions are available in most packages, such as SPSS^x and SIR.

Contingent linked variables (Figure 9.2, column c) are one of the major ways of analysing the association between the attributes of different household members. A specified individual (who is the unit of analysis) is analysed by means of 'linking' information relating to another defined household member to this individual, see Figure 9.1(iv). This, in effect, is defining a *dyad*: one partner is defined as the unit of analysis with information about the other partner 'attached'.

The most straightforward example of this is in the analysis of married couples. It is a fairly common research procedure to interrelate the characteristics of married couples: for example, studies in which the occupation, educational attainment or age of the spouses are interrelated (Goldthorpe and Payne, 1986b). Here the unit of analysis may be either the married couple, or one partner with the spouse's characteristics 'attached'. In the latter, each partner should not be a separate unit of analysis, because this would double count married couples.

In research to study women's labour force participation, using the GHS, variables relating to the woman's youngest child could be 'linked' to the woman's record: for example, the age of her youngest child, the type of school attended by the child, or who looks after the child during the holidays. In a study of the health of children, variables measuring the health of the child closest in age to the child who is the unit of analysis could be 'linked' to the latter's data. Payne's study of unemployed young people appended information about other family members to each 16–19 year old (Payne, 1987). The study used the 1980–81 GHS.

The conceptualization of linked variables may not be straightforward, as the following example illustrates. A study of the impact of the disability level of elderly people on whether they receive community nursing care must hold constant the type of household in which the elderly person lives. The analysis becomes complex where there are two or more elderly people in a household, because service receipt may be influenced *both* by the disability of the elderly person who is the unit of analysis *and* by the disability level of other elderly household members. Where there are two elderly people in the household, a variable measuring the disability level of the other elderly person could be 'linked' to the unit of analysis so that community nursing provision to *each* elderly person could be analysed in terms of the disability level of the *other* elderly household member.

However, the researcher would need to decide what to do where there are three or more elderly persons in a household. One possibility would be to define one of the other elderly persons as the individual to be 'linked' to the unit of analysis. It would probably make most sense to link with the elderly person who is the most disabled, since this person is most likely to influence service receipt. However, among those with a severely disabled dyad partner there may be households where a third elderly person is also severely disabled and households where a third elderly person has no disability. A summary contextual variable could be derived that counts the number of severely disabled elderly people in the household; this would take the values 0, 1, 2, etc. A further possibility is that variables could be added to the data file that indicate the disability level of *each* other elderly person. This would retain all the data in the flat file, but delay the decision of how to analyse the data.

Level and unit of analysis

In most research the choice of the level and unit of analysis is fairly straightforward. However, the secondary analyst, using hierarchically organized data, is able to choose the most appropriate level and unit of analysis, which may vary depending on the focus of the research. A decision about the level and unit of analysis must be made prior to the derivation of variables from hierarchically organized data.

Possible levels of analysis in the GHS were discussed in Chapter 4 (Figure 4.1). They include the household, the family unit, the individual, and an item of the individual's behaviour such as visits to a general practitioner or leisure activities.

If the choice is a higher level (for example, household or family unit) it will be necessary to aggregate up, that is, to 'attach' variables summarizing characteristics of individuals to the household or family unit (Figure 9.1(i)). If the choice is at a lower level (for example, the individual or doctor visits) characteristics from a higher level may be 'attached' to the lower level unit (Figure 9.1(ii)). If doctor visits are chosen as the level of analysis, characteristics of the individual and of the individual's household may be 'attached' to each doctor visit. The researcher will usually create a rectangular data file based on the unit of analysis, which contains various multi-level variables appended to each record.

The choice of level of analysis will be determined primarily by the theoretical purposes of the research, although it may be partly influenced by the ease of creating the relevant derived variables. The most important principle is that the analyst must be clear about the focus of the research – usually the unit of analysis will be obvious from a consideration of the main dependent variable(s). A number of examples in which alternative units of analysis may be considered, will be given as illustration:

1 A study, using the GHS, of the factors that influence whether a doctor gives a prescription during a consultation would probably define doctor consultations as the unit of analysis. If the socio-economic characteristics of the patient are theorized as influencing the doctor's decision to prescribe, information about the individual's age, socio-economic status and health status might be attached to each doctor consultation. However, it would be important to consider the clustering effects that would result from the analysis of multiple consultations by the same individual.

2 A study of the health of families could either take the family as the unit of analysis or each individual child or adult as a separate unit of analysis. It would be more complicated to take the family as the unit of analysis because there are no existing variables in the GHS that pertain to the health of families: all the existing health variables are at the level of the individual. The choice of each family member as a separate unit of analysis means that each individual's health can be analysed together with derived and 'linked' variables that measure family health or health behaviour: for example, the proportion of family members with a chronic illness, the health of the person closest in age, or the total number of cigarettes smoked by adults in the family unit.

3 A study of the impact of an elderly person on the leisure activities of younger household members could define either the elderly person, or *each* non-elderly person in the household, as a separate unit of analysis. The decision is determined primarily by the choice of dependent variable. If the analyst defines leisure activities of non-elderly household members as the dependent variable, then the most appropriate unit of analysis is each non-elderly person living in a household containing at least one elderly person. Information about the disability level of elderly household members, as well as any contextual variables about the household, would be 'linked' to each unit of analysis. This example illustrates that within a particular level of analysis, i.e. individuals, there may be a choice of *which* individual should be the unit of analysis.

The alternative of defining the elderly person as the unit of analysis would be inappropriate, however, *if* this approach were adopted, information about the leisure activities of each household member would have to be 'attached' to the elderly person's record. The problem here is that there could be any number and combination of other household members of varying ages. A general guideline is that the creation of derived variables and analysis is much easier if there is a fixed number of people to be inter-linked and much more difficult if the number varies from one case to the next.

4 To analyse the impact of an elderly household member on the labour force participation of younger household members, the researcher needs to first specify whose labour force participation is being assessed. This may vary between types of household. Where the household contains a non-elderly married couple, the focus and therefore the unit of analysis would probably be the married woman. Where the elderly person lives with a 'single' non-elderly person, the unit of analysis would be that person. Thus, the analyst might create two separate data files, one based on married women with information about the elderly person as well as non-elderly household members 'attached' to the married woman, and another where the unit of analysis was 'single' non-elderly persons living with an elderly person.

An alternative, but less sound, approach would be to take the elderly person as the unit of analysis, and 'link' to the elderly person information about the household member whose labour market participation is being assessed: for example, the married woman's employment status, working hours, type of occupation and age of youngest child (if relevant). However, there are additional problems with this approach, because in some households there will be two or more elderly people, and so, for example, a danger of double counting married women. To get over this, a possibility would be to select only the older of the elderly or the most disabled of the elderly as the unit of analysis.

The moral is that the secondary analyst should think very carefully about the advantages and disadvantages of choosing different levels and units of analysis before embarking on the derivation of variables and the specification of a data file for analysis, and should think clearly about the focus of the analysis in terms of what she is seeking to explain.

10

The derivation of variables using household-based hierarchical data

Previous chapters have discussed the potential of hierarchical surveys for secondary analysis and explored the conceptualization and measurement of derived variables using this type of data. In this chapter we continue the research process from the conceptualization stage to the point of actually creating new derived variables, using hierarchical household-based data. Again, examples will be drawn from the General Household Survey, the basic structure of which was outlined in Figure 4.1. This showed four levels of hierarchy, the highest being the *household*, which may contain one or more *family units*, which, in turn, may contain one or more *individuals*. A further, fourth level contains events such as doctor consultations which are attached to an individual but which vary in number. In this chapter we shall be dealing only with the relationships between households, families and individuals.

One of the most important features of data with this kind of structure is that the analyst is able to link information between all levels of the hierarchy (for example, between the household and the individual) and also between different people at the same level (for example, between husband and wife). However, in order to carry out any kind of analysis using standard software it is necessary to produce a 'flat' or 'rectangular' file within which all the variables are at the same level – either household, family or individual. It is only relatively recently that software has been readily available to enable the analyst to make these kinds of linkages and to select the most appropriate unit of analysis. In earlier years, it was necessary to write your own computer programs – a task which deterred a great many potential secondary analysts. However, the arrival of a number of database management packages designed for use with hierarchical data has opened up the way for the analysis of this kind of data. These packages now include SIR, P-STAT, SAS and SPSS^x – all of which were discussed in Chapter 7. In this chapter, all the examples of derived variables use SIR. The reasons for this are, first, that the GHS is available from the ESRC Data Archive in SIR format with a SIR data definition file (Schema Definition) ready prepared. Secondly, SIR is a package well suited to managing this kind of hierarchical data in a way that retains its 'household' structure and facilitates analysis at all levels. Finally, other important complex datasets, such as the National Child Development Survey, the Women and Employment Survey and the Family Expenditure Survey, are available to the secondary analyst in SIR format from the ESRC Data Archive. However, the other packages mentioned above all provide alternative methods of managing hierarchical data.

While all the examples given below use the hierarchical form of the GHS to derive variables within a SIR database, the result will always be to produce a workfile at the selected level of analysis (usually either household, family or individual) that contains all the required variables. This may be a temporary file, which exists only while tabulations or statistics are being computed. Alternatively, the variables required for analysis may be passed to an SPSS or SAS system file ($SPSS^x$ can read an old-style SPSS system file) for further analysis as flat data. In the examples given here, SIR will be used only as a database management system and not for data analysis. All the variables needed for analysis will be passed as a case by variable matrix to an SPSS system file, although if the analyst is mainly concerned with cross-tabulation, then the facilities of SIR may be preferred to those of $SPSS^x$. We have also selected examples that are relatively simple; for this reason, some of the complexities that the analyst is likely to encounter when using the GHS will not be discussed here. However, a teaching package designed to cover the more complex issues of using the GHS with SIR is available from the University of Surrey (Dale, 1986c). Before discussing detailed examples, we shall briefly outline the form of the GHS SIR files and give an overview of the way in which these are handled by SIR.

The structure of hierarchical data

The hierarchical data in these examples is household-based; thus, the household forms the case and there is one household in each case. Within each household there may be one or more families (usually only one) and within each family one or more individuals. Data is organized into 'records', where each type of record comprises variables that naturally fall together within the structure of the data. For example, those variables relating to the household may fall into the same record type (housing tenure, geographical region, housing amenities) and variables relating to the family form a separate record type. Examples of variables held in the 'family' record are: number of people in the family and number of dependent children in the family. If there are two families within the household, then each will have a family record. Variables that relate to the individual will similarly be organized into distinct record types, with a number of record types used for different kinds of information – health, income, employment. Again, each individual will hold some or all of the individual-level record types. For example, all individuals with some form of income will hold an income record. Sometimes an individual may hold more than one record within a record type: the record type for doctor consultations contains a separate record for each visit to the doctor.

It is obvious that it is crucially important to ensure that records are associated with their correct owners so that, for example, the health data for one person does not get muddled up with the income data of another. This is done by using special variables called SORT IDs. They are identification variables by which each individual can be correctly located within his or her family unit and household. The data shown in Figure 10.1 contains three SORT IDs: HOUSENO, FAMUNIT and PERNO. These provide a means of giving a unique identification to each record.

Figure 10.1 provides a simple illustration of hierarchically organized data where each case contains three different record types. Record type 1 contains household level data; Record type 2 contains variables relating to the family unit and so there will be one type 2 record for each family in the household. Record type 3 contains individual level data, with one record of this type for each person in the household.

The basics of SIR

This section provides a very brief overview of the way in which SIR handles hierarchical data. A fuller account is found in Dale (1986c) and in the SIR Primer (Schulzinger Fox, 1984) and the SIR *User's Manual* (Robinson *et al.*, 1980). A SIR database contains both the data shown in Figure 10.1 and all the associated data definition commands such as labels and missing values. As described above, the data are organized into 'record types' each of which has a number and may also have a name. Thus the record type containing basic household level variables would typically be record type 1 (REC TYPE 1) and may be named 'HHOLD'. Similarly record type 3 may be named 'INDIV'. In order to analyse the data stored in the database you extract from the database the variables of interest by means of a 'retrieval'. These variables, which comprise a *summary file* or summary record, are held in the computer's

Figure 10.1 *An example of hierarchical household based data*

```
1001 8 2
2001 1 2 0
3001 1 1 163 1
3001 1 2 252 1
100210 5
2002 1 5 3
3002 1 1 137 1
3002 1 2 233 1
3002 1 3 213 2
3002 1 4 212 2
3002 1 5 111 2
1003 7 5
2003 1 5 1
3003 1 1 155 1
3003 1 2 242 1
3003 1 3 220 2
3003 1 4 118 2
3003 1 5 112 2
```

Record type 1: HOUSENO 001; REGION 8; NPPHHOLD 2
Record type 2: HOUSENO 001; FAMUNIT 1; NPERFAM 2; NCHDEP 0
Record type 3: HOUSENO 001; FAMUNIT 1; PERNO 1; SEX 1; AGE 63; MARITAL 1
Record type 3: HOUSENO 001; FAMUNIT 1; PERNO 2; SEX 2; AGE 52; MARITAL 1

Record type 1: HOUSENO 002; REGION 10; NPPHHOLD 5
Record type 2: HOUSENO 002; FAMUNIT 1; NPERFAM 5; NCHDEP 3
Record type 3: HOUSENO 002; FAMUNIT 1; PERNO 1; SEX 1; AGE 37; MARITAL 1
Record type 3: HOUSENO 002; FAMUNIT 1; PERNO 2; SEX 2; AGE 33; MARITAL 1
Record type 3: HOUSENO 002; FAMUNIT 1; PERNO 3; SEX 2; AGE 13; MARITAL 2
Record type 3: HOUSENO 002; FAMUNIT 1; PERNO 4; SEX 2; AGE 12; MARITAL 2
Record type 3: HOUSENO 002; FAMUNIT 1; PERNO 5; SEX 2; AGE 11; MARITAL 2

Record type 1: HOUSENO 003; REGION 7; NPPHHOLD 5
Record type 2: HOUSENO 003; FAMUNIT 1; NPERFAM 5; NCHDEP 1
Record type 3: HOUSENO 003; FAMUNIT 1; PERNO 1; SEX 1; AGE 65; MARITAL 1
Record type 3: HOUSENO 003; FAMUNIT 1; PERNO 2; SEX 2; AGE 42; MARITAL 1
Record type 3: HOUSENO 003; FAMUNIT 1; PERNO 3; SEX 2; AGE 20; MARITAL 2
Record type 3: HOUSENO 003; FAMUNIT 1; PERNO 4; SEX 1; AGE 18; MARITAL 2
Record type 3: HOUSENO 003; FAMUNIT 1; PERNO 5; SEX 1; AGE 12; MARITAL 2

HOUSENO	Household identification number
FAMUNIT	Identification number of family unit
REGION	Geographical region of residence
NPPHHOLD	Number of people in the household
NPERFAM	Number of people in the family unit
NCHDEP	Number of dependent children in the family unit
PERNO	Identification number of person
SEX	Sex of person (1 = male, 2 = female)
AGE	Age of person
MARITAL	Marital status of person (1 = married, 2 = single)

memory, ready to be used either for cross-tabulation or for transmission into an SPSS system file for permanent storage. Figure 10.2(i) shows the simplest basic command structure required for data retrieval. We shall briefly explain each of the commands in turn.

Figure 10.2 *A basic SIR retrieval*

(i)

```
RETRIEVAL
PROCESS CASES
. PROCESS REC INDIV
. MOVE VARS SEX, MARITAL
. PERFORM PROCS
. END PROCESS REC
END PROCESS CASES
FREQUENCIES GENERAL=SEX, MARITAL (5)
FINISH
```

(ii)

Use of PERFORM PROCS

```
                                   Summary record    Procedure
PROCESS REC INDIV                                    (eg. frequencies)
MOVE VARS SEX      ----------->         SEX
PERFORM PROCS                                  ---------->   SEX
```

RETRIEVAL is a necessary first command line, telling SIR that the subsequent commands are all concerned with retrieving variables from the database.

PROCESS CASES denotes the beginning of the loop, within which commands are performed for each case (household) selected.

PROCESS REC INDIV This selects all records of type 3, called INDIV, which contain information about the individual. Either the name or the number of the record type may be used; the name is probably easier to remember.

The use of a dot (.) before this and following commands is for cosmetic purposes only. It enables an indentation to be used for each loop within the retrieval, while at the same time ensuring that the first column of the command line contains a character. If there is no character in the first column, SIR assumes a continuation from the previous command line.

MOVE VARS SEX, MARITAL This selects the variables required

from record type, INDIV, and moves them to the summary record – a sort of temporary file held in the computer's memory. The variables will be moved into the summary record in the order in which they are listed in the MOVE VARS command.

PERFORM PROCS When this command is encountered, the contents of the summary record are sent to the procedure section (in this case the frequencies command). If there is more than one type INDIV record in the case (if there is more than one individual in the household), then the MOVE VARS and PERFORM PROCS are repeated for each record in turn (i.e. for each person in the household). The summary record made for person 1 in the household (PERNO=1) is then replaced or over-written by the data from the second person in the household, and this, in turn, is sent to the procedure section by the PERFORM PROCS command. This is repeated until there are no more type INDIV records – no more people in the household. This is illustrated in Figure 10.2(ii).

Thus for each case (household) information about *every* person has been extracted, whether there were one, two, three or more people. The frequencies for SEX and MARITAL will represent information on these variables for all the people in the household and for each household in the database.

END PROCESS REC This denotes the end of the loop for record type INDIV, where PROCESS REC INDIV marked its beginning. It is reached after all the records of this type within the household have been processed.

END PROCESS CASES In a similar way to the END PROCESS REC command, this marks the end of the case loop. In the examples used here, it marks the end of a household.

FREQUENCIES GENERAL=SEX, MARITAL (5) The frequencies command represents a *procedure*. A procedure may, alternatively, be a cross-tabulation command or a command to generate an SPSS system file. The number 5 in parentheses indicates the maximum expected number of categories on either variable – thus MARITAL holds values from 1 to 5.

Having outlined the basic steps in a retrieval, we shall now describe the derivation of variables, using hierarchical data. All examples given will illustrate methods of retrieving variables from the database in such a way that appropriate linkages are established at the required level of analysis.

Deriving a contextual variable with the individual as the unit of analysis

In the following example, we take data from the household level and distribute it down to the individual – this information relating to the household forms a *contextual* variable. For example, housing tenure is a property of the household, but it may be distributed to the individual. In almost all analyses concerned with individuals, it will be necessary to relate to the individual some data concerning the household: for example, the type of housing occupied, the number of people living in the household, the type of amenities available. This distribution of household level variables to the individual has already been done if the 'flat' or rectangular versions of the GHS are obtained from the Data Archive; however, where the data has been obtained in hierarchical form, data distribution will usually need to be done.

Figure 10.3 illustrates the way in which, during distribution, the variable OWNHOUSE (housing tenure) becomes duplicated and attached to *each* member of the household. An example of a SIR retrieval in which this kind of distribution is achieved is shown in Figure 10.4(i). Housing tenure, a household level variable, is related to age, an individual level variable.

Figure 10.3 *Data distribution from household to individual level*

a) *before distribution*

Household level — OWNHOUSE (Data on housing tenure)

Individual level — Person 1   Person 2   Person 3

b) *after distribution*

Household level data is attached to each individual:

Individual level
Person 1 + OWNHOUSE
Person 2 + OWNHOUSE
Person 3 + OWNHOUSE

Source: Dale (1986c).

Figure 10.4 *SIR retrieval to distribute information from household to individual level*

(i)

```
RETRIEVAL
PROCESS CASES ALL
. PROCESS REC HHOLD
. MOVE VARS OWNHOUSE
.   PROCESS REC INDIV
.   MOVE VARS AGE
.   PERFORM PROCS
.   END PROCESS REC
. END PROCESS REC
END PROCESS CASE
SPSS SAVE FILE FILENAME=GHS.SF
END RETRIEVAL
```

(ii)

```
RETRIEVAL
PROCESS CASES ALL
. PROCESS REC HHOLD
. MOVE VARS OWNHOUSE
.   PROCESS REC INDIV
.   MOVE VARS AGE
.   WRITE HOUSENO, OWNHOUSE, AGE
.   END PROCESS REC
. END PROCESS REC
END PROCESS CASE
END RETRIEVAL
```

```
001 1 63
001 1 52
002 1 37
002 1 33
002 1 13
002 1 12
002 1 11
003 1 55
003 1 42
003 1 20
003 1 18
003 1 12
```

In this SIR retrieval, variables relating to housing accommodation are stored in RECORD TYPE HHOLD at the level of the household, while those relating to personal characteristics, such as age, are in RECORD TYPE INDIV. The indentation used is simply to make it easier to see the nesting of one record type within another. We first recall record type

HHOLD (PROCESS REC HHOLD), and, for the first household, move into the summary record the variable OWNHOUSE. Then, we call up REC INDIV, containing individual level variables, and move into the summary record the variable AGE for the first individual encountered within that household. The next command in the retrieval is PERFORM PROCS, which has the effect of sending the contents of the summary record to the SPSS save-file or system file. Thus, the variables OWNHOUSE and AGE are both sent to the SPSS system file for person 1. When the second person in the household is encountered, her AGE variable is moved into the summary record taking the place of, or *over-writing* that of person 1. However, OWNHOUSE remains in the summary record, and is sent again to the system file with the individual-level variable for person 2. The REC INDIV loop is repeated for each individual within the household, with the effect that the variable OWNHOUSE is attached to every individual in the household (Figure 10.3). Thus OWNHOUSE is being duplicated for each person within the household. When data for everyone in the first household has been read, then the second household is similarly processed. The SPSS system file produced in this way will contain the variables OWNHOUSE and AGE in the form of a case by variable matrix at the level of the individual. Of course, the analyst would usually be extracting a great many more variables than these two.

In retrievals using hierarchical data it is particularly important to carry out careful checks of the resulting variables to ensure that mistakes have not been made. The best way of doing this within SIR is to use the WRITE command, which is similar to the LIST CASES command described previously for $SPSS^x$. Figure 10.4(ii) demonstrates the use of the WRITE command. It may be inserted at any level within the retrieval and may appear at two different levels in the same retrieval. Neither PERFORM PROCS nor a procedure need be used with WRITE, although they may be all combined into the same retrieval. Variables named on the WRITE command do not need to be MOVEd into the summary record; they may be accessed directly from the database. Figure 10.4(ii) shows the three variables, HOUSENO, OWNHOUSE and AGE, listed for each individual in the first three households; this enables us to check that each individual within the household has been given the same value on OWNHOUSE (either (1) if owner-occupied or (2) if rented). In the example shown in Figure 10.4(ii), all individuals are in owner-occupied housing.

If the hierarchical capabilities of $SPSS^x$ were used with data which, in reality, was as simple as that shown in Figure 10.1 then distribution of the data from the household to the individual level could be simply achieved using FILE TYPE NESTED (SPSS Inc., 1986). For many kinds of relatively straightforward hierarchical data this provides a simpler alternative to SIR. However, a different method would be needed for more complex data where the individual is not the lowest level of the hierarchy. In this situation one method for distributing household level data to the individual would involve creating two separate system files, one file containing information about housing tenure and also the case definition number, written at the level of the household; and another file, written at the level of the individual, containing age, person number within household, and the case definition number. A table of housing tenure by age may then be produced by merging the two system files, using a 'match files' command, which spreads information on housing tenure in one file to individuals within the same household in the other file. A further system file may then be saved which will hold a rectangular data matrix at the level of the individual. The case definition number, present in both system files, ensures that individuals are correctly matched with the household to which they belong. It is not feasible to give the detailed construction of these commands here. However, they are available, with a great many more examples of hierarchical retrievals using SPSS^x, in Tagg (1986 and 1987).

By duplicating household level information for each individual, the sampling design is being changed to become considerably more clustered. The effect may be shown quite simply by looking at the distribution of a variable, NCHILDHH, showing number of children under 16 in the household (Figure 10.5). It is obvious that those households with more children will be over-represented when the variable is used at the individual level, and may give results that are misleading unless the analyst is quite clear that 62 per cent of *households* contain no children and that 42 per cent of *people* have no children living in their households. A similar effect, but much less marked, occurs when housing tenure is used at the level of the individual.

Although it is often essential to be able to relate household characteristics to individuals within the household, it is important to realize that, if the household has been taken as the sampling unit, then when individuals are used to describe household characteristics, the sampling error will be increased.

Figure 10.5 *Percentage distribution comparing household level and individual level data*

	NUMBER OF CHILDREN PER HOUSEHOLD	
	Individual level	*Household level*
No children	42	62
One child	18	14
Two children	22	15
Three children	12	6
Four children	4	2
Five or more	2	1
	100%	100%
N of cases	(9224)	(3324)

Source: GHS, 1976, Quarter 1.

Deriving a summary contextual variable

A contextual summary variable involves aggregation of data from some or all household members to create a variable that represents a characteristic of the household. For example, the income from paid employment of all household members may be aggregated to give a household level summary variable, TOTPAYHH. This can then be distributed back to all individuals within the household to become a summary contextual variable. This represents a 'bi-directional variable', illustrated in Figure 9.1(iii) on p. 162. Information is first aggregated to the level of the household, and then distributed back to each individual in the household. Again, a SIR retrieval is used, as shown in Figure 10.6(i), where TOTPAYHH represents the summary contextual variable and PAYWEEK represents the weekly income from employment of each adult within the household.

In order to distribute the total income from paid employment to all household members, it is first necessary to compute the sum of all values on the variable PAYWEEK for those household members who have any earned income, using the SIR function SUMR. This creates a new household level variable, TOTPAYHH. Obviously not everyone in the household will have any earned income and, in some households, there will be nobody with earned income. The function SUMR adds together the pay of all household members with valid responses on the variable PAYWEEK. (There is no need to 'MOVE' PAYWEEK into the summary record as it is not being passed to the system file.) The aggregate variable TOTPAYHH is held in the summary record. The

Figure 10.6 *SIR retrieval to derive a summary contextual variable, TOTPAYHH.*

(i)

```
RETRIEVAL
PROCESS CASES ALL
SET TOTPAYHH (0)
. PROCESS REC INCOME
.   COMPUTE TOTPAYHH=SUMR(PAYWEEK)
. END PROCESS REC
. PROCESS REC INDIV
.   MOVE VARS ALL
.   PERFORM PROCS
. END PROCESS REC
END PROCESS CASES
SPSS SAVE FILE FILENAME = GHS.SF
```

(ii)

```
RETRIEVAL
PROCESS CASES ALL
SET TOTPAYHH (0)
. PROCESS REC INCOME
.   COMPUTE TOTPAYHH=SUMR(PAYWEEK)
.   WRITE HOUSENO,PAYWEEK,TOTPAYHH
. END PROCESS REC
. PROCESS REC INDIV
.   MOVE VARS ALL
. END PROCESS REC
END PROCESS CASES
END RETRIEVAL
  001     68      68
  001     12      80
  002    110     110
  002      6     170
  003  153.8   153.8
  003   34.4   188.2
  003   84.9   273.1
  003   48.0   321.1
  004      *       *
```

Note In this retrieval we move into the summary record all the variables held in the individual record type. We could, alternatively, name only a few variables: e.g. AGE, SEX, MARITAL, HEALTH.

next step is to distribute this variable to each household member. This is done within the PROCESS REC INDIV loop, which processes each individual within the household and MOVEs individual level variables into the summary record. When the PERFORM PROCS command is encountered, the contents of the summary record (TOTPAYHH and individual level variables) are sent to the SPSS system file. This is repeated for each individual within the household. The SET command makes sure that TOTPAYHH is initialized or set to '0' at the beginning of each case (household). Although SIR is able to distinguish one household from the next, it does not automatically set TOTPAYHH to zero at the start of every household. If a household were to be encountered that contained no income records, the value on TOTPAYHH for the preceding household would still be sitting in the summary record and would be passed to the SPSS system file with the individual's variables from the new household. Therefore, setting TOTPAYHH to zero at the start of every household ensures that no data gets carried over to the wrong household.

In Figure 10.6(ii) a WRITE command is placed within the loop that sums PAYWEEK for all those who have an INCOME record (those who are 16 and over). This allows us to check that PAYWEEK is being summed correctly. The first column of the output lists the house number, the second column the weekly income from employment and the third the running total of household income from earnings. Where the individual has no income from employment, PAYWEEK is represented as an asterisk. Thus the first individual in household 001 earns £68.0 per week and this is also the total, so far, on TOTPAYHH. However, the second member of household 001 earns a further £12.0 per week, which increases TOTPAYHH to £80.0. It is not until the final income record in the household has been processed that TOTPAYHH contains the correct value. The sole member of household 004 has no income from employment and, therefore, no value on TOTPAYHH. In this example, it may also be useful to use a WRITE command in the loop for the INDIV record, in order to check that the value of TOTPAYHH is being correctly attached to each individual.

A constructed variable, where the household is the unit of analysis

Information about one or more individuals within the household may be used to construct a variable by which to characterize either the household or all members of the household, depending upon the level of analysis required. For example, to distinguish households that contain elderly people (defined as 65 and over) the analyst may wish to make a simple trichotomous categorization of households into:

1 those that contain both elderly and non-elderly people
2 those that contain only elderly people
3 those that contain only non-elderly people

The example shown in Figure 10.7 uses data relating to each individual in the household to construct this very simple categorization at the level of the household. Two WRITE commands are also used, one at the individual level and another at the household level, in the same retrieval. The output from these is given for the first two households.

Figure 10.7 *SIR retrieval to derive a constructed variable at the level of the household*

```
RETRIEVAL
PROCESS CASES
SET OLD, YOUNG (0)
. PROCESS REC INDIV
. IF (AGE GE 65)OLD=OLD+1
. IF (AGE LT 65)YOUNG=YOUNG+1
. WRITE HOUSENO, AGE, OLD, YOUNG
. END PROCESS REC
IF (OLD GT 0 AND YOUNG GT 0)HOUSTYP=1
IF (OLD GT 0 AND YOUNG EQ 0)HOUSTYP=2
IF (OLD EQ 0 AND YOUNG GT 0)HOUSETYP=3
VALUE LABELS HOUSETYP (1)Old & Young in Hhold (2)Only old in
   Hhold (3)Only young in Hhold
WRITE HOUSENO,HOUSETYP,OLD,YOUNG
PERFORM PROCS
END PROCESS CASES
FREQUENCIES GENERAL=HOUSETYP (3)/
END RETRIEVAL
001 63 0 1
001 52 0 2
001  3 0 2
002 37 0 1
002 33 0 2
002 13 0 3
002 12 0 4
002 11 0 5
002  3 0 3
```

The retrieval (Figure 10.7) begins by using the SET command to construct two new variables, YOUNG and OLD, which are initialized, or set to zero. These will be used as the basis for the categorization. PROCESS REC INDIV marks the beginning of the loop through which each individual is passed; during this stage, the variables YOUNG and OLD are incremented as an individual fulfils the required conditions. Those aged 65 and over cause the variable OLD to be incremented, and those aged less than 65 increment the variable YOUNG. At this point, the WRITE command allows us to check that each individual has been given the correct value on OLD and YOUNG.

Moving back to the level of the household, we can then categorize households into those containing both 'old' and 'young' people and those containing only 'old' or only 'young'. In practice, it would be sensible to use some further selection factors, but this example illustrates the basic idea. The exemplar in Chapter 11 gives the derivation of a more complex household typology. The WRITE command again allows us to check that the values on OLD and YOUNG have been correctly combined into HOUSETYP. The output from WRITE, therefore, will consist of one line for each individual *and* one line for each household. In Figure 10.7 the first household contains two individuals aged 63 and 52, which means that each person increments the variable YOUNG by one; thus the household contains '2' 'young' people and '0' 'old' and is given the value '3' on HOUSETYP. The value of HOUSETYP is shown in the output line written at the household level. The PERFORM PROCS command, at the level of the household, will pass the variable HOUSETYP to the frequency procedure *once* per household.

A constructed variable where the individual is the unit of analysis

If, alternatively, the analyst wishes to distribute this household categorization to each *individual* within the household, as in Figure 9.1(iii) on p.162, then a further step is required, as shown in Figure 10.8

Figure 10.8 *SIR retrieval to derive a constructed variable at the level of the individual*

```
RETRIEVAL
PROCESS CASES
SET OLD, YOUNG
. PROCESS REC INDIV
. IF (AGE GE 65)OLD=OLD+1
. IF (AGE LT 65)YOUNG=YOUNG+1
. END PROCESS REC
IF (OLD GT 0 AND YOUNG GT 0)HOUSTYP=1
IF (OLD GT 0 AND YOUNG EQ 0)HOUSTYP=2
IF (OLD EQ 0 AND YOUNG GT 0)HOUSETYP=3
VALUE LABELS HOUSETYP (1)Old & Young in Hhold (2)Only old in
   Hhold (3)Only young in Hhold/
. PROCESS REC INDIV
. PERFORM PROCS
. END PROCESS REC
END PROCESS CASES
FREQUENCIES GENERAL=HOUSETYP (3)/
END RETRIEVAL
```

Having processed each person within the household and created a categorization at the household level, we then re-read the record for each individual in the household, using PROCESS REC INDIV and with the PERFORM PROCS command moved to the individual level, so that the derived variable HOUSETYP is attached to each person as PERFORM PROCS is executed.

Deriving a linked contextual variable

In this example, the individual is still being used as the unit of analysis, but the characteristic of one member of the household (the head of household) is being linked to each individual within the household. Although the characterization of other household members by the 'head of household' is subject to much criticism (Nissel, 1980; Hunt, 1980; Stanworth, 1984), none the less it provides the basis for a straightforward example. In the GHS, information on country of birth is recorded for each individual as the variable WHBORN; in the example in Figure 10.9 we show a SIR retrieval where the country of birth (WHBORN) of the head of household is used to characterize each individual. The head of household is identified as holding the value '0' on HOHRELN.

In Figure 10.9 the contextual variable to be derived, HOHBORN, represents the country of birth of the head of household. It is set to '0' (initialized), at the beginning of each case or household. The PROCESS REC INDIV command begins the loop through which each member of the household passes. If the individual is the head of household (coded '0' on HOHRELN) then the variable HOHBORN is assigned that

Figure 10.9 *SIR retrieval to derive a linked contextual variable, HOHBORN*

```
RETRIEVAL
PROCESS CASES ALL
SET HOHBORN (0)
. PROCESS REC INDIV
. IF (HOHRELN EQ 0)HOHBORN=WHBORN
. END PROCESS REC
. PROCESS REC INDIV
. MOVE VARS ALL
. PERFORM PROCS
. END PROCESS REC
END PROCESS CASES
SPSS SAVE FILE FILENAME=GHS.SF
```

person's value on WHBORN. Because we cannot be certain that the GHS always records the head of household's data before that of any other household member, we need to construct the variable HOHBORN by first reading data for *all* individuals and then repeating the PROCESS INDIV loop in order to send each individual's variables to the SPSS system file, along with HOHBORN. Thus HOHBORN, holding information relating to one household member (the head of household) is attached, or linked, to all household members. In the diagram in Figure 9.1(iii) on p. 162, this is illustrated as bi-directional, in that the analysis moves from the level of the *individual* to the household and then back again to the individual.

In this example computing time could be reduced by using a slightly more complex retrieval. It is often possible to find ways of reducing computing time if this is important.

Deriving a contingent linked variable at the level of the family

A contingent variable holds information about *another* member of the household or family (see Chapter 9, p. 167). In the example shown in Figure 10.10 we analyse the relationship between the health of a married man and the health of his wife. The unit of analysis is the family and, for each family containing a married couple, we derive variables to represent the health of both the husband and wife. The derivation involves moving from the level of the family to that of the individual and then back again to the family. It also entails use of the SORT ID FAMUNIT, to ensure that, where a household contains more than one family unit, the wife is linked to a husband in the same family unit.

In this retrieval we first process each individual *within* their family unit (thus the REC INDIV loop is nested inside the REC FAMUNIT loop), and create a variable WIFHLTH, which is given the same value as 'HEALTH' for married women. Because it is derived within the family unit, we can be sure that, however many wives a household may contain, this variable will be derived once for *each* family containing a married woman. Because of the way in which the GHS defines a family unit, it is never possible for more than one married couple to belong to the same family unit.

If a household never contained more than one married couple, then it would be possible to take the married man as the unit of analysis, rather than the family. However, where there are two couples within a household, the variable WIFHLTH created by the first wife would be over-written when the second wife is processed. Using the retrieval shown in Figure 10.10, the variables derived for husband and wife for the first family unit will be passed to the system file before the second family unit is processed. Thus, the system file will contain a set of variables for each family that contains a married couple. The command IFNOT (HUSMAR EQ 1)NEXT RECORD ensures that, if there is no married man in the family, the program skips to the next family unit.

Figure 10.10 *Derivation of contingent variables*

```
RETRIEVAL
PROCESS CASES ALL
 · PROCESS REC FAMILY
 · SET WIFHLTH, HUSHLTH, HUSMAR(0)
 · MOVE VARS FAMUNIT
 ·  PROCESS REC INDIV WITH (FAMUNIT)
 ·  IF (MARITAL EQ 1 AND SEX EQ 2)WIFHLTH=HEALTH
 ·  IF (MARITAL EQ 1 AND SEX EQ 1)HUSHLTH=HEALTH
 ·  IF (MARITAL EQ 1 AND SEX EQ 1)HUSMAR=1
 ·  IF (MARITAL EQ 1 AND SEX EQ 1)HUSAGE=AGE
 ·  IF (MARITAL EQ 1 AND SEX EQ 2)WIFAGE=AGE
 ·  END PROCESS REC
 · IFNOT (HUSMAR EQ 1)NEXT RECORD
 · PERFORM PROCS
 · END PROCESS REC
END PROCESS CASES
SPSS SAVE FILE FILENAME=HEALTH.SF
```

Note There is no need to MOVE the variables MARITAL, SEX HEALTH, AGE from REC INDIV into the summary record as they are used only to compute new variables and are not need in the analysis.

Although many of the examples presented here are simpler than would usually be required by the secondary analyst, they may begin to give an idea of the way in which hierarchical data can be used to its full capability. Because it is very easy to specify a retrieval that is syntactically correct but that gives nonsensical results, it is very important that the analyst checks each stage of a retrieval, using the WRITE command, to ensure that the results are as expected. However, once the practicalities of managing hierarchical data have been mastered, the possibilities for analysing relationships between household members become very great indeed. So, too, does the potential for deriving variables by which to summarize the characteristics of households; this aspect will be developed further in the next chapter.

11

Exemplar: inequality of income and assets

In this chapter we go through the stages of a research project, step by step, in order to illustrate the various points that have been discussed in preceding chapters. The research described below, on inequality of income and assets, was carried out under a six-month research grant from the ESRC. Like most ESRC end-of-grant reports, the report on the project has been lodged with the British Document Supply Centre (Dale, 1985), and the work also forms the basis for a study of the stratificatory effects of lifecycle (Dale, 1987). The chapter is divided into sections, each corresponding to the logical stages of progression through the project. Of course, this has been with the benefit of hindsight, and it goes without saying that these stages were rather less clearly defined while the work was in progress! We begin by examining the theoretical basis underlying the proposed research, identifying the concepts to be used and the way in which they may be operationalized. This initial conceptualization makes it clear that the household is the appropriate unit of analysis and that a household-based data source, containing information on all household members, is necessary. Having located a suitable data source and assessed its strengths and shortcomings, we then set out a detailed research design, which leads into the derivation of variables for subsequent analysis. Finally, we illustrate the use of exploratory data analysis by giving some results from preliminary analyses.

Locating the theoretical interest of the study

The analysis of class-based inequalities has a long tradition in the sociological literature. It is usually located either within a Marxian framework (thus, Westergaard and Ressler, 1975, p.2, see class as representing 'the substance and structural sources of inequality') or in Weberian terms as deriving from the power of market forces. In both cases, it has been customary to use occupation or employment status as the basis upon which to assign class positions (Goldthorpe, 1980;

Stewart, Prandy and Blackburn, 1980). Relationship to the means of production is one of the fundamental forces structuring society, and for most people occupation is the main determinant of income, whether directly or indirectly. However, the use of occupation as a basis for allocation to class position makes it difficult to include those with no direct relationship to the occupational structure.

This project, therefore, uses two types of stratificatory measure which are not based upon occupation but which may both be representative of particular kinds of inequality. The first is *current disposable income* and the second, *assets* that can generate wealth, income, opportunity or time (for example, property, cars, consumer durables). These measures will be taken as representative of two types of inequality (both of which may be seen as ultimately deriving from the class structure) that avoid an explicit focus upon those who are in paid work. Both measures are equally applicable to those with a direct relationship to the occupational structure and those who are not in paid employment – unemployed people, the retired and housewives. Hence, a research framework may be developed which can incorporate all members of society, irrespective of their employment status, but which recognizes the major role of the class structure in determining the rewards that accrue to individuals, families and households.

Having identified these two measures of inequality, the study will focus on the relationship between the two – the extent to which income and household assets are related and the way in which they vary with household structure and stage of lifecycle. First, we consider the appropriate level of analysis.

Defining the appropriate level of analysis

While income represents the rewards accruing from an individual's relationship to the productive system – in the form either of wages paid for labour, of rent gained from property or of interest from capital assets – it does not take place in isolation from the activities of other members of the household. For example, the labour market power of any individual is either enhanced or restricted by the sexual division of labour within the home, although income paid to one individual does not necessarily take into account the unpaid labour of others within the household. Women who are responsible for the domestic care of children and family enter the labour market with less earning capacity than men who are free from such commitments. Yet both domestic work and paid employment contribute to the productive capacity of the household. Thus Haraven, in her study of Amoskeag at the turn of the century, found that:

> women who worked outside the home viewed their factory labor and their domestic tasks as complementary, if not interchangeable. It was all part of their collective family enterprise. Their domestic responsibility – the care of the children, the clothing of family members, the feeding of the family and often boarders as well – was itself a form of production. (Haraven, 1982, p. 204)

Recent UK studies have also shown that decisions about employment tend to be taken, particularly by women, in the context of the needs and earning capacity of other household members and have argued the need to take the household as the unit of production (Hunt, 1980; Yeandle, 1984; Owen 1987). The role of the household is well summarized by Mingione:

> The unit of reproduction (the household) disposes above all of working capacities which, with a limited freedom of choice, conditioned by the historical phases of development and by the socio-cultural background of the unit, it can apply either to working activities that provide a monetary income with which to purchase goods and services for subsistence, or to working activities that directly provide goods and services useful for subsistence (activities for self-consumption or domestic work). Furthermore, the unit may also be able to count on resources from outside, such as assistance from the State or from public bodies (in terms of income or of services and goods) . . . (Mingione, 1985, p.24).

This conceptualization of income as accruing from the activities of all household members clearly leads to the conclusion that the household must be the appropriate unit of analysis. Similarly, the assets to be used in this study are those that may benefit all members of the household – owner- occupied housing, cars and consumer durables. These are assets that may be converted into some form of wealth or income, time or opportunity. They differ from aspects of consumption such as holidays or alcohol consumption that, while reflecting both spending power and personal preferences, cannot be translated into a means of wealth accumulation, cannot provide access to increased income or free time, and cannot extend employment opportunities.

However, it is important to recognize that we are not able to make assumptions about the distribution of these assets *within* the household.

The work of Land (1983) and Pahl (1983) has shown that an equal distribution of resources *within* the family or household cannot be assumed, and, in fact, inequalities not just in terms of money but many other facets of life are the norm rather than the exception. None the less, it is important that research at a higher level of aggregation than the individual should be carried out, for it is at this level that the parameters are set within which individual spending is constrained. Therefore, these household level analyses will provide a base line of information within which intra-household allocation of resources can be better understood.

Data source

In order to operationalize the concepts discussed in preceding sections, we need household level data that contains detailed information about income, as well as variables that relate to housing, cars and consumer durables. We also need a dataset that is representative of all kinds of households and life-styles. The only two British national-level data sources that meet all these requirements are the Family Expenditure Survey and the General Household Survey.

Because of its greater sample size and higher response rate (about 82 per cent as opposed to about 68 per cent) the General Household Survey was chosen in preference to the FES. The GHS had a nationally representative achieved sample of about 10,000 households and a response rate of 83 per cent in 1979 (OPCS, 1981), the year used in the analysis. The choice of year was based upon that which was most recently available at the time of the research and which also contained all the information necessary to calculate a standardized measure of current disposable income. In 1979, the GHS contained a very extensive income section, in which both net and gross income from employment were recorded, as well as income from all other sources, including investments, property and housing benefits.

Choice of data form

Chapter 5 outlined the variety of forms in which the GHS is available from the Data Archive. For this study it is important to be able to use the full hierarchical capabilities of the data, as many of the variables needed must be derived from information from all household members and are not already contained within the dataset. The form in which data is available depends upon the year being used; the 1979 GHS data may be obtained from the ESRC Data Archive in hierarchical form as Surrey SIR files and also in the 'raw' form supplied by OPCS. All the examples given here are based upon the Surrey SIR files.[1]

Having selected the data, an application is then made to the ESRC Data Archive. Those wishing to use the GHS complete a special application form, in which the purposes of the research project and the methods to be used must be outlined. The Data Archive then sends this application to OPCS with a request to use the data. A positive response can usually be expected within a couple of weeks.

Identifying and operationalizing the concepts of interest

Inequalities of income – Relative Net Resources

From the previous discussion it is clear that income must be measured in a way that takes account of all sources of income within the household and that income will vary greatly with the number of people in paid employment. Because households also differ in their size and composition it is important to use a standardized form of income, which takes this into account and which reflects the level of income available after meeting basic 'needs'. To achieve this we have used income in relation to the DHSS Supplementary Benefit levels, expressed as a percentage. This measure of income is termed Relative Net Resources (RNR) and has been widely applied in the welfare economics literature (Bradshaw, 1984; O'Higgins and Bradshaw, 1984; Layard *et al.*, 1978).

Although we have decided to use the household as the unit of analysis, the DHSS does not operate on the basis of households. Rather, its assessment unit is taken to be a married couple and their dependent children under 16 (or under 19 if still in full-time education). Any unmarried person of 16 and over (or 19 and over if still in full-time education) is treated as a separate assessment unit. However, the measure of inequality based on household assets makes it impossible to differentiate the extent to which families or individuals within the household benefit from these assets. Therefore, RNR of the household, rather than of the DHSS-defined assessment unit is used. This is calculated by using the sum of the benefit entitlement of all the assessment units in the household. The formula used is:

$$\frac{\text{net weekly income of household} \times 100}{\text{supplementary benefit entitlement of household}}$$

Identifying shortcomings: Relative Net Resources

The problems associated with using income in relation to supplementary benefit level (RNR) as a measure of inequality are many and various. They include the arbitrary nature of the scale rates, especially in terms of the allowances for different ages of children and the lack of any attempt to take into account regional differences in prices, or class-based spending customs (Kincaid, 1979). Other general problems associated with using income include the impossibility of taking into account fringe benefits and payment in kind, gifts and personal services (Townsend, 1974) and the fact that it gives no indication of wealth in the form of investments in property or paintings. None the less, as a means of making standardized comparisons of the resources available for consumption, across different types of family or household, it is of value.

Although the GHS in 1979 contained all the items of information necessary to measure RNR at a reasonable level of accuracy, a few areas can be identified where shortcomings still remain.

1 The DHSS scale rates vary, depending on whether or not the recipient has householder status. Where two assessment units share a household, it has to be assumed, from the definition of a household used by OPCS (1981), that the second assessment unit does not have householder status.

2 The scale rates used to calculate RNR are those that were in operation between November 1978 and November 1979. However, wage-rates are likely to have risen during the course of the year, with the effect that those interviewed in January 1979 may have slightly lower levels of RNR than if the same people had been interviewed in December 1979. A choice must be made about whether the short-term or long-term supplementary benefit rates should be used. We decided to use long-term rates, partly to enable comparisons with the earlier work of Layard *et al.* (1978), and partly because long-term rates are designed to meet the needs of those who claim benefit for a prolonged period and are, therefore, a more realistic reflection of the amount of income needed to meet basic costs of living.

As RNR is being used as a means of *comparing* the resources available rather than making a judgement about poverty levels, the shortcomings outlined above have less importance. It is only where there are systematic differences between sectors of society that these shortcomings may cause problems – for example, the resources of higher white-collar workers will be systematically undervalued vis-à-vis manual workers if the former group receives fringe benefits of a greater value than does the latter group.

Inequalities in household assets

The household assets identified as fulfilling the criteria of bestowing wealth, income, time or opportunity are discussed in turn.

1 HOUSING TENURE

The importance of housing tenure in distinguishing inequality in lifestyle is primarily related to the inequalities in wealth that follow from home ownership as compared with renting accommodation. Murie (1983) argues that 'the potential for accumulation of wealth through individual ownership is a factor maintaining social division' (p.168). 'Differences between owners and non-owners of dwellings are not simply differences in type and value of dwelling in use, but are part of inequalities in wealth' (p.170). These inequalities are manifest through inheritance, but also in the accumulation of a capital asset through a life-time.

The geographical separation of private housing from council housing and the distinctive appearance of much council housing are argued by Ineichen (1983) to contribute to enduring and visible class differences. Added to this is the stigma that is associated with some local authority estates, such that a particular address may disadvantage a job applicant.

2 CAR OWNERSHIP

The availability of private transport makes accessible a range of facilities and services that are otherwise severely restricted for most people. The unreliability or unavailability of public transport in many areas, and at various times of the day, means that there are considerable differences in opportunity for those with and without a car. Obvious examples include: the ability to visit a supermarket to get a week's shopping; the ability to visit friends, or go to the theatre and return home late at night; the differences in travelling time for the same journey when using private and public transport.

Stanton, Cahill and Howdle (1981) found that young workers, women and the unskilled were disproportionately likely to be without access to a car and that, with the decline in bus services, this would result in less mobility and poorer access to employment opportunities. Thus, the relationship between occupation and income level and car ownership may be two-way.

3 CONSUMER DURABLES

Consumer durables such as a freezer and a washing machine may lead to household economies in both time and money. Time freed from domestic work can be used either in paid employment or in leisure activities, thereby widening the gap between those who have such appliances and those who do not.

Identifying shortcomings: assets

The fact that the analyst does not know the distribution of resources *within* the household has already been discussed. It should not be assumed that there is equality between household members; as far as usage of a car or van is concerned there is considerable evidence that there is not (Dale, 1986d). Similarly, we do not know to what extent the possession of other assets benefits the household as a whole or just some members of it. A further limitation is in the range and type of assets that are available within the GHS: for example, one might wish to include other forms of property and, perhaps, paid household help, but this information is not available in the GHS.

Incorporating household structure and stage of lifecycle into the research design

The project sets out to examine the relationship between household income expressed as RNR and household assets of the kind already described. It has been argued that these may be taken to represent two stratificatory measures; but these two measures may be expected to vary with lifecycle stage and household structure. For example, a washing machine or freezer may be totally irrelevant to a student living in a bed-sitter, but they may be of overriding importance to a family of six. We need, therefore, to construct a typology of households, which reflects not just 'typical' lifecycle stages but which also recognizes that people do not all pass through a fixed series of lifecycle stages and that a household may contain more than one lifecycle stage – for example, a 3-generational household. A typology of households, therefore, must incorporate, as far as possible, the main lifecycle stages that can be identified and also the most important kinds of household structure.

Figure 11.1 *Model of relationship between income, household assets and household structure*

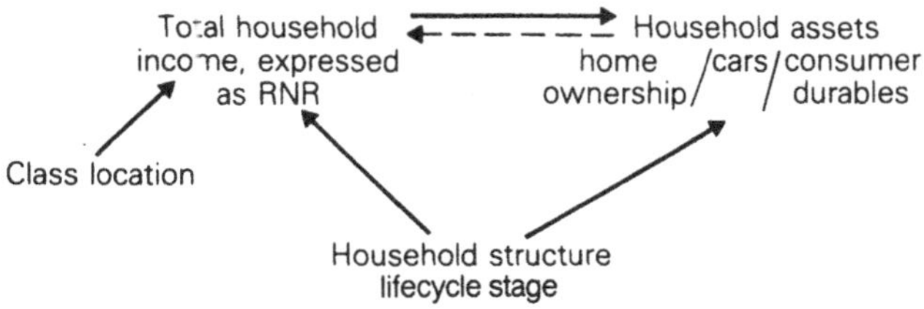

Figure 11.1 sets out the model used in this analysis and the expected directions of influence.[2]

Thus lifecycle stage/household structure is expected to have an independent effect on both RNR and assets. Therefore, we set out to establish the relationship between RNR and assets for a given type of household. Although RNR may also be expected to influence the level of assets, it is important that the research design recognizes the different time periods used to record these two concepts. Income recorded by the GHS refers to current income (usually income in the week prior to the survey, although for some kinds of income a longer time period is used), whereas household assets may have been acquired over the course of years and are unlikely to respond quickly to changes in current income. This is of value in the research design, as it means that assets may be able to give an indication of 'better times gone by' for those with low current income. Conversely, high current income but low levels of assets may relate to a stage of lifecycle where income is rising rapidly but assets have not yet been acquired. The nature of the household assets being measured means that we would not expect a direct relationship between current income and level of household asset. Items such as housing tenure and car ownership, as well as reflecting long-term earning patterns, also vary with stage of lifecycle. Thus, young couples may have moved less far along the pathway of accumulation than middle-aged couples.

The measurement of household structure

One of the disadvantages associated with secondary analysis is that we cannot influence the definitions and concepts used by those who carry out the survey. In this study, therefore, we have to accept the definition of a household that was being used by OPCS in 1979. A household is defined in the following way:

> A household can consist of one person living alone or a group of people who all live regularly at the same address and who are all catered for by the same person for at least one meal a day. Resident domestic servants are included. The members of a household need not be related by blood or marriage. (OPCS, 1981, p. 175)

For most purposes, this definition is appropriate to the study; however, it does mean that servants would be included in the same household as their employers and that lodgers, unless entirely self-catering, would also be included. Although this is unlikely to affect the results of the study in any significant way, it is none the less important to be aware of the definitions being used and any implications that they might have. Because the GHS is a household-based survey and records in detail the relationship of all household members to a predefined 'head of household', it is well suited to the construction of a typology of households. The large sample size and the representativeness of the survey mean that it is possible to distinguish households comprising groups that are numerically small in the population as a whole – for example, one-parent families.

In 1979 the GHS did not include cohabitation as a category of marital status, although the information was available from the family formation section for women aged 18–49. Where couples described themselves as married they were recorded as such; if they described themselves as single they were similarly recorded as single. In the household typology (Figure 11.2) it is likely that some households containing two 'single' adults may, in fact, represent cohabiting couples but we have no information on this.

As it will be referred to later, we also give here the definition of a family unit used by OPCS:

> A family can consist of:
> (a) a married couple on their own, or
> (b) a married couple/lone parent and their never married children, provided these have no children of their own . . . Adoptive and step-children belong to the same family as their adoptive/step-parents. Foster-children are not part of their foster-parents' family since they are not related to their foster parents (OPCS, 1981, p.175).

Figure 11.2 *A categorization of households using the GHS for 1979; HOUSETYP*

Household structure	*% all households*	*Description*
1 One person household, age < 35	2.5	60 per cent male; 80 per cent single
2 Two or more non-married adults in household	3.1	some may be co-habiting couples
3 Couple under 35, no children	4.5	These mainly represent couples at a pre-family stage
4 Couple with one or more dependent children	25.3	
5 One parent – no other adults in the household	2.5	82 per cent are female: the majority aged 23 –40; 82 per cent are divorced or separated
6 One parent with other adult	1.4	The other adult may be a co-habitee, an adult child or a widowed or divorced mother
7 Couple with dependent children + elderly person	0.5	The elderly person is typically the wife's widowed mother
8 Couple + dependent children + non-dependent 'children'	6.3	A few 'non-dependent children' are other relatives or lodgers
9 Non-elderly adults, single or married + elderly person	4.9	Most contain an elderly couple or widow with an adult 'child' living at home
10 Couple with non-dependent 'child(ren)'	6.7	A few 'non-dependent' children are other relatives or lodgers
11 One person household, 35 and over but not elderly	5.7	Men and women are equally represented; women – 49 per cent are widowed; men – 48 per cent single; 30 per cent divorced or separated
12 Couple 35 and over, no children in the household	12.8	Non-elderly couples whose children have left home or who are childless
13 Elderly couple	9.4	Includes some elderly not married
14 One elderly person	14.5	80 per cent are female; 80 per cent are widowed
Total all households	100.0	(11,486)

Definitions overleaf

Definitions for Figure 11.2

Couple The term couple is used for those describing themselves as married.

Parent A parent always has a dependent child.

Elderly Elderly is defined as over 60 for a woman and over 65 for a man. A couple is defined as elderly where the husband is over 65

Couple 35 and over The age is that of the older member of the couple; the couple is not elderly.

Dependent child A dependent child is under 16, or under 19 if still in full-time education.

Household In the GHS for 1979 a household consists of those who live at the same address and share at least one meal each day.

Derivation of variables

Figure 11.1 set out the model being used and the three variables (or groups of variables) needed in the research. The main lines of influence between household income, assets and household structure are suggested in the diagram. The derivation of each of these three variables or sets of variables will be discussed in turn. For household structure we give a full account of the rather complex procedure used to derive the variable. It should be stressed that a similar variable could be arrived at by a number of different routes, but, whatever the exact mechanism used, such a variable will require linkages to be made at both the family and individual levels of the hierarchy, with aggregation to the household level.

Level of household assets

Assets were measured in terms of:

housing tenure (OWNHOUSE)
access to a car or van (NCARS)
freezer in accommodation (FREEZER)
colour TV in accommodation (COLOURTV)
central heating (CENTHEAT)
washing machine in accommodation (WASHMACH)

These are household level variables that do not require derivation.

Household structure (HOUSETYP)

This is a constructed contextual variable to provide a typology of household structure (Figure 11.2). The variable uses information from both the family and the individual level and aggregates it to the level of the household. At its most basic, the typology is constructed from the six elements listed below, with information on the number of people in the household, the number of adults and, for one-person households, age of head of household. Some additional variables incorporating gender distinctions are also derived for later use. Variables (SINGLELD, DEPCHILD, etc.) representing the presence of these six key elements in the household are first derived.

Variable name

SINGLELD	non-married elderly person
DEPCHILD	dependent child
SINGLEAD	non-married adult (not elderly)
ECOUPLE	married couple – elderly
YCOUPLE	married couple – under 35
MCOUPLE	married couple – 35 or over, not elderly

The category of 'elderly' is defined in relation to the labour market; therefore, men aged over 65 and women aged over 60 are defined as elderly. Among married couples, the age of the husband is used to define the status of elderly on the assumption that the husband's retirement will have a greater effect on household income than his wife's. A distinction based on wife's age is made between non-elderly married couples without dependent children. It is assumed that those couples where the wife is less than 35 are at a pre-family stage (if they intend to have children), while those of 35 and over and without dependent children are either childless or have children who are no longer defined as dependent. The original research, used to produce the analyses shown later, defined age as that of the oldest member of the couple, although it subsequently became clear that wife's age would have been preferable, as this relates more closely to family formation. As later work has also used wife's age this is reflected in the SIR derivation given in Figure 11.4. Thus decisions, based upon the aims and theoretical framework of the research, are continually being made and it is important to work out a clear rationale for them. Because these decisions relate so closely to the way in which the research problem has been defined, an analyst using the data for a different theoretical purpose may make different decisions.

Figure 11.3 sets out the stages in the derivation of the variable (HOUSETYP) and indicates the levels of hierarchy and variables that are used. The first stage derives a number of variables, which measure whether or not the household contains a particular element in the typology – for example, an elderly couple, or a dependent child. The SIR retrieval used to do this is shown in Figure 11.4. Distinctions based upon gender are also incorporated into the derived variables – elderly 'single' woman, elderly 'single' man – although these are not used in defining the typology. They are, however, important at the later stage of describing the members of each category of the typology; they may also be needed in subsequent analyses where it is important to make distinctions based upon gender – for example, in analysing the provision of meals-on-wheels to elderly people living alone (Arber *et al.*, 1988).

After the hierarchical capabilities of SIR have been used to derive all the variables needed to construct the household typology, Stage 2 passes these variables (and also NPPHHOLD and NFAMHH) to an SPSS system file at the level of the household. The use of the INCLUDE command in the SIR retrieval (Figure 11.4) ensures that only those variables named are output to the system file. Thus, a rectangular data file is created, which contains one record that holds these twelve variables for each household. This can then be readily used in Stage 3 to combine the 'building blocks' in any way that the analyst chooses. In this example we used a two-stage process shown in detail in Figure 11.5.

First, these building blocks are used to establish the six basic household groupings previously listed, in a way that unambiguously defines any combination of them. This is done by assigning a value to each variable so that any of the possible combinations of the six variables will result in a unique value (Figure 11.5(i)). Thus we compute a temporary variable, which we shall call TEMPHH and which may contain values ranging from 1 to 63 (1 + 2 + 4 + 8 + 16 + 32). In this way, every combination of elements will have a different value on TEMPHH. Figure 11.5(ii) shows the results in the form of a frequency distribution of TEMPHH from a very small sub-sample of 100 households. Because of the restrictions of value labels, the term 'single' is used instead of the more accurate description of 'not currently married'. One of the frustrations of the limitation on the length of value labels is that we are continually being forced into using shorthand, inaccurate and often pejorative descriptions!

From Figure 11.5(ii) it is apparent that most households will fall into a small number of readily identifiable categories: single elderly (code 1); young couple with dependent children (code 18; 16 + 2 = 18). The number of categories will, of course, increase when a full sample of

Figure 11.3 *Stages in the derivation of a typology of household structure*

Target variable	: HOUSETYP
Type of variable	: A contextual 14 category variable at the level of the household (Figure 11.2)
Aim of variable	: To provide a broad categorization of households based upon lifecycle stages and composition of household

Stage 1 Using SIR to derive contextual variables

SIR is used to derive a number of contextual household level variables. From these, the presence of the six basic elements shown in the left-hand column are computed.

Basic elements	*Contextual variables*	
SINGLELD	ELDFEM	– number of elderly 'single' women; over 60
	ELDMAN	– number of elderly 'single' men; over 65
DEPCHILD	NDEPCHHH	– number of dependent children
SINGLEAD	SINGLEM	– number of adult non-elderly 'single' men
	SINGLEF	– number of adult non-elderly 'single' women
ECOUPLE	ELDCUP	– couple, husband over 65
YCOUPLE	YOUNGCUP	– couple, wife aged less than 35
MCOUPLE	MIDCUP	– couples, wife 35 and over but couple not elderly
	HOHAGE	– age of head of household (one-person households)
	NADULTS	– number of adults in household
	NPPHHOLD	– number of people in household
	NFAMHH	– number of family units in household

The levels of the GHS and the variables within each, which are used to derive these variables, are shown below. The SIR retrieval used is given in Figure 11.4.

Household	
NPPHHOLD	Number of people in household
NFAMHH	Number of family units in household
Family	
FAMUNIT	Family unit number
Individual	
AGE	Age of individual
SEX	Sex of individual
MARITAL	Marital status of individual
Adult	
AGELFTS	Age of leaving school (coded 99 if still at school)
EDUCNOW	Whether in full-time education (yes = 1)

Stage 2 :

All the contextual variables above, derived at the level of the household, are passed to an SPSS system file.

Stage 3:

$SPSS^X$ is then used to compute the variables representing the presence or absence of the six main elements and to combine then into a temporary variable TEMPHH which unambiguously defines each possible combination (Figure 11.5(i)).

Stage 4

The final step constructs the 14-category household typology (HOUSETYP) using the temporary variable from stage 3 and three other household level variables – NPPHHOLD, HOHAGE and NADULTS (Figure 11.5(iii)).

Figure 11.4 *Derivation of household structure variables using SIR*

SIR Retrieval to derive variables used in household structure typology

```
RETRIEVAL
COMMENT This retrieval uses data for the GHS 1979 to construct the
   elements needed for a typology of household structure. Data is written to
   an SPSS system file at the level of the household.
PROCESS CASES
SET DEPCH, WIFAGE, HUSAGE, HOHAGE, DEPCHLD1,
  YOUNGCUP, MIDCUP, ELDCUP, SINGLEM, SINGLEF, ELDFEM,
  ELDMAN (0)
PROCESS REC HHOLD
MOVE VARS NPPHHOLD, NFAMHH
PROCESS REC FAMILY
MOVE VARS FAMUNIT
 · PROCESS REC INDIV WITH (FAMUNIT)
 · MOVE VARS PERNO, AGE, MARITAL, SEX
 · IF (HOHRELN EQ 1) HOHAGE=AGE
 · IF (AGE LT 16)DEPCHLD1 = DEPCHLD1+1
 · IF (MARITAL EQ 1 AND SEX EQ 1)HUSAGE=AGE
 · IF (MARITAL EQ 1 AND SEX EQ 2)WIFAGE=AGE
 · IF (MARITAL EQ 1 AND HUSAGE GT 65)ELDCUP=ELDCUP+1
 · IF (MARITAL NE 1 AND AGE GT 60 AND SEX EQ 2)ELDFEM=
   ELDFEM+1
 · IF (MARITAL NE 1 AND AGE GT 65 AND SEX EQ 1)
   ELDMAN=ELDMAN+1
 · IF (MARITAL EQ 1 AND WIFAGE GE 35 AND HUSAGE LE 65)
   MIDCUP=MIDCUP+1
 · IF (MARITAL EQ 1 AND WIFAGE GT 15 AND WIFAGE LT 35 AND
   HUSAGE LT 65) YOUNGCUP=YOUNGCUP+1
 ·  PROCESS REC ADULT WITH (FAMUNIT,PERNO)
 ·  MOVE VARS AGELFTS, EDUCNOW
 ·  IF (AGE GE 16 AND AGE LE 18 AND (AGELFTS EQ 99 OR
    EDUCNOW EQ 1)DEPCH=DEPCH+1
 ·  IF (AGE GT 18 OR (AGE GE 16 AND AGE LE 18 AND AGELFTS NE 99
    AND EDUCNOW NE 1)AND SEX EQ 2 AND MARITAL NE 1 AND AGE
    LE 60)SINGLEF=SINGLEF+1
 ·  IF (AGE GT 18 OR (AGE GE 16 AND AGE LE 18 AND AGELFTS NE 99
    AND EDUCNOW NE 1) AND SEX EQ 1 AND MARITAL NE 1 AND
    AGE LE 60)SINGLEM=SINGLEM+1
 ·  END PROCESS REC
 · COMPUTE NDEPCHHH=DEPCH+DEPCHLD1
 · END PROCESS REC
END PROCESS REC
END PROCESS REC
COMPUTE NADULTS=NPPHHOLD-NDEPCHHH
INCLUDE ELDFEM, ELDMAN, NDEPCHHH, SINGLEM, SINGLEF,
  YOUNGCUP, MIDCUP, ELDCUP, HOHAGE, NADULTS, NPPHHOLD,
  NFAMHH
PERFORM PROCS
END PROCESS CASES
SPSS SAVE FILE FILENAME=HOUSETYP.SF
```

Note that only those variables named by the INCLUDE command will be passed to the system file.

households is used. However, this method of derivation enables the analyst to identify very complex households: for example, a household that contains an elderly 'single' person, a middle-aged couple with dependent children and a 'single' adult. This would take the value on TEMPHH of (1 + 32 + 2 + 4 = 39).

The fourth and final step in the procedure uses the variables NPPHHOLD, HOHAGE and NADULTS together with this temporary variable TEMPHH to construct the final 14-category variable. The derivation of the first few categories is shown in Figure 11.5(iii). Thus category 1 on HOUSETYP comprises a one-person household (NPPHHOLD EQ 1) where that household member is an adult under the age of 35. The second category, HOUSETYP=2, contains households with more than one member (NPPHHOLD GT 1) but all of whom have been categorized as 'single adults' (TEMPHH EQ 4). The third category comprises households containing only 'young' couples, where the wife is under 35.

However, classifying households is not always as straightforward as the examples shown in Figure 11.5(iii) suggest. In order to restrict the typology to a manageable number of categories, it is necessary to combine several different household groupings (with different values on TEMPHH) into the same category of HOUSETYP. This requires the analyst to have thought very carefully about the basis on which households should be grouped. It is always necessary to strike a balance between deriving a typology that is small enough to be usable and one that accurately represents every possible household situation. Decisions are continually needed, and it is important to be clear about the framework that underlies the research in order to make them in an informed way. For example, should we make separate categories for households containing elderly people living alone, elderly married couples, and two or more elderly non-married people? In this research, married couples were combined with households containing two or more non-married elderly people on the basis that, as the research focus was the relationship between total household income and household assets, the most important effect on level of assets and income was likely to be the number of people within the household. However, in other research which focused exclusively upon the elderly (Dale *et al.*, 1987; Gilbert *et al.*, 1986), the distinction between these three groups was made explicit and found to be important. Other classificatory decisions need to be made; for example, where a household contains a single adult with a dependent child and also a single elderly person – should this be classified as category 6, or category 9 on HOUSETYP (Figure 11.2)? In this case, a decision was made to allocate the household to category 6

Figure 11.5 *Derivation of HOUSETYP and temporary variable TEMPHH, using $SPSS^X$*

(i)

	LABELS
COMPUTE SINGLELD=0	Single elderly
COMPUTE DEPCHILD=0	Dependent child
COMPUTE SINGLEAD=0	Single adult
COMPUTE ECOUPLE=0	Elderly couple
COMPUTE YCOUPLE=0	Young couple
COMPUTE MCOUPLE=0	Middle-aged couple

```
IF (ELDFEM OR ELDMAN GT 0) SINGLELD=1
IF (NDEPCHHH GT 0)DEPCHILD=2
IF (SINGLEM GT 0 OR SINGLEF GT 0)
  SINGLEAD=4
IF (ELDCUP GT 0)ELDCUP=8
IF (YOUNGCUP GT 0)YCOUPLE=16
IF (MIDCUP GT 0)MCOUPLE=32

COMPUTE TEMPHH = SINGLED + DEPCHILD + SINGLEAD +
  ECOUPLE + YCOUPLE + MCOUPLE
```

(ii) Frequencies of TEMPHH for 100 households

CATEGORY LABEL	CODE	ABSOLUTE FREQ
SINGLE ELDERLY	1.	29
SINGLE ADULT	4.	10
SINGLE ADT+SINGLE ELD	5.	6
SINGLE ADT+DEP.CHILD	6.	6
ELDERLY COUPLE	8.	11
YOUNG COUPLE	16.	2
YOUNG CPLE+DEP.CHLD	18.	12
MID-COUPLE	32.	11
MID-COUPLE+DEP.CHLD	34.	8
MID-CPLE+SINGLE ADT	36.	2
MID-CPLE+DEP.CH+ADT	38.	2
MID-CPLE+YOUNG CPLE	48.	1
	TOTAL	100

(iii)

```
COMPUTE HOUSETYP=0
IF (NPPHHOLD EQ 1 AND HOHAGE GT 15 AND HOHAGE LT 35)
  HOUSETYP=1
IF (NPPHHOLD GT 1 AND TEMPHH EQ 4) HOUSETYP=2
IF (TEMPHH EQ 16) HOUSETYP=3
IF (TEMPHH EQ 18 OR TEMPHH EQ 34) HOUSETYP=4
IF (TEMPHH EQ 6 AND NADULTS EQ 1) HOUSETYP=5
IF (TEMPHH EQ 6 AND NADULTS GT 1) HOUSETYP=6
IF (TEMPHH EQ 19 OR TEMPHH EQ 35) HOUSETYP=7
etc.
```

'one parent with other adult', although had the research been focusing explicitly on the elderly, this decision might have been different. It is not feasible to establish separate categories for groups that comprise a very small proportion of all households, as the resulting typology would extend to at least 50 categories! For this reason, it is essential to be clear about the underlying aim of the research, as there are no 'right' answers.

Although the only family relationship used in *defining* the typology is marital status, it is none the less useful to establish the family relationship of members of each category in the typology. This then enables us, for example, to describe members of category 5 on HOUSETYP (Figure 11.2) as a 'one-parent household' rather than 'single adult + dependent child'. This can most simply be done by checking the number of family units per household (NFAMHH) for households in category 5. With very few exceptions, there will be only a single family unit. Knowing the way in which the GHS defines a family unit enables us to describe this category as 'one-parent households'. However, if in later analyses it becomes important to distinguish any households where a child is living with an aunt, foster-parent or guardian (and is therefore allocated to a separate family unit), then we are able to do this. Similarly, category 10 in Figure 11.2 may be labelled as 'couple with non-dependent children' once it has been established that, in the overwhelming majority of cases, the single adult shares a family unit with the married couple. It is, however, important to note that in a small proportion of these households the single adult will not be related to the married couple.

Relative Net Resources (RNR)

Relative Net Resources is a contextual summary variable measured at the level of the household. It is calculated by using the formula:

$$\frac{\text{total net weekly income of household} \times 100}{\text{long-term supplementary benefit entitlement of household}}$$

It is composed, therefore, of two separate household-level variables; total net weekly income, which includes all sources of income from all members of the household, and long-term supplementary benefit entitlement, which uses information on household composition in conjunction with the published DHSS scale rates for 1978–9. Each of these two variables involve aggregation of information from the individual to the household level. Each variable will be considered in turn.

1 To calculate supplementary benefit entitlement, the following categories are derived, within each household:

number of married couples
number of single adults of householder status
number of non-dependent adults in the household
number and age of dependent children

The household structure derivation described earlier forms the basis for this, with some extra distinctions incorporated. The appropriate amount from the published DHSS long-term scale rates is then allocated to each category. Additionally, for each person aged 80 and over, add the appropriate extra amount (50 pence in 1979). The total sum of all these inputs will give the supplementary benefit entitlement of each household, using long-term rates, but excluding any 'additional requirements'.

2 To calculate net weekly household income, it is firstly necessary to establish all sources of income. In the GHS in 1979 the available sources are:

Net income from employment
Self-employment
A second job or casual work
Child benefit
Child benefit increase
Family Income Supplement (FIS)
National Insurance Retirement pension, Old Age pension or Widow's pension
National Insurance sickness benefit or Industrial Injury benefit
Supplementary pension, benefit or allowance
Unemployment benefit
Other National Insurance or state benefits payable for a short-term
Other National Insurance or state benefits payable for a long-term
occupational pension
Rent from property
Interest from Building Society
Bank Account
Savings or investments
All other forms of regular income – including maintenance payments, private pensions, educational grants, government training allowances
Rent rebate

Rate rebate

Taxation paid direct to the Inland Revenue – a negative form of income

All forms of income (and also taxation paid) refer to the individual, with the exception of rate and rent rebate, which are given for the household.

All forms of income must be changed to refer to the same time unit – in this case a week – and then summed across all members of the household. Rent and rate rebates can then be added to the household level income variable. This variable is a more complex form of that shown in Figure 10.6 (p.190), which sums just one form of income for all household members.

At this stage further shortcomings in the data, not obvious at an earlier stage, become apparent. For example, although most sources of income are net of tax, income from self-employment and income from property are given before deductions for taxation. The only information on the amount of tax paid on these forms of income comes from the amount of tax paid directly to the Inland Revenue. While this must be deducted from income, clearly there is scope for inaccuracy, particularly as tax paid in one year often reflects earnings from several years earlier.

MISSING VALUES

Only those households in which all adult members reported all items of income were included in the derivation of RNR. This meant that 13.5 per cent of all households with completed interview schedules were omitted from analyses involving RNR. The decision to deal with missing values in this way was taken when it became apparent that the inclusion of households with missing values on some income items reduced the median levels of RNR quite considerably and, therefore, were likely to give misleading results. However, it was important to establish whether those with missing values were disproportionately drawn from one particular category of household. Therefore, a comparison was made between those households containing any missing income information and all households. From this it was evident that, in terms of their distribution on the household typology variable, those with missing income information were not seriously over-represented in any one category of household. Generally, single person households were somewhat less likely to record missing values than multi-person households, presumably reflecting the fact that the chances of encountering missing information increase with the number of people in the household.

Checking derived variables

Having derived the variables of interest the next stage is to carry out extensive testing and checking to ensure that no mistakes have been made. In this project the following checks were made.

1 HOUSEHOLD STRUCTURE

The WRITE facility in SIR forms a vital stage in checking this variable as it allows us to list, for each individual, those variables used to define the elements of the household typology (AGE, SEX, etc.), and the values of the elements themselves (ELDFEM, ELDMAN, etc.). Further checks were then made with published statistics to compare the frequencies of major groups such as the 'single' elderly. Finally, a series of cross-tabulations was run at the level of the individual, in which household structure was cross- tabulated against marital status, number of children in the household and similar variables.

2 RELATIVE NET RESOURCES

Again, the WRITE facility in SIR allows the component variables to be checked against the final derived variable at all stages of the procedure. This was particularly important for a few households located at either extreme of the distribution of RNR.

Additionally, the distribution of RNR levels was compared with other available material; this included figures obtained from DHSS calculations on Low Income Families (DHSS, 1983) and based upon the Family Expenditure Survey, and also figures published by Layard *et al.* (1978) as part of the Royal Commission on the Distribution of Income and Wealth. Finally, a number of cross-tabulations were run, using RNR recoded into conventional categories (e.g. supp. ben. level and below; up to 120 per cent of supp. ben. level) and variables such as housing tenure and household structure to make sure that the results made *sense.*

It is, perhaps, worth stressing that the length of time spent making checks is likely to equal the length of time needed to carry out the original derivation of complex variables.

Documentation of derived variables

Several different methods of documentation were used. First, a log of work on the project was kept, and each stage of variable derivation and analysis was written up fully as it was completed. Secondly, all variables in the original dataset were already fully labelled, and newly derived variables were similarly labelled. Thirdly, as each extra section of computer code was added, documentation was inserted into the file recording what that code was attempting to do. Finally, a 'hard' copy of the file containing the variable derivation was printed and the file was also archived on the mainframe computer.

The initial reading and thinking that preceded work with the data was also written up fully and referenced. This early stage in the research process is vital, as it ensures that a suitable theoretical framework is developed within which to carry out subsequent analyses. Also, at the final stage of producing a report or paper, it is a great relief to find that the introductory section has already been written.

Analysis

To give an indication of the kinds of results obtained by the project, the first stage of analysis in which methods of exploratory data analysis were used to examine the structure of the data are reported here. Figure 11.6 shows the distribution of RNR by household structure. It uses box and whisker plots (Velleman and Hoaglin, 1981; Tukey, 1977; Erickson and Nosanchuk, 1979) to show, for each category of household, the median value of RNR and also the range of levels of RNR; 10 and 90 per cent cut-off points have been used in order that the distribution is not unduly influenced by odd and perhaps misleading values at each end of the range. It is immediately apparent that both the median levels of RNR and its range vary greatly with different categories of household.

Figure 11.7 shows the relationship between RNR and household assets for each category of household. In this figure a coded table is used to indicate the distribution of each sort of asset among household categories (Velleman and Hoaglin, 1981, p.201). The right-hand column makes a similar comparison in terms of RNR. Although this form of presentation lacks the accuracy of a table in which exact percentages are recorded, it has the advantage of giving an immediate picture of the similarities and differences both among and between household types. For example, it is apparent that there is a tendency for households of a particular category to have similar levels of each sort of asset, although there are also some interesting differences. Thus, elderly couples have a lower level of most assets than households generally, with the exception of home ownership on which they fall into the median range. The figure shows little direct relationship between levels of assets and level of RNR; rather, stage of lifecycle and, in particular,the number of people living in a household seem to be of particular importance in determining the distribution of assets. For example, although households comprising one person under 35 (category 1) have median levels of RNR that are similar to couples with children (category 4) (both are just above the median level for all households), it is clear that there are very marked differences between the level of household assets of these two categories. The next stage in the analysis, not reported here, relates the level of RNR and assets *within* particular household categories.

Concluding comments

By moving through the stages of this project we have brought together the numerous separate elements that, together, make up secondary analysis and have tried to indicate the way in which they interrelate. The examplar presented in this chapter may also suggest ways in which the secondary analysis of an existing large-scale dataset may be used to address important research topics, which would otherwise be beyond the resources of most social researchers. The availability of high-quality datasets, such as the General Household Survey and Family Expenditure Survey, enables academic researchers to carry out fundamentally important research on relatively low budgets. Where datasets have already been processed to make them readily accessible to the analyst (as with the Surrey version of the GHS used here) the amount of preparatory work needed is considerably reduced. In terms of cost-effectiveness, it is difficult to envisage any other methodology that has greater potential. However it is clear that a price is paid for using data that is not collected to your own specification – for example, you are unable to specify the topics included in the survey or to control the categorization of responses. It would also be foolish to suggest that secondary analysis is the only research methodology of value – it needs to be used as one important method among many others.

One important contribution of secondary analysis to social research may be as a means of establishing broad parameters and providing a full description of a social phenomenon that had hitherto been only partially acknowledged. For example, the re-analysis of the National Training Survey by Elias and Main (1982) provided the first detailed analysis of women's work-histories, using longitudinal data at a national level. Although the use of a secondary source meant that there were some areas that could not be addressed as adequately as may have been desired (for example, the survey recorded only whether there was a child in the household, and not the relationships within the household) none the less, the research gave an important overview of women's working lives, which was then enlarged upon and clarified further with the

Figure 11.6 *Box plots to show the range and level of RNR for different household categories (Data source: GHS, 1979)*

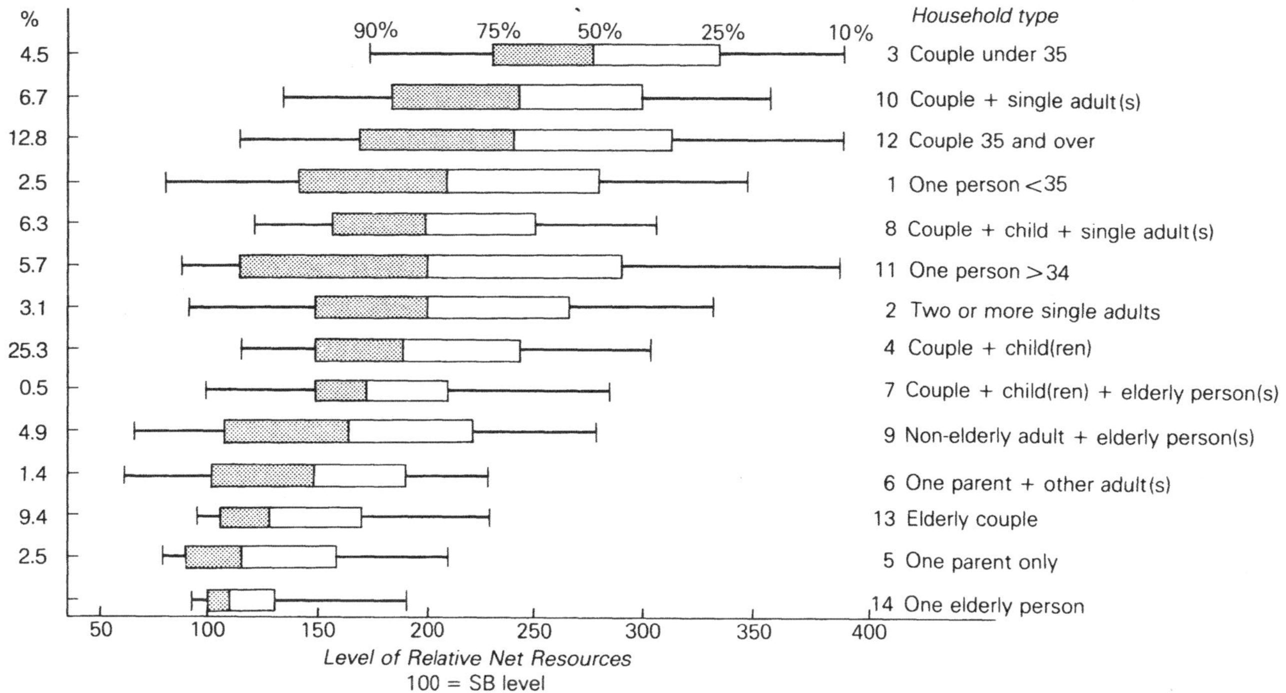

Note: the category number associated with each household type relates to the numbers used in Figure 11.2.

Figure 11.7 *Household type by possession of household assets*

Household type	*Household has* Washing machine	Colour TV	Car	Central heating	Own house	Freezer	RNR
14 One elderly person	---	---	----	-	--	----	---
11 One person >34	---	--	--	-	--	---	+
1 One person <35	----	---	-	-	--	----	+
5 One-parent household	*	-	---	*	---	--	--
2 Two or more non-married adults	--	-	*	-	--	--	+
13 Elderly couple	-	-	--	-	*	--	--
6 One parent + other adult(s)	+	*	--	--	---	--	-
9 Non-elderly adult + elderly person(s)	*	*	*	-	-	-	*
12 Couple 35 and over	+	+	++	*	*	++	++
3 Couple under 35	+	*	++	+	++	+	+++
10 Couple + single adult(s)	++	++	++	*	*	+++	++
8 Couple + child + single adult(s)	++	++	++	+++	*	+++	+
4 Couple + child(ren)	++	++	+++	++	++	+++	+
7 Couple + child(ren) + elderly person(s)	++	++	++++	++	+++	++++	++

In each category of household, the percentage possessing each item is coded by comparison with the distribution for all households:

Key:

----	type of household falls into the range of the lowest 11 per cent of all households.

--	
-	
*	type of household falls into median range, between 44.5 and 55.5 per cent of all households.
+	
++	
+++	
++++	type of household falls in the highest 11 per cent of all households.

analysis of the Women and Employment Survey (Martin and Roberts, 1984a).

Secondary analysis may also provide the detailed national-level evidence for a firmly established topic such as poverty and income inequality. Through the General Household Survey and the Family Expenditure Survey, a great deal of very detailed information is available on both income and expenditure. Until recently this has been used principally by economists (Fieghan, Lansley and Smith, 1977; Atkinson, Micklewright and Sutherland, 1983; Layard *et al.*, 1978). However, the potential of this household-based data for other branches of social research is now becoming realized and provides an exciting prospect for the future. By establishing linkages within families and households it is possible to explore relationships between household members in terms of health, employment, income and education, as well as doing more conventional research in which the individual is analysed using only a limited number of family or household variables to provide a context for the analysis.

The increasing number of applications being made to the ESRC Data Archive suggests that social scientists in the UK are beginning to realize the potential of secondary data sources. In this book, we have tried to show that these sources can be used to produce research that is not only soundly based and theoretically informed but which can also address issues of importance to policy-makers and academics alike. At the same time we have begun the somewhat neglected task of establishing some guidelines and tools for those who use secondary analysis as a research method.

Notes

1 The derivation of variables discussed here uses the database management system, SIR. The original research was carried out using the rectangular GHS files and the Crosslinker program (Gilbert, 1982). For this reason the derivation of the household structure variable (HOUSETYP) differs slightly from the original research.

2 Saunders (1986) provides an extensive discussion of the relationship between the spheres of production and consumption.

References

Airey, C. and Potts, A. (1981), *Workplace Industrial Relations Survey: An Initial Report* (London: Social and Community Planning Research).

Alexander, K. and Eckland, B. R. (1975), 'Contextual effects on High School attainment process', *American Sociological Review*, vol. 40, pp. 402–16.

Arber, S. L. (1988), 'Gender and class inequalities in health:understanding the differentials', in A. J. Fox (ed), *Inequalities in Health in European Countries* (Aldershot: Gower).

Arber, S., Dale, A., Gilbert, G. N. and O'Byrne, J. (1984), 'Surrey GHS files', *ESRC Data Archive Bulletin*, vol. 27, pp. 7–8.

Arber, S., Gilbert, N. G., Dale, A. and Rajan, L. (1984), *Exploring British Society: Social Science Teaching using the General Household Survey* (Guildford: Department of Sociology, University of Surrey).

Arber, S., Gilbert, G. N. and Evandrou, M. (1988), 'Gender, household composition and receipt of domiciliary services by the elderly disabled', *Journal of Social Policy*, (forthcoming).

Armstrong, D. (1986), 'The invention of infant mortality', *Sociology of Health and Illness*, vol. 8, pp. 211–32.

Atkins, E., Cherry, N. M., Douglas, J. W. B., Kiernan, K. E. and Wadsworth, M.E. (1981), 'The 1946 British Birth Cohort Survey: An Account of the Origins, Progress and Results of the National Survey of Health and Development', in S. A. Mednick and A. E. Baert (eds), *Prospective Longitudinal Research in Europe* (Oxford: Oxford University Press).

Atkinson, J. (1984), *Flexibility, Uncertainty, Manpower Management*, Institute of Manpower Studies, Report No. 89 (Brighton: Institute of Manpower Studies).

Atkinson, M. (1978), 'Coroners and the categorisation of deaths as suicides: changes in perspectives as features of the research process', in C. Bell and H. Newby, (eds), *Doing Sociological Research* (London: Allen and Unwin), pp. 31–46.

Atkinson, M. and Heritage, J. (1984), *Structures of Social Action* (Cambridge: Cambridge University Press).

Atkinson, A. J., Micklewright, J. and Sutherland, H. (1983), *Who are the Low Paid? A Preliminary Look at the Evidence from the FES*, Low Pay Unit Discussion Paper No. 3 (London: Low Pay Unit).

Barker, R. and Roberts, H. (1987) *Social Classification Scheme for Women* LS Working Paper No. 51, Social Statistics Research Unit (London : City University).

Barton, A. (1970), 'Comments on Hauser's "Context and consex"', *American Journal of Sociology*, vol. 76, pp. 514–20.

Bebbington, A. C. and Davies, B. P. (1983), 'Equity and efficiency in the allocation of the personal social services', *Journal of Social Policy*, vol. 12, pp. 309–30.

Blau, P. (1960), 'Structural effect', *American Sociological Review*, vol.25, pp. 178–93.

Blaxter, M. (1986), 'Longitudinal studies in Britain relevant to inequalities in health', in R. G. Wilkinson (ed.), *Class and Health: Research and Longitudinal Data* (London: Tavistock), pp. 125–215.

Blumer, H. (1956), 'Sociological analysis and the variable', *American Sociological Review*, vol. 21, no. 6, pp. 683–90.

Bone, M. (1981), 'What makes a survey complex?' *Survey Methodology Bulletin*, no. 12, pp. 2–11.

Booth, C. (ed.) (1889), *Labour and Life of the People of London*, 17 vols, (London: Macmillan).

Bott, E. (1971), *Family and Social Networks* (New York: Free Press).

Bowley, A. L. (1915), *The Nature and Purpose of the Measurement of Social Phenomena*, 2nd edn (London: P. S. King and Son).

Boyd, L. H. and Iversen, G. R. (1979) *Contextual Analysis: Concepts and Statistical Techniques* (Belmont, Calif.: Wadsworth).

Bradshaw, J. (1984), 'Families sharing poverty: an analysis of the living standards of single and multi-unit households', ESRC Social Security Workshop, March 1984.

Bradshaw, J., Cooke, K. and Godfrey, C. (1983), 'The impact of unemployment on the living standards of families', *Journal of Social Policy*, vol. 12, pp. 433–52.

Braverman, H. (1974), *Labor and Monopoly Capitalism* (New York: Monthly Review Press).

British Association Study Group (1979), 'Does research threaten privacy or does privacy threaten research?', in M. Bulmer (ed.), *Censuses, Surveys and Privacy* (London: Macmillan), pp. 37–54.

Britten, N. and Heath, A. (1983), 'Women, men and social class', in E. Garmarnikov *et al.* (eds), *Gender, Class and Work* (London: Heinemann), pp. 46–60.

Britton, M. and Birch, F. (1985), *1981 Census Post-Enumeration Survey* (London: HMSO).

Brown, A. and Fox, J. (1984), 'OPCS longitudinal study: ten years on', *Population Trends*, no. 37, pp. 20–2.

Brown, A. and Kiernan, K. (1981), 'Co-habitation in Great Britain: evidence from the GHS', *Population Trends*, vol. 25, Autumn, pp. 4–10.

Brown, C. (1984), *Black and White Britain: The Third PSI Survey* (London: Heinemann Educational).

Brown, G. W. (1987), 'Statistical interaction and the role of social factors in the aetiology of clinical depression', *Sociology*, vol. 20, pp. 601–6.

Brown, G. W. and Harris, T. O. (1978), *Social Origins of Depression: A Study of Psychiatric Disorder in Women* (London: Tavistock).

Bryman, A. (1984), 'The debate about quantitative and qualitative research', *British Journal of Sociology*, vol. 35, pp. 75–92.

Bulmer, M. (1979), *Censuses, Surveys and Privacy* (London: Macmillan).

Bulmer, M. (1982), *Social Research Ethics* (London: Macmillan).

Bulmer, M. (1986), *Social Science and Social Policy* (London: Allen and Unwin).

Burgess, R. (ed.) (1986), *Key Variables in Social Investigation* (London: Routledge and Kegan Paul).

Burrows, R. (1987), 'Some notes towards a realistic realism: the practical implications of realist philosophies of science for sociological research methods', paper presented to the British Sociological Association Conference, 6–9 April, 1987, University of Leeds.

Butcher, B. (1986), 'Use of the Postcode Address File as a sampling frame', mimeo, OPCS.

Butcher, B. and Dodd, P. (1983), 'The electoral register – two surveys', in *Population Trends*, vol. 31, pp. 15–19.

Butler, N. R., Golding, J. and Howlett, B. C. (eds) (1985), *From Birth to Five: A Study of the Health and Behaviour of a National Cohort* (Oxford: Pergamon).

Butler, N. R., Haslum, M. N., Barker, W. and Morris, A. C. (1982), *Child Health and Education Study*, First Report to the Department of Education and Science on the Ten-year Follow-up (Bristol: Department of Child Health, University of Bristol).

Casey, B. (1988), *Temporary Employment Relationships in Britain*, Policy Studies Institute Report No. 669, (London : PSI).

Casterline, J. B. (ed.) (1985), *The Collection and Analysis of Community Data* (Voorburg, Netherlands: International Statistical Institute).

Cavendish, R. (1982), *Women on the Line* (London: Routledge and Kegan Paul).

Center for Human Resource Research (1981), *The National Longitudinal Surveys Handbook* (Columbus, Ohio: Center for Human Resource Research, The Ohio State University).

Cicourel, A. V. (1964) *Method and Measurement in Sociology* (New York:Free Press).

Coleman, J.S. (1961) *The Adolescent Society* (Glencoe, Ill.: Free Press).

Coxon, A. P. M. (1977), 'Recent developments in social science software', *SSRC Newsletter*, no. 33, pp. 6–9.

Coxon, A. P. M. (1982), *The User's Guide to Multidimensional Scaling* (London: Heinemann).

CPAG (1984), *Whose Poverty?*, Newsletter of the Child Poverty Action Group (London: CPAG).

Craig, C., Garnsey, E. and Rubery, J. (1985), *Payment Structures and Smaller Firms: Women's Employment in Segmented Labour Markets*, Department of Employment Research Paper No. 48 (London:DE).

Craig, C., Rubery, J., Tarling, R. and Wilkinson, F. (1982), *Labour Market Structure, Industrial Organisation and Low Pay* (Cambridge: Cambridge University Press).

Cutler, S. J. (1978), 'Instructional uses of the General Social Survey', *Contemporary Sociology*, vol. 7, pp. 541–5.

Dale, A. (1985), 'Family poverty in Great Britain', End-of-grant report to ESRC (London: British Document Supply Centre).

Dale, A. (1986a), 'Social class and the self-employed', *Sociology*, vol. 20, pp. 430–4.

Dale, A. (1986b), 'Labour market participation and household dynamics', mimeo (Guildford: University of Surrey).

Dale, A. (1986c), *A Teaching Package for the Database Management System SIR* (Guildford: University of Surrey).

Dale, A. (1986d), 'A note on differences in car usage by married men and married women', *Sociology*, vol. 20, pp. 91–2.

Dale, A. (1987a), 'The effect of lifecycle on three dimensions of stratification', in A. Bryman, W. Bytheway, P. Allatt and T. Keil (eds) *Rethinking the Life Cycle* (London: Macmillan), pp.170–97.

Dale, A. (1987b), 'The structure of the UK labour market: evidence from occupational mobility', *Work and Occupations*, Vol. 14, No. 4, pp. 558–80.

Dale, A. and Bamford, C. (1987), 'The peripheral work-force: evidence from the Labour Force Survey', mimeo (Guildford: Department of Sociology, University of Surrey).

Dale, A., Bamford, C., Arber, S. and Gilbert, G. N. (1987), 'A time-series dataset from the General Household Survey 1973–1982', *General Household Survey Newsletter* (University of Essex: ESRC Data Archive), pp. 15–16.

Dale, A., Evandrou, M. and Arber, S. (1987), 'The household structure of the elderly in Britain', *Ageing and Society*, vol. 7, pp. 37–56.

Dale, A., Gilbert, G. N. and Arber, S. (1983), *Alternative Approaches to the Measurement of Social Class for Women and Families*, Report to the Equal Opportunities Commission (University of Surrey).

Dale, A., Gilbert, G. N. and Arber, S. (1985), 'Integrating women into class theory', *Sociology*, vol. 19, no. 3, pp. 384–409.

Daniel, W. W. and Millward, N. (1983), *Workplace Industrial Relations in Britain. The DE/PSI/ SSRC Survey* (London: Heinemann).

Davie, R. (1966), *Summary of the National Child Development Study* (London: National Bureau for Co-operation in Child Care).

Davis, J. (1961), *Great Books and Small Groups*, (Glencoe, Ill.: Free Press).

Denzin, N. K. (1978), *The Research Act in Sociology* (London: Butterworth).

Department of Employment (1983), *New Earnings Survey 1983, Part C, Analyses by Industry* (London: HMSO).

De Vaus, A. (1986), *Surveys in Social Research* (London: Allen and Unwin).

Dex, S. (1984), *Women's Work Histories: An Analysis of the Women and Employment Survey*, Department of Employment Research Paper No. 46 (London: DE).

Dex, S. (1986), 'The secondary analysis of data on women's employment', *Equal Opportunities Commission Research Bulletin*, no. 10, (Manchester: EOC), pp. 20–7.

Dex, S. (1987), *Women's Occupational Mobility* (Basingstoke: Macmillan).

Dex, S. and Shaw, L. (1986), *British and American Women at Work* (London: Macmillan).

DHSS (1983), *Low Income Families – 1981*, mimeo (London: DHSS).

Douglas, J. W. B. (1964), *The Home and the School* (London: MacGibbon and Kee).

Dunnell, K. (1979), *Family Formation Survey 1976*, Office of Population Censuses and Surveys (London: HMSO).

Durkheim, E. (1952), *Suicide: A Study in Sociology* (London: Routledge and Kegan Paul).

Edgell, S. (1980), *Middle Class Couples* (London: Allen and Unwin).

Elias, P. and Main, B. (1982), *Women's Working Lives: Evidence from the National Training Survey* (Coventry: Institute for Employment Research, University of Warwick).

Elliot, D. (1982), 'A study in occupation and social class coding – summary of results', *OPCS Survey Methodology Bulletin*, no. 14, pp. 48–9.

Elliot, D. and Thomas, R. (1983), 'Further thoughts on weighting survey results to compensate for non-response', *OPCS Survey Methodology Bulletin*, no. 15, pp. 2–11.

Entwisle, B. and Mason, W. M. (1985), 'Multilevel effects of socioeconomic development and family planning programs on children ever born', *American Journal of Sociology*, vol. 91, no. 3, pp. 616–49.

Equal Opportunities Commission (1986), 'Methodological issues in gender research', *Equal Opportunities Commission Research Bulletin*, no. 10 (Manchester: EOC).

Erickson, B. H. and Nosanchuk, T. A. (1979), *Understanding Data* (Milton Keynes: The Open University Press).

Erickson, R. (1984), 'Social class of men, women and families', *Sociology*, vol. 18, no. 4, pp. 500–14.

Erickson, R., Goldthorpe, J. and Portocarero, L. (1982), 'Social fluidity in industrial nations', *British Journal of Sociology*, vol. 33, pp. 1–34.

Erickson, R., Goldthorpe, J. and Portocarero, L. (1983), 'Intergenerational class mobility and the convergence thesis', *British Journal of Sociology*, vol. 34, pp. 303–43.

ESRC Data Archive (1984), *Notes for Enquirers and Users* (Colchester: ESRC Data Archive).

Evandrou, M., Arber, S., Dale, A. and Gilbert, G. N. (1986), 'Who cares for the elderly? Family care provision and receipt of statutory services', in C. Phillipson, M. Bernard and P. Strang (eds), *Dependency and Interdependency in Old Age – Theoretical Perspectives and Policy Alternatives* (London: Croom Helm), pp. 150–66.

Evers, M. and McGee, J. (1980), 'The trend and pattern in attitudes towards abortion: 1965–1976', *Social Indicators Research*, vol. 7, pp. 251–67.

Family Policy Studies Centre (1983), *An Ageing Population: Fact Sheet* (London: FPSC).

Family Policy Studies Centre (1986), *Family Trends and Social Security Reform* (London: FPSC).

Farkas, G. (1974), 'Specification, residuals and contextual effects', *Sociological Methods and Research*, vol. 2, no. 3, pp. 333–63.

Fiegehan, G. C., Lansley, P. S. and Smith, A. D. (1977), *Poverty and Progress in Britain 1953–73*, National Institute of Economic and Social Research (Cambridge: Cambridge University Press).

Fielding, N. G. and Fielding, J. L. (1986), *Linking Data* (Beverly Hills, Calif.: Sage).

Finch, J. (1984), '"It's great to have someone to talk to": the ethics of interviewing women', in C. Bell and H. Roberts (eds), *Social Researching: Politics, Problems and Practice* (London: Routledge and Kegan Paul), pp. 70–87.

Finch, J. (1987), 'Family obligations and the life course', in A. Bryman, W. Bytheway, P. Allatt and T. Keil (eds), *Rethinking the Life Cycle* (London: Macmillan) pp. 155–68.

Fogelman, K. (1984), 'Exploiting longitudinal data: examples from the NCDS', in A. R. Nicol (ed.), *Longitudinal Studies in Child Psychology and Psychiatry* (Chichester: Wiley).

Fowler, H. W. (1965), *A Dictionary of Modern English Usage*, 2nd edn (Oxford: Clarendon Press).

Fox, J. and Goldblatt, P. (1982), *Longitudinal Study 1971–75*, Longitudinal Series, No. 1, OPCS (London: HMSO).

Galtung, J. (1967), *Theory and Methods of Social Research* (London: Allen and Unwin).

Gershuny, J., Miles, I., Jones, S., Mulings, C., Thomas, G. and Wyatt, S. (1986), 'Time budgets: preliminary analyses of a national survey', *Quarterly Journal of Social Affairs*, vol. 2, no. 1, pp. 13–39.

Gilbert, G. N. (1981), *Modelling Society* (London: Allen and Unwin).

Gilbert, G. N. (1982), *The XLKer: A User's Manual*, mimeo (Guildford: University of Surrey).

Gilbert, G. N., Dale, A. and Arber, S. (1982), 'The Crosslinker: a computer program for the analysis of hierarchical datasets from non-hierarchical analysis packages', *SSRC Data Archive Bulletin*, no. 22, pp. 7–10.

Gilbert, G. N., Dale, A. and Arber, S. (1983), 'The General Household Survey as a source for secondary analysis', *Sociology*, vol. 17, no. 2, pp. 255–9.

Gilbert, G. N., Dale, A., Arber, S., Evandrou, M. and Laczko, F. (1986), 'Resources in old age: ageing and the life course', ESRC Workshop on Ageing, University of Surrey, September 1986.

Glass, D. V. (1954), *Social Mobility in Britain* (London: Routledge and Kegan Paul).

Glenn, N. (1978), 'The General Social Surveys: editorial introduction to a symposium', *Contemporary Sociology*, vol. 7, pp. 532–4.

Goldthorpe, J. H. (1980), *Social Mobility and Class Structure in Modern Britain* (Oxford: Clarendon Press).

Goldthorpe, J. H. (1983), 'Women and class analysis: in defence of the conventional view', *Sociology*, vol. 17, no. 4, pp. 465–88.

Goldthorpe, J. H. (1984), 'Women and class analysis: a reply to the replies', *Sociology*, vol. 18, no. 4, pp. 497–9.

Goldthorpe, J. H., Lockwood, D., Bechhofer, F. and Platt, J. (1969), *The Affluent Worker in the Class Structure* (London: Cambridge University Press).

Goldthorpe, J. H. and Payne, C. (1986a), 'Trends in intergenerational class mobility in England and Wales 1972–1983', *Sociology*, vol. 20, no. 1, pp. 1–24.

Goldthorpe, J. H. and Payne, C. (1986b), 'On the class mobility of women: results from different approaches to the analysis of recent British data', *Sociology*, vol. 20, no. 4, pp. 531–55.

Graham, H. (1983), 'Do her answers fit his questions? Women and the survey method', in E. Gamarnakow, D. Morgan, J. Purvis and D. Taylorson (eds), *The Public and the Private* (London: Heinemann Educational), pp. 132–46.

Hakim, C. (1982), *Secondary Analysis in Social Research* (London: Allen and Unwin).

Hakim, C. (1984), 'Employers' use of homework, outwork and freelances', *Employment Gazette*, vol. 92, pp. 144–50.

Hakim, C. (1985), *Employers' Use of Outwork*, Department of Employment Research Paper No. 44 (London: DE).

Hakim, C. (1987a), *Home-based Work in Britain*, Department of Employment Research Paper No. 66 (London: DE).

Hakim, C. (1987b), *Research Design: Strategies and Choices in the Design of Social Research* (London: Allen and Unwin).

Haraven, T. (1982), *Family Time and Industrial Time* (Cambridge: Cambridge University Press).

Harris, C. C., Lee, R. M. and Morris, L. D. (1985), 'Redundancy in steel: labour market behaviour, local social networks and domestic organisation', in R. Finnegan, D. Gallie and B. Roberts (eds), *New Approaches to Economic Life* (Manchester: Manchester University Press).

Hartwig, F. and Dearing, B. (1979), *Exploratory Data Analysis*, Sage University Paper (Beverly Hills, Calif.: Sage).

Hauser, R. M. (1970), 'Context and consex: a cautionary tale', *American Journal of Sociology*, vol. 75, pp. 645–64.

Hauser, R. M. (1974), 'Contextual analysis revisited', *Sociological Methods and Research*, vol. 2, no. 3, pp. 365–75.

Hauser, R. M., Dickinson, P. J., Travis, H. P. and Koffel, J. N. (1975), 'Structural changes in occupational mobility among men in the United States', *American Sociological Review*, vol. 40, pp. 585–98.

Heath, A. (1981), *Social Mobility* (Glasgow: Fontana).

Heath, C. (1986), *Body Movement and Speech in Medical Interaction* (Cambridge: Cambridge University Press).

Hellevik, O. (1984), *Introduction to Causal Analysis* (London: Allen and Unwin).

Hornsby-Smith, M. P. and Dale, A. (1988), 'Occupational assimilation of the Irish in England', *British Journal of Sociology* (forthcoming).

Hughes, J. A. (1976), *Sociological Analysis: Methods of Discovery* (London: Nelson).

Hunt, A. (1968), *A Survey of Women's Employment* (London: HMSO).

Hunt, A. (1980), *Some Gaps and Problems arising from Government Statistics on Women and Work*, Equal Opportunities Commission Research Bulletin No. 4, pp. 29–42 (Manchester: EOC).

Hunt, P. (1980), *Gender and Class Consciousness* (London: Macmillan).

Hyman, H. H. (1954), *Interviewing in Social Research* (Chicago: University of Chicago).

Hyman, H. H. (1955), *Survey Design and Analysis* (Glencoe, Ill.: Free Press).

Hyman, H. H. (1972), *Secondary Analysis of Sample Surveys* (New York: Wiley).

ICPSR (1986), *Guide to Resources and Services 1985–1986* (Ann Arbor, Mich.: Inter-University Consortium on Political and Social Research).

Ineichen, B. (1983), 'Council housing and disadvantage: the allocation of council housing and its relation to social stratification', in M. Brown, *The Structure of Disadvantage* (London: Heinemann), pp. 153–71.

Irvine, J., Miles, I. and Evans, J. (1979), *Demystifying Social Statistics* (London: Pluto Press).

Jones, G. (1986), 'Youth in the social structure: transitions to adulthood and their stratification by class and gender', PhD Thesis (Guildford: University of Surrey).

Jones, G. (1987), 'Young workers in the class structure', *Work, Employment and Society*, vol. 1, no. 4, pp. 487–508.

Joshi, H. (1984), *Women's Participation in Paid Work: Further Analysis of the Women and Employment Survey*, Department of Employment Survey Research Paper No. 45 (London: DE).

Jowell, R. and Airey, C. (1984), *British Social Attitudes: The 1984 Report* (Aldershot: Gower).

Jowell, R. and Witherspoon, S. (eds) (1985), *British Social Attitudes: The 1985 Report* (Aldershot: Gower).

Kemsley, W., Redpath, R. and Holmes, M. (1980), *Family Expenditure Survey Handbook*, Office of Population Censuses and Surveys (London: HMSO).

Kiecolt, K. J. and Nathan, L. E. (1985), *Secondary Analysis of Survey Data*, Sage University Paper (Beverly Hills, Calif.: Sage).

Kincaid, J. (1979), 'Poverty in the Welfare State', in J. Irvine, I. Miles and J. Evans (eds), *Demystifying Social Statistics* (London: Pluto Press), pp. 212–19.

Laczko, F., Dale, A., Arber, S. L. and Gilbert, G. N. (1988), 'The social implications of early retirement and redundancy', *Journal of Social Policy* (forthcoming).

Land, H. (1983), 'Poverty and gender: the distribution of resources within the family', in M. Brown, *The Structure of Disadvantage*, pp. 49–71 (London: Heinemann).

Layard, R., Piachaud, D. and Stewart, M. (1978), *The Causes of Poverty*, Royal Commission on the Distribution of Income and Wealth, Background Paper No. 5 (London: HMSO).

Lazarsfeld, P. F. and Menzel, H. (1961), 'On the relationship between individual and collective properties', in A. Etzioni (ed.) *Complex Organizations* (New York: Holt, Rinehart and Winston).

Lievesley, D. and Waterton, J. (1986), 'Measuring individual attitude change', in R. Jowell and S. Witherspoon (eds), *British Social Attitudes: The 1985 Report* (Aldershot: Gower).

Lipset, S. M., Trow, M. and Coleman, J. (1956), *Union Democracy: The Inside Politics of the International Typographical Union* (New York: Free Press).

Madron, T. W., Tate, C. N. and Brookshire, R. G. (1985), *Using Microcomputers in Research*, Sage University Papers on Quantitative Applications in the Social Sciences, series no. 07-052 (Beverly Hills and London: Sage).

McDill, E. L. and Rigsby, L. C. (1973), *Structure and Process in Secondary Schools: The Impact of Educational Climates* (New York: Johns Hopkins).

McKee, D. and Vilhjalmsson, R. (1987), 'Life stress, vulnerability, and depression: a methodological critique of Brown *et al.*', *Sociology*, vol. 20, pp. 589–99.

Marsh, A. and Matheson, J. (1983), *Smoking Attitudes and Behaviour: An Enquiry for the DHSS* (London: HMSO).

Marsh, C. (1979a), 'Opinion polls – social science or political manoeuvre?', in J. Irvine, I. Miles and J. Evans (eds), *Demystifying Social Statistics* (London: Pluto Press), pp. 268–88.

Marsh, C. (1979b), 'Problems with surveys: method or epistemology?', *Sociology*, vol. 13, pp. 293–305.

Marsh, C. (1982), *The Survey Method* (London: Allen and Unwin).

Marsh, C. (1988), *Exploring Data: An Introduction to Data Analysis for Social Scientists* (Cambridge: Polity Press) (forthcoming).

Marshall, G., Rose, D., Vogler, C. and Newby, H. (1988), *Social Class in Modern Britain* (London : Hutchinson).

Martin, J. and Bone, M. (1986), 'OPCS surveys of disabled people in Great Britain', *Survey Methods Bulletin*, no. 18, pp. 45–55.
Martin, J. and Roberts, C. (1984a), *Women and Employment: A Lifetime Perspective*, Department of Employment/Office of Population Censuses and Surveys (London: HMSO).
Martin, J. and Roberts, C. (1984b), *Women and Employment: Technical Report* (London: OPCS).
Mason, K. O., Czajka, J. L. and Arber, S. (1976), 'Change in US women's sex-role attitudes, 1964–1974', *American Sociological Review*, vol. 41, no. 4, pp. 573–96.
Mills, C. W. (1959), *The Sociological Imagination* (Harmondsworth: Penguin).
Millward, N. (1983), 'Workplace industrial relations: results of a new survey of industrial relations practices', *Employment Gazette*, vol. 91, no. 7, pp. 280–9 (London: Department of Employment).
Millward, N. and Stevens, M. (1986), *British Workplace Industrial Relations 1980–1984: the DE/ESRC/PSI/ACAS Surveys* (Aldershot: Gower).
Minford, P. (1985), *Unemployment: Cause and Cure* (Oxford: Blackwell).
Mingione, E. (1985), 'Social reproduction and the surplus labour force', in N. Redclift and E. Mingione (eds), *Beyond Employment: Household, Gender and Subsistence* (Oxford: Blackwell), pp. 14–54.
Moser, C. A. and Kalton, G. (1971), *Survey Methods in Social Investigation* (London: Heinemann Educational).
Moser, K. A., Fox, A. J. and Jones, D. R. (1986), 'Unemployment and mortality in the OPCS Longitudinal Study', in R. G. Wilkinson (ed.), *Class and Health: Research and Longitudinal Data* (London: Tavistock).
Moylan, S., Millar, J. and Davies, R. (1984), *For Richer, for Poorer? DHSS Cohort Study of Unemployed Men* (London: HMSO).
Murie, A. (1983), *Housing Inequality and Deprivation* (London: Heinemann).
Murphy, M. (1983), 'The life course of individuals in the family: describing static and dynamic aspects of the contemporary family', in *The Family*, British Society for Population Studies Occasional Paper No. 31 (London: OPCS), pp. 50–69.

Nissel, M. (1980), *Women and Government Statistics: Basic Concepts and Assumptions*, Equal Opportunities Commission Research Bulletin No. 4, pp. 5–28 (Manchester: EOC).

Oakley, A. (1981), 'Interviewing women: a contradiction in terms', in H. Roberts (ed.), *Doing Feminist Research* (London: Routledge and Kegan Paul), pp. 30–61.
Oakley, A. and Oakley, R. (1979), 'Sexism in official statistics', in J. Irvine, I. Miles and J. Evans (eds), *Demystifying Social Statistics* (London: Pluto Press), pp. 172–89.
OECD (1985), *Labour Force Statistics 1963–1983* (Paris: Organisation for Economic Co-operation and Development).
O'Higgins, M. and Bradshaw, J. (1984), 'Life cycle income inequality' (University of Bath: unpublished paper).
OPCS (1970), *Classification of Occupations 1970* (London: HMSO).
OPCS (1980), *Classification of Occupations 1980* (London: HMSO).
OPCS (1981), *The General Household Survey 1979* (London: HMSO).

OPCS (1982), *Labour Force Survey 1981* (London: HMSO).

OPCS (1983), *The General Household Survey 1981* (London: HMSO).

OPCS (1985), *The General Household Survey 1983* (London: HMSO).

OPCS (1986), *The Labour Force Surveys 1983, 1984* (London: HMSO).

Owen, S. J. (1987), 'Household production and economic efficiency: arguments for and against domestic specialization', *Work, Employment and Society*, vol. 1, pp. 157–78.

Pahl, J. (1983), 'The allocation of money and the structuring of inequality within marriage', *Sociological Review*, vol. 31, pp. 237–62.

Pahl, R. (1984), *Divisions of Labour* (Oxford: Blackwell).

Payne, J. (1985), 'Changes in the youth labour market, 1974–1981', *Oxford Review of Education*, vol. 11, no. 2, pp. 167–79.

Payne, J. (1987), 'Does unemployment run in families? Some findings from the General Household Survey', *Sociology*, vol. 21, no. 2, pp. 199–214.

Platt, J. (1986), 'Functionalism and the survey: the relation of theory and method', *Sociological Review*, vol. 34, pp. 501–36.

Platt, J. (1987), 'Research dissemination: a case study', *Quarterly Journal of Social Affairs*, vol. 3, pp. 181–98.

Pollert, A. (1981), *Girls, Wives and Factory Lives* (London: Macmillan).

Popay, J., Rimmer, L. and Rossiter, C. (1983), *One Parent Families: Parents, Children and Public Policy*, Occasional Paper No. 12 (London: Study Commission on the Family).

Procter, M. J. and Abell, P. (eds) (1985), *Sequence Analysis* (Aldershot: Gower).

Rainwater, L., Smeeding, T. M. and Schmaus, G. (1985), *User's Guide to LIS: The Luxembourg Income Study*, mimeo, CEPS, Case Postale 2, L-7201 Walferdange, Luxembourg.

Rauta, I. (1985), 'A comparison of the census characteristics of respondents and non-respondents to the 1981 GHS', *Statistical News*, no. 71, pp. 12–15.

Redclift, N. and Mingione, E. (1985), *Beyond Employment* (Oxford: Blackwell).

Redpath, R. (1986), 'Family Expenditure Survey: a second study of differential response, comparing Census characteristics of FES respondents and non-respondents', *Statistical News*, February, pp. 72.13–72.16.

Report of the Committee on Data Protection (1978) (chairman, Sir Norman Lindop), Cmnd 7341 (London: HMSO).

Ritchie, J. (1986), 'Researching the unaskable', paper given to an SRA Conference, April 1986.

Roberts, H. (1984), 'Putting the show on the road: the dissemination of research findings', in C. Bell and H. Roberts (eds), *Social Researching: Politics, Problems and Practice* (London: Routledge and Kegan Paul), pp. 199–212.

Roberts, H. (1986), 'The social classification of women', *Equal Opportunities Commission Research Bulletin*, no. 10, pp. 47–70 (Manchester: EOC).

Robinson, B. N., Anderson, G. D., Cohen, E., Gazdzik, W. F., Karpel, L. C., Miller, A. H. and Stein, J. R. (1980), *SIR Scientific Information Retrieval User's Manual, Version 2* (Evanston, Ill.: SIR Inc.)

Rose, D., Marshall, G., Newby, H. and Vogler, C. (1987), 'Goodbye to supervisors?', *Work, Employment and Society*, vol. 1, pp.7–24.

Rowntree, S. (1902), *Poverty: A Study of Town Life* (London: Longman).
Rutter, M., Maughan, B., Mortimore, P. and Ouston, J. (1979), *Fifteen Thousand Hours: Secondary Schools and their Effects* (London: Open Books).

Saunders, P. (1986), *Social Theory and the Urban Question*, 2nd edn (London: Hutchinson).
Schlackman Research Organisation (1979), *Women and Unemployment: A Qualitative Preliminary Research Report* (London: Q-Search, Schlackman Research Organisation).
Schulzinger Fox, J. (1984), *The SIR/DBMS Primer* (Madison, Wis.: University of Wisconsin, Madison Academic Computing Center).
Scott, C. and Chidambaram, V. C. (1985), 'World fertility survey: origins and achievements', in J. Cleland and J. Hobcraft (eds), *Reproductive Change in Developing Countries* (Oxford: Oxford University Press), pp. 7–26.
SCPR Working Party (1979), 'Survey research and privacy', in M. Bulmer (ed.), *Censuses, Surveys and Privacy* (London: Macmillan).
Selvin, H. and Stuart, A. (1966), 'Data dredging in survey analysis', *The American Statistician*, June, pp. 20–3.
Shanas, E. and Madge, J. (1968), *Methodological Problems in Cross-National Studies in Aging* (Basle: Karger).
Shanas, E., Townsend, P., Wedderburn, D., Henning, F., Milhoj, P. and Stehouwer, J. (1968), *Old People in Three Industrial Societies* (London: Routledge and Kegan Paul).
Shepherd, P. M. (1986), *The NCDS5 Development Programme*, Working Paper No. 17, (Social Statistics Research Unit, London: City University).
Silverman, D. (1985), *Qualitative Method and Sociology* (Aldershot: Gower).
Smith, T. (1982), *Who, What, When, Where and Why: An Analysis of the GSS 1972–1982*, General Social Survey Technical Report no. 37 (Chicago: National Opinion Research Center).
Smith, T. (1983), 'The role of the General Social Survey in the social sciences', *SCPR Survey Methods Newsletter*, pp. 7–8.
Social Research Association (1985), *Register of Members* (London: SRA).
Sonquist, J. A. and Dunkelberg, W. C. (1977), *Survey and Opinion Research: Procedures for Processing and Analysis* (Englewood Cliffs, NJ: Prentice-Hall).
SPSS Inc. (1984), *SPSS^x Basics* (New York: McGraw Hill).
SPSS Inc. (1986), *SPSS^x User's Guide* (New York: McGraw Hill).
Stacey, M., Batstone, E. and Bell, C. (1975), *Power, Persistence and Change: A Second Study of Banbury* (London: Routledge and Kegan Paul).
Stanton, D., Cahill, M. and Howdle, M. (1981), *Mobility within Local Labour-Markets*, Department of Employment Research Paper No. 24 (London: DE).
Stanworth, M. (1984), 'Women and class analysis: a reply to John Goldthorpe', *Sociology*, vol. 18, no. 2, pp. 159–70.
Stewart, A., Prandy, K. and Blackburn, R. (1980), *Social Stratification and Occupations* (London: Macmillan).
Stewart, D. W. (1984), *Secondary Research: Information Sources and Methods* (Beverly Hills, Calif.: Sage).

Stinchcome, A. L., Adams, R., Heimer, C. A., Scheppele, K., Smith, T. W. and Taylor, D. G. (1980), *Crime and Punishment: Changing Attitudes in America* (San Francisco: Jossey-Bass).

Stouffer, S. A., Suchman, E., De Vinney, L., Star, S. and Williams, R. (1949), *The American Soldier*, vol. 1 (Princeton, NJ: Princeton University Press).

Stouffer, S. A. (1963), *Communism, Conformity, and Civil Liberties* (Gloucester, Mass.: Peter Smith).

Tagg, S. (1986), *Analysis of GHS data using SPSS*[x], mimeo (Glasgow: University of Strathclyde).

Tagg, S. (1987), 'Taking SPSS-X to the limit: processing raw GHS data files', *ESRC Data Archive Bulletin*, no. 38, pp. 52–4

Taylor, M. F. (1986), *ESRC Data Archive Catalogue*, vols. 1 and 2 (Cambridge: Chadwyck-Healey).

Todd, J. and Butcher, B. (1982), *Electoral Registration in 1981* (London: Office of Population Censuses and Surveys).

Townsend, A., Blakemore, M., Nelson, R. and Dodds, P. (1986), 'The National On-Line Manpower Information System (NOMIS)', *Employment Gazette*, vol. 94, pp. 60–4.

Townsend, P. (1974), 'Poverty as relative deprivation: resources and style of living', in D. Wedderburn, *Poverty, Inequality and Class Structure* (Cambridge: Cambridge University Press) pp. 15–42.

Townsend, P. (1979), *Poverty in the United Kingdom* (Harmondsworth: Penguin).

Tsui, A. O. (1985), 'Community effects on contraceptive use', in J. B. Casterline (ed.), pp. 77–99.

Tukey, J. (1977), *Exploratory Data Analysis* (Reading, Mass.: Addison-Wesley).

van den Eeden, P. and Hüttner, H. J. M. (1982), 'Multi-level research', *Current Sociology*, vol. 30, no. 3, pp. 1–181.

Van Slooten, R. and Coverdale, A.D. (1977), 'The characteristics of low income households', *Social Trends*, 8, pp. 26–39.

Velleman, P. F. and Hoaglin, D. C. (1981), *Applications, Basics, and Computing of Exploratory Data Analysis* (Boston, Mass.: Duxbury Press).

Wadsworth, M. E. J. (1986), 'Serious illness in childhood and its association with later-life achievement', in R.G. Wilkinson (ed.), *Class and Health: Research and Longitudinal Data* (London: Tavistock), pp. 50–74.

West, J. (1982), *Work, Women and the Labour Market* (London: Routledge and Kegan Paul).

Westergaard, J. and Resler, H. (1975), *Class in a Capitalist Society* (Harmondsworth: Penguin).

Wilkinson, R. G. (ed.) (1986), *Class and Health: Research and Longitudinal Data* (London: Tavistock).

Wilson, P. (1981), 'Improving the methodology of drinking surveys', *OPCS Social Survey Methodology Bulletin*, no. 12.

Wright, E. O., Costello, C., Hachen, D. and Sprague, J. (1982), 'The American class structure', *American Sociological Review*, vol. 47, pp. 709–26.

Wright, J. D. and Wright, S. R. (1976), 'Social class and parental values for children: a partial replication and extension of the Kohn thesis', *American Sociological Review*, vol. 41, pp. 527–37.

Yeandle, S. (1984), *Women's Working Lives* (London: Tavistock).

Yeandle, S. (1986), 'Married women at midlife: past and present patterns of labour', paper given to the British Sociological Association Annual Conference, Loughborough, April 1986.

Index

For Product Safety Concerns and Information please contact our EU representative GPSR@taylorandfrancis.com Taylor & Francis Verlag GmbH, Kaufingerstraße 24, 80331 München, Germany